A Treatise of the Life of Faith

Thomas Manton

Christian Focus

© Christian Focus Publications
ISBN 1 85792 271 9
Published in 1997 by Christian Focus Publications, Geanies House, Fearn, Ross-shire, IV20 1TW, Great Britain.
Cover design by Donna Macleod

Contents

Foreword by *Maurice Roberts* 7

Introduction 17

1. The Life of Faith and Justification 32

2. The Life of Faith and Sanctification 51

3. The Life of Faith and Glorification 69

4. Living By Faith, as to the promises
and blessings of the present life. 89

5. The Life of Faith and the Temptations of Satan 120

6. The Life of Faith and the Temptations of the World 139

7. The Life of Faith and Afflictions 156

8. The Effects of Faith 182

9. The Life of Faith in Prayer 200

10. The Life of Faith in Hearing the Word 217

FOREWORD

The book which the reader now has in his hands is an exposition of the life of faith. These studies, or discourses, to use the word in vogue at the time when they were first written, were originally prepared by their distinguished author as outlines of sermons to be delivered in the pulpit. This fact will explain to the reader who is unfamiliar with the sermonic literature of the Puritan period why the writer of this book has set his material out in a rather unfamiliar way, with divisions and subdivisions.

Any such unfamiliarity of form and presentation, it needs to be said, is quickly forgotten once the reader begins to get into the book and its theme.

No subject is more relevant to our life in this world than the life of faith. Though some three centuries have elapsed since these sermons were first heard by their eager audiences, probably in London first, they are fresh and relevant in the highest degree.

The Puritans of seventeenth-century Britain (and here the writer would include the Scottish as well as of the English divines of the period) were by common consent a most remarkable body of men. No less an authority on historical matters than Lord Macaulay could say of them that they were: 'Perhaps the most remarkable body of men which the world has ever produced.' The learned and celebrated Erasmus of Rotterdam is said to have expressed his enthusiasm for the English Puritans in this way: 'O sit anima mea cum Puritanis Anglicanis!' (O let my soul be with the English Puritans!) The great J. C. Ryle, first Bishop of Liverpool, estimated their contribution in the following terms: 'The Puritans, as a body, have done more to elevate the national character than any class of Englishmen that ever lived.'

Such praise is high praise indeed. But it is no more than the sober truth. For the genius of Puritanism was just this: to live unto God and to instill into the hearts of men that God is to be set first in every aspect of man's life in this world: in the private life; and in the family, church and state. In Puritanism therefore we have a Christianity which aims to be thoroughly and consistently biblical in every aspect of man's life. And the engine which drove this concept of man's life on earth was the Puritan pulpit.

Among Puritan pulpit giants, none was more esteemed than Thomas Manton, the author of these sermons. If proof of this assertion were needed it could be given at length. Perhaps it will suffice in this context to say that the most formative and representative of all the documents produced in the Puritan age was published with a commendatory Epistle from Thomas Manton. We refer here to the Westminster Confession and the two accompanying Catechisms – documents which have gone through the earth and which have helped to shape the character of churches and nations. It is Dr. Manton's name which appears at the end of the original Preface to these monumental theological writings. Clearly, Manton was deemed by his fellows in that theologically literate age to be the fittest person to recommend the Westminster standards to the Christian public at large. No single fact could more fully demonstrate the esteem in which he was then held. This should not surprise us, for it was said of Manton that he never preached a poor sermon!

Thomas Manton

Manton was born in Somersetshire, in the year 1620. Educated at Wadham College, Oxford, he was admitted to deacon's orders by Bishop Joseph Hall (later of Norwich), but he never took ordination as a 'priest' because he judged that he had been 'properly ordained' to the ministerial office. He commenced his ministry at Stoke Newington near London, and then took a charge in the city of London itself as successor to Obadiah Sedgewich, at Covent Garden.

During the Commonwealth period he was one of Cromwell's chaplains and offered the prayer at the latter's installation in 1657. At this period he preached frequently before Parliament.

At the Restoration he welcomed Charles II to the throne in 1660 and took part in the famous Savoy Conference. However in 1662 he was deprived of his living along with two thousand other ministers of Puritan conviction who, with Manton, were sufferers for conscience under the Act of Uniformity of that year.

When Manton then began to preach in his own rooms he was arrested. The imprisonment which followed was not as severe as that suffered by many of the other Puritan preachers ejected from their pulpits by the 1662 Act. He was in fact permitted to preach to a small gathering of persons who came to his prison.

Thomas Manton passed to his eternal rest on October 18th 1677, at the age of fifty seven. He was buried at Stoke Newington and the funeral sermon was preached by a fellow Puritan minister of great fame, Dr. William Bates.

Biographical details of Manton's life are few. Suffice to say that he was incessant in the ministerial labours which he loved and in which he excelled. His collected writings (including an index) comprise twenty two volumes of closely printed sermons. The sermons which make up this little volume are therefore but a small fragment of the total output of this learned and prolific preacher, of whom it could truly be said that from his own day until ours 'his praise is in all the churches'.

Manton must be called a 'preacher's preacher'. He has had a formative influence on those who have excelled since his day in the great work of the pulpit. George Whitefield, for instance, and C. H. Spurgeon had a high regard for Manton, as also did Dr. D. Martyn Lloyd-Jones. 'Manton's work is most commendable,' says Spurgeon, in reference to the volumes of sermons on Jude. The comment is typical.

It must be a significant tribute too to the honour and worth of Manton that he is currently in print in two editions, one American and the other British. All over the world he is being read today and is being increasingly appreciated as a 'master in Israel' in his ability to open out the riches of Holy Scripture.

To begin to read the great Puritan writers like Owen, Sibbes, Flavel, Brooks and Manton is to enter into a world of thought and spirituality which it is almost impossible to find in other writers. This is not to overstate the case. Indeed, to 'discover' the Puritans can be almost to feel that they are, as a friend of the writer's once put it, 'more spiritual than the Bible itself'! This of course is an impossibility. But what is meant by those who have this experience is that they have come to discover that the Bible is a far more wonderful book than they had before realised.

To say what we have just said requires some explanation of how the standard Puritan writers, whose names we

FOREWORD

have given examples of above, came to be so eminent in their ability to open out the treasures of the Word of God.

For one thing, the Puritans (and here it is in place to state that Thomas Manton was in the ripe third generation) were brought up to love and to learn the Bible with 'their mother's milk'. Their writings abound with a profusion of biblical references from every part of the Word of God. For the Puritan mind a clear text from the Bible settled all controversy. Happily, they lived in that 'pre-critical age' when it had not yet become the habit of theologians and preachers to question the authority or the divine origin and sufficiency of scripture. The finality and inerrancy of the Bible were to them an unquestioned assumption, just as they ought to be ours. All that they believed therefore was tested by scripture and proved by scripture. What the Bible did not teach they did not include among articles of their faith. What scripture taught was to them binding, whether for faith or life, or both.

Then, we must appreciate that the mainline Puritans, of whom Manton was one *par excellence*, were committed to the Augustinian or Calvinistic system of theology. This underlying acceptance of the teachings of John Calvin as the true theology of the Bible was taken by them for granted. Of course they might differ on secondary matters. But they were of one mind in their commitment to what we now call 'Westminster' theology.

Thirdly, among reasons why they were so profound in their preaching, we must state that they excelled in practical and experimental religion. By this is meant that they made a close study of the human heart and its spiritual working as well as of the pastoral problems which they found among their hearers, both converted and otherwise;

that they applied themselves to understand the wiles and methods of the devil; and that they viewed this life, as no Christians before or since have done better, as a time of probation and preparation for eternity.

To the above observations ought too to be added another: the Puritan way of looking at the Moral Law. As evangelicals, of course, they knew that salvation is by grace and through faith alone in Christ. But they were of the belief that the Ten Commandments have a place of great importance in the life of the believer since they are the rule for life in this world. We are not 'under the law' as a covenant of life, as they would put it. But we are as Christians under the Moral Law as a rule to show us how to glorify and enjoy God. No analysis of the religion of these men is adequate which does not take full account of this element in their thinking.

They would regard as Antinomian the forms of recent evangelicalism which fail to give a place to the Moral Law which we have described here. All thought that we are saved to enjoy an undefined 'freedom', as some modern writers have put it, would be anathema to them. Their love was to live 'by rule'. This did not mean that they taught salvation by the law, as we have said already. But it did mean that they insisted that the believer is to spend his energies in understanding how to please God in every way. In so doing he must work out the implication of the Decalogue. That this was their view is clear from the place they give to the Moral Law in their writings. They have been accused by some of being 'legalists'. But they were in fact no such thing. They were orthodox, evangelical believers, who lived to glorify and enjoy God.

There was in the genius of Puritanism an instinctive

FOREWORD

aptitude for pithy and memorable expressions. Perhaps this was the fruit of their mastery of the Latin writers, who formed a chief element in the educational system of their day. But, however it was, they were masters of the epigram and the memorable phrase.

The question might occur to the mind of one not familiar with the Puritan writers: Why should a volume of sermons as old as this be republished today when there must surely be many books on this subject which are up-to-date and which deal with the same theme? The answer to this, in the opinion of the present writer, can be summed up in one word: profundity.

There is a depth of treatment here which will be very difficult indeed to match, whether in terms of biblical knowledge or of an understanding of the human heart with its proneness to fall into the snares of Satan. After all is said and done, there is no reason for us to imagine that the people of this modern world are any better at fighting the devil than our fathers were in the seventeenth century! Observation suggests indeed that we are a good deal less so. We are a technically expert age but we have not the remotest idea of how to go about the basic duties of life: marriage, social justice and the love of God. We live in a world which has been aptly called a 'Techtopia'. There is today everything to live with, but almost nothing to live for. It is there that the Puritans have so much to teach us. At the point at which we are so weak, they were strong. Our design in life, they would tell us, should be to live unto and upon God.

A few words must be said about the best way to read the Puritans. In this edition the reader will find that difficult words have been explained by the use of square brackets, in which the best modern equivalent word or term is given. The editor is solely responsible for these suggestions and he will have to bear the blame where it can be shown that he has missed the true meaning. However he believes that at least in most cases he has given the true sense of an obscure word. Here and there in the book Manton uses Greek, Latin and Hebrew words which in the original appear in their respective alphabets. Here it has been thought best to give these words in the approximate English transliteration and to place a translation after them. Obscure historical references too have been elucidated by a note (see page 254).

How to read the Puritans

1. The reader must understand that this Puritan discourse was a series of sermons preached on passages of scripture. The preacher's aim was to open up the meaning of the passage in its setting; and then to show his audience the principles which are of permanent validity; and finally to point to the practical lessons which the believer should attempt to apply in his own life.

2. The opening sentences are usually brief. They give the main headings of the passage and indicated originally to the hearers the form in which the preacher would divide up the text. This analysis is worth taking a little time over. Once its outline is grasped the reader can go ahead confident that he knows the general direction of the preacher's thoughts.

3. The points made at the end of each sermon under the heading of 'Uses' are the practical ways in which the author believes that the passage which he has expounded demands to be worked out by Christians in their everyday

FOREWORD

lives. Often such thoughts are put down in a seminal form. No doubt the preacher developed these points more fully in the course of his spontaneous remarks in the pulpit. A sermon after all is a thing of life and not a set piece to be read in the pulpit.

It is believed that the above guidelines will be of some assistance to the reader who may not have ventured before into our older spiritual literature. We wish him well as he now sets off. If there are initial difficulties arising from unfamiliarity of language or of style, let him remember that there are also treasure islands ahead for him and a vast store of spiritual gold to be carried off by the time the end is reached!

Introduction

And the life which I now live in the flesh, I live
by the faith of the Son of God (Gal. 2:20).

There are two parts of a Christian's duty – dying to sin and living to God. They are both in the text; the first part, dying to sin, in that mysterious expression, 'I am crucified with Christ'; the second branch, living to God, in the following clauses, in which a spiritual and holy riddle is propounded, and then solved and opened: 'I am crucified, yet I live', and though I live, yet I live not, 'for Christ liveth in me'; and then he openeth the whole riddle and mystery in the latter part: 'And the life which I live in the flesh, I live by the faith of the Son of God.'

Many things might be observed:

1. They that are crucified with Christ nevertheless live. They that partake with Christ in one act partake with him in all; if they are mortified with Christ, they are also quickened by him.

2. In the spiritual life of a Christian, Christ hath the greatest hand and stroke: 'Not I, but Christ liveth in me.'

3. Believers live in the flesh after they are called to grace, but they do not live after the flesh.

4. That besides the animal life, there is a spiritual life, and these two are distinct. The animal life is the life of the rational soul void of grace, accommodating itself to the interests of the body: 'Sensual, having not the spirit' (Jude 19); and to the power and pomp of the world, highness of rank and place, riches, pleasures, honours; it consists in the exercise of the senses. The spiritual life is a principle that enableth us to live unto God, to act and move towards God as our last and utmost end, to serve his glory as our great scope, and

enjoy his favour as our chief good. Both these two lives are governed by a distinct guide and ruler: the animal life by sense, the spiritual life by faith; so that man's reason is either brutified and debased by sense, or refined, sublimated, and raised by faith. If a man be debased by sense, he walloweth in all manner of brutish sensuality, he liveth in pleasure, and maketh the profits and pleasures of the world his only scope and aim; if refined and elevated by faith, his soul worketh after God, and is carried out to the concernments of the world to come. But quitting all these, here is a life within a life, and a life overruled by a life, and that overruling life is called the life of faith.

Doctrine: Those only live spiritually that live by faith; or, the great means on our part whereby we receive the influences of the spiritual life is faith in Christ.

Living by faith is a point of large and universal concernment, therefore I shall in a few discourses insist upon it. And I shall treat of it: (1) In the general, and (2) In particular, in all duties, acts and conditions of this life.

1. In the general. Here I shall inquire: (1) What faith is; (2) Why and how we are said to receive life from it; (3) Give you some observations concerning this life.

What is this faith by which the just shall live?
Faith is a grace by which we believe God's word in the general, and in a special manner do receive Christ, and rest upon him for grace here and glory hereafter. This may serve for a short definition or description of faith. Here is assent, consent, and affiance [trust].

1. There is *assent*, by which we believe God's word in general: 'Believing all things which are written in the law and the prophets' (Acts 24:14). There is the first work of faith, which is to assent to the scriptures and all things contained therein. The general faith goeth before the particular; there is no building without a foundation.

2. There is *consent*. Faith doth in a special manner receive Christ; that is, the faith that saveth: 'To as many as received him, to them gave he power to become the sons of God, even to them that believe on his name' (John 1:12). When I take him as God offereth him, and to the ends for which he offereth him, that he may do that for me, and be that to me, what God hath appointed him to do and be in the gospel.

3. There is *affiance* [trust]. Faith doth rest upon him; besides choice, there must be a recumbency: 'Thou wilt keep him in perfect peace whose mind is stayed on thee; because he trusteth in thee' (Isa. 26:3). That is a special work of faith. Now, what do we rest upon him for?

(a) For grace here, all kinds of grace, justification, sanctification: 'Him hath God exalted with his right hand to be a Prince and a Saviour, to give repentance to Israel, and remission of sins' (Acts 5:31). For privileges, qualification, duties, Christ is all to us.

(b) And then for glory hereafter: we are said to 'believe on him to life everlasting' (1 Tim. 1:16). There is the end which faith aimeth at, or the main blessing with it seeketh, and upon the hopes of which the life which it begetteth is carried on: 'Receiving the end of your faith, the salvation of your souls' (1 Pet. 1:9). Those that fly to Christ by faith do eye this as the prime benefit to be had by him, by which temptations of sense are defeated.

How and why we are said to live by it

Distinct graces have their distinct offices; in scripture speech we are said to live by faith, but to work by love; there must be life before operation. Now we are said to live by faith:

1. *Because it is the grace that doth unite us to Christ.* Other graces make us like Christ, but this maketh us one with Christ principally and primarily. For the understanding of this reason, you must know that the author and fountain of the spiritual life is Christ. He is called 'the Prince of life' (Acts 3:15). Christ liveth in a believer, and a believer liveth in Christ; he is in us by his Spirit. Before we can have anything from Christ, we must first have Christ himself: 'He that hath the Son hath life' (1 John 5:12). We have Christ when we are united to him, as members to the head, from whence they receive sense and motion: 'And not holding the head, from which all the body by joints and bands having nourishment ministered, and knit together, increaseth with the increase of God' (Col. 2:19); as the root to the branches from whence they receive sap and influence: 'I am the vine, ye are the branches; he that abideth in me, and I in him, the same bringeth forth much fruit, for without me ye can do nothing' (John 15:5). Christ is the principle and motion, as united to us by the Spirit on his part. But what is the bond on our part but faith? 'That Christ may dwell in our hearts by faith' (Eph. 3:17).

Jesus Christ doth make his first entry into, and dwelleth in believers by his Spirit: 'Hereby we know that we dwell in him, and he in us, because he hath given us of his Spirit' (1 John 4:13). Whereby he uniteth them to himself, and quickeneth them, and worketh the grace of faith in them; as bees first make their cells, and then dwell in them. And when faith is so wrought, we do thereby lay hold upon Christ, and receive daily supplies from him, and make use of him as a fountain of life and grace upon all occasions. This uniteth us to him, and keepeth him with us, and us with him, so that he never withdraweth that influence which is necessary to the being and life of grace. The habit of faith in our hearts is the pledge of his presence, and as it is exercised daily, it draweth from him strength and comfort, to support us in all conditions, and to excite and enable us in every duty.

2. *Because all other graces are marshalled and ranked under the conduct of faith.* As the stars in their order fought against Sisera, so all graces are brought up in their order and season. There are several divine qualities that have their office and use in the spiritual life; but all are regulated and quickened by faith; and therefore the whole honour is devolved upon this grace: 'Add to faith, virtue; to virtue, knowledge; and to knowledge, temperance; and to temperance, patience; and to patience, godliness; and to godliness, brotherly-kindness; and to brotherly-kindness, charity' (2 Pet. 1:5-7). Saving faith, which taketh hold of Christ for pardon and strength, and daily flieth to him for both, is the root which must be cherished, increased, and kept in exercise by all that would thrive in any other grace, and be fit for any duty. That is the first stone in the spiritual building, to which all the rest are added. Without faith virtue would languish, our command over our passions be weak, and the back of patience quite broken, and our care of the knowledge of divine things very small. It is faith acting upon Christ and heaven, and the hopes of a better life, that sets all the wheels at work in the soul; temperance, in moderating sensual delights; patience, in bearing the miseries of the present life: 'By faith the elders obtained a good report' (Heb. 11:2). In every verse it is said, By faith, by faith.

Some of the effects there spoken of do directly and more formally belong to other graces; but though the private soldiers do worthily in the high places of the field, yet we say the general won the day; the honour of the victory is put upon him, because it was achieved under his conduct. So it is here; all graces have their use in the holy life. Love worketh, hope waiteth, patience endureth, zeal quickeneth to own God's truth and cause, obedience urgeth to duty; but faith, remembering us of our obligations to Christ, and presenting the hopes of a better life, hath the greatest stroke in all these things. 'Faith worketh by love' (Gal. 5:6); 'faith feedeth hope' (Heb. 11:1): 'faith is the substance of things hoped for'; faith teacheth patience to wait and submit to God's will for the present; it is but a little time: 'Now the just shall live by faith, but if any man draw back, my soul shall have no pleasure in him' (Heb. 10:38). So that faith is like a silken string that runs through a chain of pearl; or rather, like the spirits [life in man] that run with the blood through all the veins. If love constraineth, it is faith working by love; if hope be exercised, it is faith that showeth it the riches of the glory of the world to come; if patience be contented to tarry God's leisure, it is because faith assureth us of the blessing to come.

3. *Because whatever is ascribed to faith redoundeth to the honour of Christ.* The word lieth in the object, as the ivy receiveth strength from the oak about which it windeth. Faith doth all, not from any intrinsic worth and force in itself, but all its power is in dependence upon Christ: *Fidei mendica manus* ['The dragging hand of faith']. We are said to live by faith, as we are said to be fed by the hand; it is the instrument. It is very notable what the apostle saith of the miraculous work of faith: 'And the prayer of faith shall save the sick, and the Lord shall raise him up' (Jas. 5:15). Faith is said to do it, because the Lord doeth it, and faith setteth his power a-work. The like concurrence and use of faith there is in other gracious works: 'This is the victory that overcometh the world, even our faith; and who is he that overcometh the world, but he that believeth that Jesus is the Son of God?' (1 John 5:4, 5). Christ hath and will overcome the world; therefore faith, that apprehendeth this, and encourageth us by it, is said to do it. Christ is the fountain, and faith the pipe and conveyance; it is the grace that bringeth most honour to him.

4. *Because faith removeth obstructions, and openeth the passages of grace, that it may run more freely.* Expectation is the opening of the soul: 'Open thy mouth wide, and I will fill it' (Ps. 81:10). He hath power and readiness to give us abundance of all things, if we could come and depend upon him for it. It is the narrowness of our faith which hindereth our felicity [blessedness]; we are not straitened in God, but in ourselves; we will not enlarge our expectations to take in and seek as much as God offereth. Unbelief *ponit obicem*, puts a bar in the way: 'And he could do no mighty work there' (Mark 6:5). It is like a dam to a river, it hindereth the passage of grace. God's grace is given out to the creature according to its expectation. Unbelief is a kind of restraint to almightiness; he could not because he would not; for so it is, 'And he did not many mighty works there, because of their unbelief.' That power which we distrust is justly hidden from us; but confidence opens a free passage for grace into our souls.

Observations concerning this life

Observation 1. This life must be extended, not only to spiritual duties, and acts of immediate worship, but to all the actions of our natural and temporal life: 'The life which I now live in the flesh'. That natural life which we live and those things which concern that life are ordered by a virtue drawn from Christ by faith in him. A true believer sleepeth and eateth and drinketh in faith; and in the lawful occasions of his calling, as well as religion, faith hath an influence to order them to God's glory, and with respect to eternal happiness: 'Whether ye eat or drink, or whatsoever ye do, do all to the glory of God' (1 Cor. 10:31); and 'Who through faith subdued kingdoms, fought battles' (Heb. 11:33). Take God's directions, and order all things to his glory: 'Whatsoever ye do in word of deed, do all in the name of the Lord Jesus Christ, giving thanks to God and the Father by him' (Col. 3:17). Every action must be influenced by religion, looking to the promises: 'By faith Sarah received strength to conceive seed' (Heb. 11:13); by her faith in the promise. Christians are not left to their own nature, either in things necessary or in things indifferent in their own nature, either in words or deeds; they are to look to Christ's command, and to be looking for his help, and aiming at his glory, still consulting with God, and seeing God in every little work of his. There is not a gnat, nor pile of grass, but discovers [reveals] its Author. And as there is a providential influence, so a gracious influence; as when we use such holy fear and heavenly-mindedness that every one may see heavenly-mindedness in all our actions, and so the poorest servant, being under this divine influence, liveth by faith as well as the greatest monarch.

Observation 2: We never act nobly in anything till we live the life of faith. There is a two-fold life: the animal life, and the spiritual and divine life: 'The natural man receiveth not the things of the Spirit of God' (1 Cor. 2:14). The human soul accommodateth itself to the interests and concernments of the body, but the divine life is animated by heavenly things, and is carried out to look after more noble things than back and belly concernments [bodily things].

Observation 3: We never live comfortably till we live by faith. While we are guided by sense, we are tossed to and fro, according to the variety of accidents in the world; but a believer in the greatest straits [difficulties] doth not only make a poor and sorry shift to live, but hath a comfortable means of subsistence [livelihood]: 'The just shall live by his faith' (Hab. 2:4). For whilst he dwelleth under the shadow of imputed righteousness, to cover all his defects and sins, and to hide him from death and wrath, and can draw virtue from Christ to enable him to do every good word and work, and hath the power of God to make use of for his inward and outward support, and the hopes of glory to comfort him when this life is ended, what should hinder his rejoicing even in the hardest dispensations [circumstances]? He is well at ease that hath wholly given up himself to this kind of life: 'Now the just shall live by faith' (Heb. 10:38); that is, in the hardest trials, when they suffer the spoiling of their goods, and look for loss of life every day. By life we are to understand a happy and a comfortable life: *non est vivere, sed valere vita* [Life is not mere existence but well-being]. We are enabled to hold on cheerfully and comfortably in a holy course, notwithstanding troubles.

Observation 4: That the life of faith is glory begun. First we live by faith, and then by sight (2 Cor. 5:7). Faith now serveth instead of sight and fruition: 'Faith is the substance of things hoped for and the evidence of things not seen' (Heb. 11:1). Though it doth not affect us to the same degree that the life of glory or the beatifical vision will, yet somewhat answerable it doth. The life of glory is inconsistent with any misery; but the life of faith maketh us to rest as quietly upon God and his gracious promise as if there were no misery, where it hath any efficacy and vigour, so as no allurements or terrors can turn us aside, but we follow our Lord in all conditions with delight and cheerfulness. The expectation cannot affect us as the enjoyment; but in some measure it doth: 'We rejoice in hope of the glory of God; and not only so, but we glory in tribulations also' (Rom. 5:2, 3). We are contemptible in the world, but we hope for a glorious estate, and so can forego those transitory contentments which worldlings so much magnify. This quieteth and comforteth God's children in the meanest condition.

The use of this is to persuade you to live this life of faith, if you would live indeed, and live nobly and happily. To this end:

(1) Take care that this life be begun in you.

(2) Improve this life to a cheerful walking with God in all conditions. So then:

First, If you would have this life begun in you:

1. *Study the grounds of faith*; for if the foundation be not well laid, all the building will be like a bunching [bowing] wall or a tottering fence. Now what are the grounds of faith? The promises of the gospel. Therefore consider seriously (a) what is said in the gospel: (b) to whom, and (c) by whom.

1.1 *What is said in the gospel.* The sum of the gospel is abridged and contracted to our hands [in a short form] in many places of scripture; these especially: 'This is a faithful saying, and worthy of all acceptation, that Jesus Christ came into the world to save sinners, of whom I am chief' (1 Tim. 1:15). Is this true indeed, that God hath sent his Son to save us from hell, and to pay our debt and procure salvation for us? And why shall I stand out? The gospel excludeth none; why should I exclude myself? I am sinner enough. Shall this discourage me from looking after Christ? That will be in effect as if a beggar should say, I am too sick to go to the physician; or as if one should say, I am too filthy to be washed, or too cold to go to the fire. Your discouragement should be a motive; I am the chief of sinners, and therefore I will put in for a share. God inviteth us, not because we are worthy, but that we may be worthy.

So Acts 10:43: 'To him give all the prophets witness, that through his name whosoever believeth in him should receive remission of sins.' What do all the prophets and holy men of

God give witness to? That there is such a benefit prepared for all that will lay hold of it; and I profess to believe the scriptures, and shall I not put in for a share? Lord, I have sins to be pardoned as well as others, and I believe thou art the Son of God, and the Lamb of God that came to take away sin.

So Hebrews 5:9: 'He is become the author of eternal salvation to all that obey him.' Will Christ give eternal life to all that obey him? I have too long stood out against thee, Lord. I now lay down the weapons of my defiance, and say 'Here I am; what wilt thou have me to do?'

1.2 *To whom God offereth this mercy.* To every creature: 'Go ye into all the world and preach the gospel to every creature' (Mark 16:15). And am not I in the rank of creatures? But to whom especially? To 'the weary and heavy laden' (Matt. 11:28). To them that are lost: 'I am not come to call the righteous, but sinners to repentance' (Matt. 9:13). To such as have most feeling of their sins. I have a burden too heavy for me to bear; since Christ calleth me, I will come to him for ease.

1.3 *Who is it that calleth*: Christ, who is able, willing, and faithful. Able; for all authority and power is given to him in heaven and earth (Matt. 28:18); 'All judgment is given the Son' (John 5:22). They said to the blind man, 'Be of good comfort; arise, he calleth thee' (Mark 10:49). The 'he' here is the One who hath the disposal of every man's eternal state. And willing he is: 'Not willing that any should perish, but that all should come to repentance' (2 Pet. 3:9); if you will believe him on his call: 'I have no pleasure in the death of the wicked, but that the wicked turn from his way and live' (Ezek. 33:11). And you have God's truth for it: 'He that magnified his word above all his name' (Ps. 138:2). Now take him at his word; nay, we have this oath: 'That by two immutable things, in which it was impossible for God to lie, we might have strong consolation' (Heb. 6:18). His word was enough; but since he hath added his oath, what contumely [insult] do you do him to refuse his offers! 'He that believeth not God, hath made him a liar' (1 John 5:10).

2. *Wait for God's power to settle your hearts upon these grounds*: Faith is his gift (Eph. 2:8); and 'To you it is given on the behalf of Christ to believe in him' (Phil. 1:29). And he worketh it: 'Looking unto Jesus, the author and finisher of our faith' (Heb. 12:2). Without him it cannot be done: 'No man can come unto me except the Father, which hath send me, draw him' (John 6:44). And this by his almighty power: 'And what is the exceeding greatness of his power to us-ward who believe, according to the working of his mighty power' (Eph. 1:19).

3. *Look not for a transient act*; that his Spirit should work upon us as a stranger, but dwell in us as an inhabitant. After believing, the Spirit cometh to dwell in us and work in us, as a pledge and earnest of eternal life: 'After ye believed, ye were sealed with that Holy Spirit of promise, which is the earnest of our inheritance' (Eph. 1:13, 14). He remaineth constantly, and flitteth not, but taketh up a fixed and unmovable habitation, not as a wayfaring man for a night: 'Know ye not that your body is the temple of the Holy Ghost that is in you?' (1 Cor. 6:19). He dwelleth there not as an inmate or underling, but as lord of the house, and is worshipped and reverenced there. This is the great evidence: 'Hereby we know that we dwell in him, and he in us, because he hath given us of his Spirit' (1 John 4:13). Magnificent words! Who may entitle themselves to such a privilege? They that have the Spirit, not to come upon them at times, but to remain there as a principle of life:

INTRODUCTION

'Whosoever drinketh of the water that I shall give him, shall never thirst; but the water that I shall give him shall be in him a well of water springing up into everlasting life' (John 4:14). It shall quench his thirst after [for] vanity and earthly delights, and make them tasteless; they not only get a draught, but the Spirit of Christ is as a fountain to make this grace enduring in itself and in its effects. It is not a stream or a pond, that may be dried up; but a well, and a springing well, and maketh us fruitful in all well-doing; yea, at length [in the end] it becomes an ocean.

4. *Look for the effects of it.* If you have such a life begun in you as the life of faith, then you will have:

4.1 *Spiritual senses, taste and feeling*: 'If so be ye have tasted that the Lord is gracious' (1 Peter 2:3); and Psalm 119:103: 'How sweet are thy words unto my taste! yea sweeter than honey to my mouth!' You will relish spiritual things, which to others have no savour; then promises begin to be savoury [attractive] and to rejoice the heart, when others are no more moved with them than with common histories. You will be sensible [aware] of good and evil suitable to that life [which] you have; more sensible of sin than any affliction: 'Oh wretched man that I am! who shall deliver me from this body of death?' (Rom. 7:24). More sensible of God's hiding his face. It was as a sword in David's bones (Ps. 42:10). More sensible of providence: Thou hast stricken them, but they have not grieved' (Jer. 5:3).

4.2 *Spiritual affections, being dead to sin and the world, and alive to God*: 'Now we have received, not the spirit of the world, but the spirit which is of God, that we might know the things which are freely given to us of God' (1 Cor. 2:12);

desiring to be with Christ (Phil. 1:23); and having an heart set on things above (Col. 3:1).

4.3 *You have spiritual strength*: 'We are his workmanship, created in Christ Jesus to good works, which God hath before ordained that we should walk in them' (Eph. 2:10); and 'I can do all things through Christ that strengtheneth me' (Phil. 4:13).

Secondly, *Improve this life to a cheerful walking with God in a course of obedience*. To this end:

1. *Meditate on the promises*: 'Godliness is profitable to all things, and hath the promise of this life and that which is to come' (1 Tim. 4:8); and Psalm 84:11: 'He is a sun and shield; the LORD will give grace and glory, and no good thing will he withhold from them that walk uprightly'; and Psalm 34:9: 'There is no want to them that fear him'; and Romans 8:28: 'All things work together for good to them that love God.' We shall have whatever is expedient to bring us safely to heaven. God hath made promise of more than we could ask or think: protection from all evil, a comfortable supply of all blessings, temporal, spiritual, and eternal. Consult with these promises: 'Thy testimonies also are my delight and my counsellors' (Ps. 119:24); 'Walk about Zion, and go round about her; tell the towers thereof; mark ye well her bulwarks, consider her palaces' (Ps. 48:12, 13).

2. *Set not your right at the throne of grace*. There the promises are put in suit [to be asked of God]: 'Let us come with boldness to the throne of grace, that we may obtain mercy, and find grace to help in the time of need' (Heb. 4:16). Promises are given us, not only to plead with ourselves, but to put them in suit, and plead them with God.

3. *What is wanting in the creature, see it made up in God.* That is living by faith: 'He that dwelleth in the secret place of the Most High shall abide under the shadow of the Almighty' (Ps. 91:1); 'Having nothing, yet possessing all things' (2 Cor. 6:10). In every strait do this: make God all in all: 'Because thou hast made the LORD which is my refuge, even the Most High, thy habitation' (Ps. 91:9). This is not a senseless stupidity, but a lively exercise of faith.

4. *Counterbalance things like this*: set God against the creature: 'Fear not them which kill the body, but are not able to kill the soul; but rather fear him who is able to destroy both body and soul in hell' (Matt. 10:28).

Set the covenant against providence [that is, do not go by what you see but by what God says]: 'When I thought to know this, it was too painful for me, until I went into the sanctuary of God, then understood I their end' (Ps. 73:16, 17).

Set things eternal against things temporal: 'I reckon that the sufferings of this present time are not worthy to be compared to the glory which shall be revealed in us' (Rom. 8:18,) So 2 Corinthians 4:18: 'While we look not to the things that are seen, but to the things which are not seen are eternal.' Set the use and profit of afflictions against the present smart [pain] of them: 'Now no chastening for the present seemeth to be joyous, but grievous, nevertheless afterwards it yieldeth the peaceful fruit of righteousness unto them which are exercised thereby' (Heb. 12:11). All trouble [to the believer] cometh from not right sorting and comparing things: seeking that on earth which is only to be had in heaven, and seeking that in the creature which is only to be had in God, and looking for that from self which is only to be found in Christ, and seeking that in the law which is only to be had in the gospel.

1

The Life of Faith and Justification

Now I come particularly to treat of the life of faith; let us see how this life of faith is exercised and put forth. The life of faith may be considered either:

First, with respect to its object, the promises of the new covenant; as our justification, sanctification, the supplies of the present life, or everlasting blessedness.

Secondly, with respect to its trials, or the opposite evils that seem to infringe the comfort of these promises; as deep afflictions, great temptations from the devil, the world, and the flesh.

Thirdly, with respect to its effects, as holy duties and the exercises of grace. As with respect to the ordinances by which it is fed and increased, as the word, prayer, and sacraments. And the duties of charity, of public and private relations, as to the honouring God in our generation or in our callings.

First, To begin with the life of faith as to justification, or those promises wherein Jesus Christ and his righteousness is offered to us for the pardon of our sins and our acceptance with God. Here I shall do three things:

1. Prove that justification is one main or chief part of the life of faith.
2. I shall show you how we live by faith, or what is the work of faith in order to justification.
3. What we must do that we may so live.

1. That justification is a main part of the life of faith

1. It is included in the expression, as it is applied and expounded by the apostle. I shall bring two places [quote two texts]: 'For therein is the righteousness of God revealed from faith to faith; as it is written, The just shall live by faith' (Rom. 1:17). He giveth a reason why he was not ashamed of the gospel, because of that great blessing revealed in it, the righteousness of God; that righteousness which God imputeth without the works of the law, by virtue of which we are accepted with God; and how doth he prove it, that there is such a righteousness of God? He proves it by that saying, 'It is written, The just shall live by faith.' The other place is Galatians 3:11: 'But that no man is justified by the law in the sight of God is evident; for the just shall live by faith.' So that we cannot handle living by faith, unless we take in the branch [aspect].

2. There are many promises made of this benefit. Now it is faith that receives the promises: 'I will forgive their iniquities, and will remember their sins no more' (Jer. 31:34). Now, wherever there is a promise there must be faith; for as the law, with its threatenings to the fallen creature, is the strength of sin (1 Corinthians 15:56, 'The strength of sin is the law'), so the gospel, with its promises, is the strength of faith; and therefore our comfort thence ariseth. If we would live and act comfortably on the promises, we must live by faith.

3. Because there is a daily use of faith for the continuance and the increase of the sense of this benefit, therefore this is a great part of our living by faith. It is said in Romans 1:17 that 'the righteousness of God is revealed from faith to faith'; from first to last, from one degree of faith to another; not only the beginning of justification is by faith, but the whole progress of it. Many think that this kind of faith on God's free justifying grace in Christ is necessary to give comfort at our first conversion, as if then it had finished all it should or could be; at other times faith is laid aside, unless we fall into some notable decay, or may be plunged into some deep doubts, or fall into some great offences, or be exercised with some sharp afflictions, when we are forced, as it were, to begin all again. Oh no! there is a continual use of it; for faith is not only obstetrix, the midwife to the new birth, but nutrix, the continual nurse and cherisher of it, and of all the comfort and peace that we have thereby; it is still necessary to our communion with God, and continuance and increase of comfort; for as soon as we take off our eye from Christ, the remembrance of former sins will trouble and vex the conscience. And therefore we must every day humble ourselves for sin, and seek pardon, and cry out with David: 'Enter not into judgment with thy servant, O Lord, for in thy sight no man living shall be justified' (Ps. 143:2). Neither the greatest sinner, nor the best saint, either before regeneration nor after. There is no other way of maintaining comfort but by flying to grace, and seeking favour and pardon according to the new covenant. Yea, those evils mentioned before, as notable decays, great offences, deep doubts, sharp afflictions, they are all occasioned by the discontinuance of the exercise of faith, and because we do not cherish a warm sense of the love of God in pardoning our sins for Christ's sake. The more we keep the grounds of comfort in constant view, the more uniform and even we are in our course of walking with God; as fire once kindled is better kept burning than when it is often quenched [put out] and often kindled again. And therefore this should be our daily task, to live by faith with respect to justification.

4. Because this is the ground of all other parts of the life of grace, take it either for the life of sanctification, or our present living to God, or take it for the life of glory, or our living with God hereafter.

4.1 It is the way to the life of sanctification, or our present living to God and converse with him. Take it either for his influence upon us, or our duty to him; for Christ lives in us by his Spirit, and we live in him by faith, as Christ liveth in us by the Spirit, and we receive his influences. The holy God will have no communication with us while the guilt of sin standeth in the way: 'Your iniquities have separated between you and your God, and your sins have hid his face from you' (Isa. 59:2). Sin, and nothing but sin, doth raise up a wall of separation between us and God; poverty, sickness and reproaches are evils, but none of these shall separate us from the love of God in Christ. But sin breedeth a strangeness [estrangement] between us and God; so that till sin be taken away, there can be no communion between God and us, and we are cut off from the blessed influences by which the life of grace might be maintained: 'Your sins have withheld good things from you' (Jer. 5:25). Till sin be removed, the cock [tap] is, as it were, turned, and the course [flow] of the blessing stopped. But take it for our acting grace, and living to God; we are careless of our duty unless we be interested in this benefit; the more love we have to God, the more sense we have of his pardoning mercy: 'There is forgiveness with thee, that thou mayest be feared' (Ps. 130:4). We can neither have hand nor heart to serve and obey God without this encouragement; the more we believe him to be gracious, the more we fear to offend him; and by experience none are so cautious of sin, as those that seek after daily pardon. Who is more careful not to run into new arrearages [debts] than he that desireth to have his debts paid and cancelled and blotted out? So they that are solicitous to make even reckoning [have their sins all pardoned] between

God and their souls are most cautious that they do not interrupt their peace with new sins; and whilst they plead so hard for mercy, they have the greater sense of duty and obedience. So that we cannot carry on the life of sanctification without looking after the life of justification.

4.2 For the life of glorification, we are incapable of that, and cannot hope for it with any comfort till we are pardoned: 'The free gift came upon all to justification of life' (Rom. 5:18). Life follows justification, as death doth condemnation. All men by nature are dead in law, and by justification this sentence is repealed, and men are invested with a new right to everlasting life: 'He that heareth my word, and believeth on him that sent me, hath everlasting life, and shall not come into condemnation, but is passed from death to life' (John 5:24). They are not only put into a living condition by sanctification, but have a sentence of life passed in their favour, for justification is a sentence of life; so that if we would live the life of grace, or hope for the life of glory, we must be put into a condition for both by justification.

2. What doth faith do with respect to this benefit?
1. It assents to the truth of the gospel offering this benefit to us, and causeth the soul to be fully persuaded that God is appeased in Christ with all those that cast themselves upon his grace, and seek God's favour in and through him. This is the work of faith, to believe that it is the good pleasure of God revealed in the gospel to pardon and justify all them that do believe in Christ: 'This is a faithful saying, and worthy of all acceptation, that Christ Jesus came into the world to save sinners' (1 Tim. 1:15). Assent goeth before pursuit; first we must believe that this is a true and faithful saying, before we shall look after such a benefit from him. So Hebrews 11:13:

'They saw the promises afar off, and were persuaded of them, and embraced them.' When a man can be persuaded that it is even so, that God will be gracious to them that believe in Christ, then he will hug and embrace these precious promises. And Ephesians 1:13: 'In whom also ye trusted, after ye heard the word of truth, the gospel of your salvation.' You see under what notion they took up the gospel; first we must be persuaded that the gospel is a word of truth, before we stir either hand or foot to look after any benefit by it. I do the rather press this, because the justification of a sinner is the great secret revealed in the gospel, which was hidden from nature till God revealed it. And therefore doth the apostle so operously [carefully] prove the truth of this in the three first chapters to the Romans. His argument stands thus, that all the world being guilty before God, they must either be condemned and that will not consist with the mercy and goodness of God, or there must be some way of justifying a sinner; but his wisdom hath found out that way: 'But now the righteousness of God without the law is manifested, being witnessed by the law and the prophets; even the righteousness of God, which is by faith of Jesus Christ unto all and upon all that believe; for there is no difference: for all have sinned, and come short of the glory of God' (Rom. 3:21-23). All the world was at a loss about this, how the sinful creature should get rid of the dread of God's justice; for every man that hath a conscience knoweth that it implies a law, and a law implies a judgment for the breach of the law. Now all the world was afraid of this judgment of God; the apostle proves this both of Jews and Gentiles. Now faith looks into the gospel; and therefore, whenever the gospel is spoken of, and this mystery of justification, you shall find there is some addition or note of assurance added, that it is a word of truth, or a faithful saying, because the heart of man is apt to doubt of the truth of this glorious mystery.

2. Faith exciteth us to put in for this benefit of being justified in God's sight. We fell from God by unbelief, and nothing exciteth us to seek after God again but faith. Now this faith doth by setting before us, on the one side, our own sinful and cursed estate; and on the other side, God's promises of pardon and free justification by Christ. In Hebrews 6:18, the heirs of promise are described to be those 'who fly [flee] for refuge to lay hold upon the hope that is set before them.' This is a plain allusion to the avenger of blood and the city of refuge. A man that had killed another, if he were taken before he came to the city of refuge, was to be put to death; now such a man, when his life was concerned, would fly to the city of refuge. Such are the heirs of promise; they run to take hold of the hope set before them; the curses of the law drive them, and the promises of the gospel draw and allure them; and we never put in seriously and in good earnest for a share in this benefit till faith stirreth up active and lively thoughts about these things, and then we never leave till we see ourselves interested therein.

2.1 Faith worketh in us a serious thoughtfulness about our sinful and cursed estate; that driveth us to Christ, as the other consideration draweth us, and sweetly allureth us to close with him. The first consideration of our sinful and cursed estate driveth us out of ourselves, when we consider how 'all the world is become guilty before God' (Rom. 3:9); and liable to the curse, 'As many as are of the works of the law, are under a curse' (Gal. 3:10); that we are 'children of wrath' (Eph. 2:3); that this curse is no slight one; that it is an eternal separation from God, and being cast out with the devil and his angels into everlasting fire. Now, when this is represented by faith, the sinner beginneth to 'flee from the wrath to come' (Matt. 3:7), which otherwise is looked upon but as a fable and vain scarecrow. Sense and natural reason cannot judge aright either of its own misery, or of the way or recovery from it. But faith, improving the scriptures, shuts up the sinner, that he hath no evasion, nor way of escape: 'The scripture hath concluded all under sin' (Gal. 3:22); shut them up as in a prison, as the word signifieth. This is the work of faith. Conscience will tell men of a law, and a law of a judge and a judgment-day, and that he doth not stand upon sound terms with this judge, that he dareth not seriously to think of death and the world to come, without horror and amazement; but faith, working upon scripture, doth make him more distinctly to understand it, and to be most sensibly affected with it: 'The people of Nineveh believed God, and proclaimed a fast, and put on sackcloth, from the greatest of them to the least of them' (Jon. 3:5). There is a faith required to believe the threatenings of the law, as well as the promises of the gospel, to convince men of their cursed estate by nature, without which it is not effectual.

2.2 It draweth us to close with [trust in] Christ by the promises of pardon. It spreadeth before the soul all the melting offers of the word, and his invitations of sinners to return to him; such as that in Isaiah 55:7: 'Let the wicked forsake his way, and the unrighteous man his thoughts; and let him return unto the LORD, and he will have mercy on him; and to our God, for he will abundantly pardon him.' And he prays us to be reconciled to him: 'Now then we are ambassadors for Christ, as though God did beseech you by us; we pray you in Christ's stead, be ye reconciled to God' (2 Cor. 5:20). And shall all this be spoken in vain? 'We beseech you, receive not the grace of God in vain' (2 Cor. 6:1). Shall all the sweet offers of grace in the gospel be as dry chips or withered flowers to me? This makes a poor distressed creature to stir up himself, to believe if this be certain, that God is not willing that any should perish, but rather that they should repent, and be converted, and healed.

And hath he made such a general offer, that I am sure that I am contained under it? Why shall I hang back and not come to him for pardon, and wait for his grace? I am condemned already, and shall I pull upon myself new woes, by despising God's mercy so freely offered to sinners? Shall my unbelieving heart draw back when God inviteth me to come to him? What did Peter mean when he said in Acts 10:43: 'To him give all the prophets witness, that through his name whosoever believeth on him should receive the remission of sins'? Wherefore did Christ send abroad his apostles with the glad tidings of salvation in their mouths? 'And that repentance and remission of sins should be preached in his name among all nations' (Luke 24:47). What is said 1 John 2:1, 2? 'If any man sin, we have an advocate with the Father, Jesus Christ the righteous; and he is the propitiation for our sins.' Surely God did not intend to flatter and delude his creature with a vain hope, nor to entice and court him into a fool's paradise; certainly he is in earnest in what he saith. I need mercy, and he hath promised to give it; I thirst after it, and he will give it me, for he is faithful; therefore let me see what God will do for my poor soul.

2.3 It directeth us to use the means which God hath appointed; namely, to humble ourselves before God, and to sue out [plead for] this blessing: 'Lord, be merciful to me a sinner' (Luke 18:13); and 'If we confess our sins, he is faithful and just to forgive us our sins' (1 John 1:9). It is a great part of faith to put God's bonds in suit [plead God's promises]: 'I am merciful; only acknowledge thine iniquity' (Jer. 3:12, 13). This is God's prescribed course, and we must use it in faith; he cannot be offended with that which himself commandeth, nor deny what he hath promised. Doth not he command thee thus to come into his presence, yea, beseech thee? And why art thou afraid? Hath he not said, that if we cast ourselves at his feet with brokenness of heart, confessing our sins, he will forgive them, and cast them into the depths of the sea? Refusal of means argueth despair; therefore go and plead the promises with him, and urge him upon his own word.

2.4 The work of faith is to make application; not only to see that sin may be pardoned, and how, but that our sins are or shall be pardoned for Christ's sake. There are degrees in this application; sometimes God's children apply promises in the humbling way, and creep in at the backdoor of a promise: 'Christ came into the world to save sinners, of whom I am chief' (1 Tim. 1:15). There I can put in for a share; I am sure I am sinner enough, if Christ came to save sinners. They put their mouths in the dust, yet look up because there is hope. And sometimes they express their confidence for the future; though they are not persuaded of their good estate at present, yet they hope they shall at length be pardoned and accepted: 'As for our transgressions, thou shalt purge them away' (Ps. 65:3). He can and will do it. So Micah 7:19: 'He will turn again, he will have compassion on us, he will subdue our iniquities; thou wilt cast all their sins into the depth of the sea.' At other times they express their confidence of pardon as an act past: 'Thou forgavest the iniquity of my transgression' (Ps. 32:5); and 'Thou hast cast all my sins behind thy back' (Isa. 38:17). To say so is an act of experience of a sinner now justified by faith; and though every self-condemned sinner cannot thus apply his pardon, nor thus lay hold upon this benefit, and apply it to himself, yet he should endeavour it.

2.5 It is a work of faith to wait the Lord's leisure, though comfort doth not succeed and flow as soon as we would have it. You must not throw up all, as if God were beholden to you [obliged to you], or at your beck and command. As soon as you have used the means, you must be satisfied and contented with his word till the promise be made good. Many give the lie to God when they find not at first what they hope for; but we must be satisfied with God's word till it be made good to us: 'In the way of thy judgments we have waited for thee; the desire of our souls is to thy name, and to the remembrance of thee' (Isa. 26:8). Whatever desires we have after comfort and the enjoyment of this benefit, we must be contented to tarry the Lord's leisure; though we be not answered, his word is sure; though we do not presently feel the comfort and effect of it, his word is gone forth in truth. 'I shall yet praise him for the help of his countenance' (Ps. 42:5). There may be a grant where there is no sense of it. We do not live by sense or actual comfort, but by faith.

3. What must we do that we may so live and set faith a-work?

To this end and purpose directions are several, according to the different state and posture of the soul. As for instance, if the heart be sluggish, and your desires cold and dull towards this benefit, then there is one course to be taken; but if the heart be comfortless and dejected, then there is another course to be taken; and then, if you find your hearts too slight in the work of pardon, and you make a small matter of it, another course must be taken.

3.1 *If the heart be sluggish, and your desires cold and faint*, and you cannot be earnest in the pursuit of so considerable a blessing, then you must quicken and awaken the heart by considering the danger on the one side, and the profit and utility on the other.

(i) *The danger of security* [complacency], or not prizing of a pardon, and of the comforts of a justified estate. Let me tell you, it is as ill [bad] a sign as can be when a man esteemeth not of pardon, or of God as a pardoner. It argues deep carnality and security in those that were never acquainted with God, and a strange witchery and fascination of soul [as if they had fallen under a spell] that is fallen upon them that are regenerate, and will in time cause them to smart for it.

(a) It argues deep carnality and security in those that are strangers to God. For this is the first notion that rendereth God amiable, because he is so necessary to our consciences. Guilt and bondage are natural to us; but it is a sign men are hardened in fleshy delights when they have lost their actual sense of this, and are past feeling. Therefore consider how dangerous their condition is, if God puts the bond of the old covenant in suit, and requires their souls at their hands: 'Thou fool, this night thy soul shall be required of thee' (Luke 12:20). O, miserable they! when they shall be haled to hell, and the direful sentence shall be executed upon them, 'Go ye cursed, into everlasting fire.' And consider, there is nothing but the slender thread of a frail life between you and this; and how soon is that fretted asunder [worn away]!

(b) Or if this evil should fall upon God's own children, a man that is spiritual, that he be listless and careless about his justification, it argueth some sore spiritual disease, and it will cost them much bitterness before they get rid of it; and if the Lord meaneth them mercy, they shall again taste the vinegar and gall of the law's curse; and it is nothing to you to be liable to the wrath of God?

(ii) *To awaken the sluggish heart*, consider the utility and profit of it; if once you could clear up your justification, what sweet, happy lives might you lead! 'Blessed is the man whose transgression is forgiven, whose sin is covered' (Ps. 32:1, 2). In the original it is, Oh! the blessedness of the man. But the blessedness of such a man is more fully set forth by the apostle: 'Being justified by faith, we have peace with God through Christ' (Rom. 5:1-5).

(a) The very first-fruit of it is *peace with God*. Sin had broken off all friendship and amity, and procured enmity between God and the creature; and is it nothing to have God for an enemy, and to be in dread of him every day, lest he should bend his bow, and shoot his arrows at us? If all the world were at war with you, and God were your friend, you were happy men; but if all the world be at peace with you, and God your enemy, you may be soon miserable enough. Till you can make a wall between you and heaven, you can never be secured. All that is truly good and truly evil dependeth upon our peace and war with God. I shall illustrate it by that place in Acts 12:20: 'The men of Tyre and Sidon had offended Herod, but they made Blastus their friend, and desired terms of peace, because their country was nourished by the king's country.' Tyre was an island on the sea, and could not subsist without supplies from the king's country. Certainly we cannot subsist a moment without God, and therefore it concerns us to be at peace with him. Till we are justified, we are utterly out of God's favour, and liable to his indignation; but when we are justified, there is an everlasting peace concluded between us and him.

(b) *Free and cheerful access to God*. So it follows: 'By whom also we have access by faith into this grace wherein we stand' (Rom. 5:2). If you have any dealings with God, and know anything of this kind of traffic [prayer], you will be glad to hear how you may think of him comfortably, and come to him with assurance of welcome. Wicked men cannot endure to think of God; their thoughts of God are a torment to them. But to have a free access to him upon all occasions, and cheerfully to lay forth your whole case to him, is not this a blessed privilege? To be in like favour with God as Joseph was with

Pharaoh, to ask and have, and be assured of welcome whenever we come to him, that, ask what we will, we may be assured it shall be done for us.

(c) *Joy of salvation.* So it follows, 'We rejoice in hope of the glory of God' (Rom. 5:2). Though our estate be poor and contemptible in the world, yet there is glory enough provided for us in heaven; and seemeth it a light thing to be the King's son-in-law? To be heirs to God, and co-heirs with Christ? Well may we forego all transitory preferments, which worldlings so magnify, for these hopes. Well may we despise the shame, and endure the cross, if such a glory be set before us. To have a glimpse of it here in the world is very comfortable; the very preparatives are sweet. Now this glory is but revealed to us, and our hearts have received a little of it; what will it be when this glory shall be revealed in us? 'I reckon that the offerings of this present life are not worthy to be compared with the glory that shall be revealed in us' (Rom. 8:18), when we shall have glorious bodies, glorious souls, glorious company, glorious sights, glorious exercises. Nothing can be desired here to be compared with it.

(d) *Comfort in afflictions*: 'We glory in tribulations' (Rom. 5:3). Some make it an enlargement of what he had said before: 'We rejoice in the hope of the glory of God'; and tribulation doth not weaken this joy. And others interpret it, 'We do not only rejoice in the glory of God, which is the best part of our estate, but, which is much more admirable, we find matter of rejoicing in our afflictions and tribulations, which are the worst part of our estate: 'My brethren, count it all joy when you fall into divers temptations, knowing this, that the trial of your faith worketh patience' (Jas. 1:2, 3); and 'I take pleasure in my infirmities, in reproaches, in necessities, in persecutions, in distresses for Christ's sake; for when I am weak, then I am strong' (2 Cor. 12:10). Those things that are so unwelcome to the natural man, that spoil all his rejoicings, they are the matter of a godly man's rejoicing. A wicked man will part with God, and Christ, and peace and conscience, and the hopes of eternal life, and all to shun the cross; but such is the temper of a godly man that he cleaves closest to God in the worst of times, and finds matter of rejoicing in the worst condition.

(e) And this is backed with a reason, which makes a fifth benefit: *a further increase of patience*: 'Tribulation worketh patience' (Rom. 5:3). Grace is so welcome that they are willing to exchange outward comforts for inward grace. By nature we are like untamed heifers, very unruly at first yoking, but after a while we come quietly to bear the yoke: 'Knowing this, that the trial of your faith worketh patience' (Jas. 1:3). At first a new cart squeaks and creaks, but afterwards goes away silently under a heavy load. At first we complain the cross is very heavy and burdensome to us, but afterwards we quietly submit to the will of God.

(f) And this bringeth on another benefit, and that is *experience*: 'And patience, experience' (Rom. 5:4). We learn many sweet experiences of God by afflictions. A man that hath been at sea, and endured storms and tempests in foul weather, is not so easily dismayed nor afraid of the rolling of every wave and the tossing of the ship as one that never hath been at sea. So when we have had experiences of God and ourselves, and of the course and issues of things, we are not so easily discouraged as others are.

(g) *The hopes of everlasting life are increased and strengthened*, and so we are the better able to bear the inconveniences of the present life. If a poor man be robbed of twenty or thirty shillings, no wonder if he cry and take on, because he hath no more to help himself with; but now, if a rich man be robbed of such a sum, he is not much troubled, because he hath more at home. So a man that is justified by

THE LIFE OF FAITH AND JUSTIFICATION

faith, and hath assurance of the favour of God, he can comfortably bear up against all the troubles and crosses he meets with in his way to heaven.

(h) *Sweet tastes of God's fatherly love*: 'The love of God is shed abroad in their hearts' (Rom. 8:5). God hath his comforts for his afflicted ones. His people are never so assured of his love as then, for there is love seen in their afflictions. Oh! it is no mean thing to live by faith. Come and see; will you be a stranger to all this?

3.2 *If the heart be dejected and comfortless:*

(i) Consider what ground we have to hope for pardoning mercy from the Lord.

Partly from *the nature of God*: 'Who is a God like unto thee, that pardoneth iniquity, and passeth by the transgression of the remnant of his heritage? He retaineth not his anger for ever, because he delighteth in mercy' (Mic. 7:18). Never did we take more pleasure in the acting and committing of sin, than he in the pardon of it. No man is backward to do that he delights in. God's purpose is to make his grace glorious: 'To the praise of the glory of his grace' (Eph. 1:6). He everlastingly purposed this within himself, and, as a wise God, accordingly hath suited means to that end. His justice cannot complain, having received full satisfaction in Christ, who paid the full price: 'Being justified freely by his grace, through the redemption that is in Jesus Christ' (Rom. 2:24); 'Therefore will the LORD wait, that he may be gracious unto you; and therefore will he be exalted, that he may have mercy upon you: for the LORD is a God of judgment: blessed are all they that wait for him' (Isa. 30:18).

And partly from *the name of God*: 'Who is among you that feareth the LORD, that obeyeth the voice of his servant, that walketh in darkness, and hath no light? Let him trust in the name of the LORD, and stay himself upon his God' (Isa. 50:10). Now the name of God is at large described: 'The LORD, the LORD God, gracious and merciful, long-suffering, and abundant in goodness and truth ...' (Exod. 34:6, 7). These names are given to God that we may take notice of his graciousness, and that we might stay our hearts on the name of God. Why doth he invite us with such earnestness? He that waiteth upon thee when thou wentest astray, will he not pardon thee when thou returnest?

(ii) *To answer all discouragements*: What is it that keepeth thee off? Thy unworthiness? That indeed maketh us the fitter objects of his grace and mercy. God giveth this freely without worth; for grace doth all things gratis [freely]; without any worth in us. If we were not unworthy, how should God show forth the riches of his grace? And when we have a sense for it, and a heart broken for it, it is a good preparation to the work. If any man were bitten with the fiery serpent, he might look up to the brazen serpent and be healed. It matters not what the disease be, if Christ is the physician. If any feel sin a burden, and do truly and earnestly desire to be eased of it, he is invited to ask, that by asking he may receive: 'Come unto me, all ye that are weary and heavy laden, and I will give you rest' (Matt. 11:28). Oh! but, saith the poor troubled, humbled soul, I am not humbled enough. Remember, it is not the deepness of the wound, but the soundness of the cure that we should look after. If you are weary of sin, and unfeignedly willing to part with it, and everything that would separate between you and Christ; if Christ be precious to you, and you are willing to give up yourselves to the Lord's use, the end is wrought [aim is achieved]. Humiliation is not required for itself, but for these ends.

THE LIFE OF FAITH AND JUSTIFICATION

3.3 If you have cause to suspect that your hearts are too slight in the estimation of pardon, and that you make too easy a work of it, and pass it over too lightly, then consider:

(i) *What it cost the Lord Jesus Christ to bring it about.* It cost the precious blood of the Son of God: 'Being justified by his blood, we shall be saved from wrath through him' (Rom. 5:9). Did it cost the blood of Christ to procure it, and shall I have slight and mean thoughts of it? The apostle did urge this as an argument to press ministers to have a care of the flock, because 'they were purchased by the blood of God' (Acts 20:28). It was not an imposter that died at Jerusalem, but the very Son of God. By the same argument we may press men to look after justification by faith in Christ, because Christ hath purchased it with his precious blood.

(ii) *It is a work wherein eternity is concerned*; justification is but that act done privately which you expect God will do publicly at the last day: 'Repent, that your sins may be blotted out, when the times of refreshment shall come from the presence of the Lord' (Acts 3:19). Your act is nothing, unless it be ratified by Christ at that day. Everywhere the scripture puts us upon this task. Boldness at his coming is made the test of the strength of our faith: 'And now, little children, abide in him, that when he shall appear, we may have confidence, and may not be ashamed before him at his coming' (1 John 2:18).

(iii) If you go about this work with brokenness of heart, you cannot be slightly [half-hearted] in it, if indeed the heart be wounded for sin; there is no dallying with broken bones; surely such [people] will mind [really desire] a cure.

(iv) Take heed of an heart purposing to continue in sin: 'Let is draw near with a true heart, in full assurance of faith, having our hearts sprinkled from an evil conscience, and our bodies washed with pure water' (Heb. 10:22). If you have fallen into sin, you must humble your souls deeply before the Lord: 'Take away all iniquity, and receive us graciously' (Hos. 14:2, 3). You will not beg that God would take away this plague, but take away this sin. Your prayer will be, not that you may not sin again, but that you may be more serious than ever you have been, that you may have a new heart, and that sin may never live in you more.

2

The Life of Faith and Sanctification

Secondly, I shall speak of the life of faith as it respects sanctification. This also must be regarded.

1. These two must not be severed; justification and sanctification must carefully be distinguished, but not separated: 'Such were some of you, but you are washed, but you are justified, but you are sanctified, in the name of the Lord Jesus, and by the Spirit of our God' (1 Cor. 6:11); 'Who of God is made unto us wisdom, and righteousness, and sanctification and redemption' (1 Cor. 1:30). They always go together in God's dispensations [dealings]: 'If we confess our sins, he is faithful and just to forgive us our sins, and to cleanse us from all unrighteousness' (1 John 1:9).

Sin is considerable in the guilt and filth of it, as it renders us obnoxious to God's justice, or as it tainteth our faculties and actions, and indisposeth us for his service; and both must be done away. Christ came to do both; he was sent into the world to restore God's image in us; but the image of God consisteth in the participation of holiness, as well as the participation of blessedness. For God, who is happy and blessed, is also holy and good; the filth of sin is opposite to holiness, and the guilt of it to blessedness. So that Christ must restore but half the image of God, or he must give us this double benefit; if he should free us from the guilt of sin, and give us impunity [pardon] without holiness, then *bonum physicum*, a natural good, would be consistent with *malum morale*, a moral evil; and if he should give us sanctification, and deny impunity [pardon], the highest natural evil would be consistent with a moral good. And therefore he giveth us both; he justifies that he may sanctify, and he sanctifies that he may glorify.

It is not consistent with God's wisdom and justice to give us pardon and let us alone in our sins, nor with his wisdom and mercy to give us holiness without pardon. Yea, justification (if it could be said to be alone) would only give us freedom from hell; but without sanctification we should remain unqualified for heaven or the life of glory. It is true, such an one would be exempted from *poena sensus*, the punishment of sense, but not from *poena damni*, the punishment of loss. We cannot enjoy heaven, nor see the face of God till we are sanctified: 'For without holiness no man shall see the Lord' (Heb. 12:14).

And therefore both must go together; and wounded souls, those that are affected with their condition, look for both; as he that hath his leg broken desireth not only to be eased of the present pain, but to have it set right again. Those that are sensible of their condition before God would not only have their sins pardoned, but would have their hearts enlarged to serve God with more cheerfulness and freedom. Well, then, both are desired by a broken heart, and Christ is made both to us: 'He is made of God unto us wisdom, and righteousness, and sanctification and redemption' (1 Cor. 1:30). And it is his work not only to turn away God's wrath, but to turn us from our sins: 'Unto you first, God having raised up his Son Jesus, sent him to bless you, in turning away every one of you from his iniquities' (Acts 3:26); and Acts 5:31: 'Him hath God exalted with his right hand, to be a Prince, and a Saviour, to give repentance to Israel, and forgiveness of sins.' Now, what Christ giveth, faith receiveth; and therefore if we would live by faith, faith must be exercised in this great blessing of sanctification.

THE LIFE OF FAITH AND SANCTIFICATION

2. Sanctification is the greatest benefit of the two, if you compare them together. Many will cry up [speak well of] justification, but neglect sanctification, but preposterously; for, of the two, sanctification is the greater privilege. I prove it thus:

2.1 Justification freeth us a *malo naturali* [natural evil], from pain and suffering; but sanctification a *malo moralo*, from sin and pollution; for sin is worse than misery, and holiness is to be preferred before impunity; and therefore justification, which frees us from misery, is not so great a privilege as sanctification, which frees us from sin. And the saints here have chosen the greatest sufferings rather than the least sins; as Moses 'chose rather to suffer affliction with the people of God, than to enjoy the pleasures of sin for a season' (Heb. 11:25). And God hateth sin as being against his very nature. God may inflict punishment, but he cannot infuse sin. Now, as misery and punishment is less than sin, so justification, which frees us from misery and punishment, is not so great a blessing as sanctification, which frees us from sin.

2.2 The end must needs be more noble than the means. Now, sanctification is the end of justification, as glorification is the end of sanctification. God's end in justifying is to sanctify, or to promote holiness; and therefore Christ is said to 'purge our conscience from dead works, that we may serve the living God' (Heb. 9:14); and 'He hath delivered us out of the hands of our enemies, that we might serve him without fear, in holiness and righteousness before him all the days of our lives' (Luke 1:74, 75). Therefore we are purged from the sentence of death, therefore we are delivered from the curse of the law, and from hell. Certainly the end must needs be more noble than the means: now the wisdom of God hath appointed justification to promote sanctification.

2.3 This is that which is nearest to the life of glory. Ends are more noble, as they are nearest the last end. Justification is the pledge of the life of glory; but sanctification is not only a pledge, but a beginning. Indeed justification is *causa removens prohibens* [a cause which removes what prevents]; it takes away that which hinders, namely, guilt, or the sentence of condemnation, which is that which hinders our entering into glory; but sanctification beginneth that life which is perfected in glory, and differeth from it as an infant from a man. When we know God perfectly, and love God perfectly, then our happiness is completed, and not till then. Complete holiness and conformity to God is the great thing that God designeth; and therefore, the more of that the more are we advanced towards eternal happiness: 'Christ loved the church, and gave himself for it, that he might sanctify and cleanse it with the washing of water by the word, that he might present it to himself a glorious church, not having spot or wrinkle, or any such thing; but that it should be holy and without blemish' (Eph. 5:25-27). First he doth cleanse and sanctify, and then he doth perfect all in glory; when they are fully freed from all sin, then they are fully freed from all misery.

2.4 Real perfections are above relative [those affecting our relationship]. Sanctification is a real moral perfection, but justification is but a relative one; our state is changed by it, but not our hearts; that is done by this other privilege of sanctification. Real moral perfections make us like God: 'God is glorious in holiness' (Exod. 15:11); he counts that his highest and chiefest glory. Moral perfections exceed natural; and of all moral perfections, holiness is the greatest. It is better to be wise than to be strong, and to be holy than to be wise. Beasts have strength, and man hath reason, and the devils have cunning and knowledge; but angels are holy, and God is glorious in holiness; that is their perfection, and herein we most resemble God, in that which is his chiefest glory.

2.5 This is that which renders us most amiable in the eyes of God, and therefore it is the greatest privilege. Now God loveth us for holiness; he delighteth in it, as the reflex of his own image upon us; he doth not love us as pardoned, but as holy. We love him indeed for pardoning: 'She loved much, because much was forgiven her' (Luke 7:47); but God delights in the pure and upright. God is the first object of his own love: and next, 'the saints and excellent ones upon earth, in whom is his delight' (Ps. 16:3). So that though we love him for pardoning, yet he loveth us for holiness. There is *amor complacentiae* [love of complacency], as the scripture witnesseth, 'Such as are upright in their way are his delight' (Prov. 11:20).

2.6 God's interest and honour is to be preferred before our comfort and personal benefit. Justification, though it sets forth the glory of God's grace, yet it doth more immediately concern our comfort. In sanctification, besides our personal benefit, which is the perfection of our nature, God's honour and interest is concerned in our subjection to him; and this, besides the honour of his grace for our sanctification, springs only from grace, as our justification doth, and is the fruit of Christ's merits. Well, then, we need to look after this benefit, as well as justification, which is of such use and service to us, lest the main disease be left uncured.

3. It is a great part of the glory which God expecteth from us, to believe in him as the only Holy One of Israel, and the sanctifier of his people, viz., that he will sanctify our natures, and enable us to practice of that holiness which he requireth of us: 'I am the God that sanctifieth you' (Lev. 20:8); and 'I am the

LORD, your holy one' (Isa. 43:15); and 'Art not thou from everlasting, O LORD my God, my holy one?' (Hab. 1:12). He is not only our merciful one, to pardon us; but our holy one to sanctify us; and he taketh it to be a principal part of his honour and glory to be so.

4. It is needful to exercise faith upon this privilege of sanctification, that we may not be discouraged, and grow cold and negligent, when we find the difficulties of obedience. There is none that hath had to do with God and his own heart, but he finds strong oppositions, little prevailing against his lusts, and the work of God is often interrupted. Now if there were not promises to bear him up, he would throw off all as impossible, and be discouraged, that he should never bring his heart to any good purpose in the things of God. And therefore God hath undertaken in his promises, as sin is filthy, to cleanse and purge it out:

> 'Then will I sprinkle clean water upon you, and ye shall be clean; from all your filthiness and from all your idols will I cleanse you. A new heart also will I give you, and a new spirit will I put within you; and I will take away the stony hearty out of your flesh, and I will give you an heart of flesh. And I will put my Spirit within you, and cause you to walk in my statues, and ye shall keep my judgments and do them' (Ezek. 36:28-29).

And as there is strength in it, so he hath promised 'He will turn again, he will have compassion upon us, he will subdue our iniquities' (Mic. 7:19). A Christian may encourage himself in his God; he will help him. Our own strength is too weak to govern our hearts, to conquer our lusts, to defeat temptations; but God will do it for us: and therefore we should not give over all as a desperate case, but cheer up our hearts in the sense of God's love and help; though we can never hope to overcome sin in our own strength, yet God will do it for us.

THE LIFE OF FAITH AND SANCTIFICATION

My next business is to show how faith doth concur, or what influence it hath upon sanctification. I shall first speak of sanctification in general, then of the parts of it: mortification and vivification.

What influence it hath upon sanctification in general. I shall show you that in two distinctions. Sanctification may be considered as to its beginning, or as to its increase and progress.

As to *the beginning of sanctification*, what influence hath faith upon the first work? Certainly there is need of faith; for the first work falls under a promise: 'This is the covenant that I will make with the house of Israel after those days, saith the Lord; I will put my laws into their hands, and write them in their hearts' (Heb. 8:10). There are promises of grace, and promises to grace, that where he hath given grace, he will give more – absolute and conditional promises. Faith and the promises are correlatives. Now all the business [a Christian's concern] is to know what use we can make of these absolute promises of grace: the conditional promises point out what we must do; but as to the absolute promises what shall we do there?

1. These absolute promises show the power of God to all those who take hold of his covenant, and his [God's] willingness to make use of his power for their good; for God will use his power this way, so that we may come to him, and plead as the leper did, 'Lord, if thou wilt, thou canst make me clean' (Matt. 8:2). God can do it, and therefore there is some comfort; and we have to reason to despair, as if the work were impossible. So that what difficulties do arise, they should drive us to God to put these promises in suit [into prayer]. Though we do not know how it will succeed with us; though we have such sinful hearts, that we do not know which way they should be subdued, and our headstrong corruptions mortified; yet the Almighty, who hath promised it, is able to do it for us, as that place [text] showeth: 'With God all things are possible' (Mark 10:27). God can change our crooked, perverse hearts, and make them willing in the day of his power (Ps. 110:3).

2. These absolute promises encourage us to come to God, and set his power a-work by prayer; as Ephraim: 'Turn thou me, and I shall be turned; for thou art the LORD my God' (Jer. 31:18). Though Ephraim had a stubborn and rebellious heart, like a bullock unaccustomed to the yoke, yet he was encouraged to go to God because he was the Lord his God. These absolute promises may be pleaded in prayer.

3. These absolute promises engage us to wait upon God till they be accomplished. God hath undertaken to take away the old heart; so that we may say, as in Psalm 123:2, 'Behold, as the eyes of servants look unto the hand of their masters, and as the eyes of a maiden are unto the hand of her mistress, so our eyes wait upon the LORD our God, until that he have mercy upon us.' They engage us to persevere with diligence in the use of means, though we do not know what will come of it. So Proverbs 8:34: 'Blessed is the man that heareth me, watching daily at my gates, waiting at the posts of my doors.' Though it be long ere [before] God look upon us, long before we find any preparation towards this work, yet this engageth us to lie at the pool [like the man in John 5].

4. These absolute promises engage us to wait with hope, looking up still with confidence that he will accomplish the things promised. But you will say, 'What hope can a man have of the absolute promises?' There is this hope, that I am not excluded; that I as well as others am invited to take hold of God's cov-

THE LIFE OF FAITH AND SANCTIFICATION

enant; and there is the same favour shown to me that there is to all; and in some hopeful presage [omen], that God hath inclined my heart to look after [for] it; that I am weary of my sins, that I am troubled with my lusts, though it be but a natural weariness, because of the inconveniency of them; that I desire grace, though it be but a natural desire of ease and happiness; that, I pray, though it be but literally, and not spiritually: 'Take with you words, and turn unto the LORD, and say unto him, Take away all iniquity, and receive us graciously' (Hos. 14:2). It is well that there is some affection and natural fervency; we are in grace's way [in the way of grace], and lie more obvious [open to] to the Lord's grace.

But, most of all, there is this hope, that we have a general confidence of God's all-sufficiency; as the woman that had an issue of blood twelve years: 'And came behind Christ and touched the hem of his garment; for she said within herself, If I may but touch the hem of his garment, I shall be made whole' (Matt. 9:21). When all remedies fail, and we are still troubled and burdened with our lusts, yet we have this general propositional persuasion, that if we come to Christ, and get into him, we shall be the better for him; though we have tried many means, and have been nothing the better, but rather the worse, yet when we thus do, there is some hope. Thus these promises have their use; for God doth not only propound them to faith, but by them worketh faith: 'Whereby are given unto us exceeding great and precious promises, that by these you might be partakers of the divine nature, having escaped the corruption that is in the world through lust' (2 Pet. 1:4); enabling a graceless sinner to believe and apply the pardon, grace, and blessedness offered in them. So soon as a sinner gets grace to believe and apply them, the Lord worketh in the heart the things promised, and infuseth those divine qualities in which the life of grace consisteth.

5. There are many considerations as means which may uphold and encourage our hearts in waiting for this work of grace to be begun in us, and faith makes use of them. These are examples:

5.1 That many that have been as vile and obstinate against God, and as much hardened in a way of sin as we are, yet the promise hath taken hold of them. Men that have been bondslaves to the devil and their own lusts, yet they have been caught in their month [in God's time], and the Lord hath wrought upon them; as Zaccheus, who had formerly lived in a course of oppression (Luke 19:8, 9); Mary Magdalene, who had lived in whoredom[1] (Luke 7:37); and Saul, a persecutor and blasphemer, and an injurious person (1 Tim. 1:13). Instances and examples encourage faith as well as promises, for they are patterns of what God will do: 'For this cause I obtained mercy, that in me first Jesus Christ might show forth all long-suffering, for a pattern to them that should hereafter believe on him to life everlasting' (1 Tim. 1:16). These instances are as masterpieces of grace. As artists hang up their masterpieces in their shops to draw customers, so God sets forth these instances to show what he will do for poor returning sinners.

5.2 There is an encouragement that Christ hath purchased the spirit of grace for us, to promote this work in our hearts: 'For their sakes I sanctify myself, that they also might be sanctified by the truth' (John 17:19). He hath set apart himself as a sin-offering, that we might be sanctified; all the means of grace are sprinkled with the blood of Christ that promote and help on the work of grace in our hearts: 'He gave himself for the church, that he might sanctify and cleanse it with the washing of water by the word' (Eph. 5:26). Christ hath given himself as a sacrifice and offering to God, that we might come to duty not only in obedience, but in faith, and that we may with the

THE LIFE OF FAITH AND SANCTIFICATION

more comfort depend upon him in the use of the means of grace that he hath appointed.

5.3 He hath filled himself with all grace for the same end, that we might be filled with the abundance of that grace which is in him: 'He hath received gifts for men, yea, for the rebellious also, that the LORD God might dwell among them' (Ps. 68:18); not to keep them to himself alone, but to communicate them to us. So it is said, 'Of his fulness have we all received grace for grace' (John 1:16). There is a fountain of grace set up in our nature, that we might repair to him [Christ]. He is God that freely giveth life to all things, and he is God in our nature, that we might not think him strange to us.

Let us consider sanctification in its progress and increase; and there let us see what promises are made to faith, and what faith must do with these promises.

1. *Let us see what promises are made to faith.* And so it is a great relief and encouragement to poor creatures, that are troubled with the relics of sin and the remainders of corruption, to consider what is propounded to faith. Christ hath undertaken to subdue sin wholly, and to sanctify us throughout:

> And the very God of peace sanctify you wholly; and I pray God your whole spirit and soul and body may be preserved blameless to the coming of our Lord Jesus Christ. Faithful is he that calleth you, who also will do it (1 Thess. 5:23, 24).

The work is but begun, but God will carry it on to perfection:

> Being confident of this very thing, that he that hath begun a good work in you will perfect it unto the day of Jesus Christ (Phil. 1:6).

The same power that began will finish it. It was said of the foolish builder, that he began and could not make an end; but the work of grace hath its beginning, progress, and final consummation and accomplishment from God. And where God hath begun his work in any heart, it is a pledge that he will do more. And so the apostle propounds it as a precept [duty]: 'Let not sin reign in your mortal body, that ye should obey it in the lusts thereof' (Rom. 6:12); and after it is propounded as a promise, 'Sin shall not have dominion over you; for you are not under the law, but under grace' (verse 14). Well, then, these are the promises, so that if we would increase and grow up in this holiness intimated in the promises, we must increase in faith, and believe that Christ will be as good as his word.

2. *Let us see what faith must do as to these promises.*
2.1 The work of faith is to encourage us in our conflicts. We are many times wrestling with sin, and find it too hard for us; but then the believer should look up to the power of God engaged and assisting in this work, and so can triumph in victory before the battle. In outward cases the chance of war is uncertain, and that is a good caution, 'Let not him that puts on his harness boast as he that puts it off'; but it is not so in the spiritual warfare. Paul mingleth thanksgivings with his very groans (Rom. 7:24, 25). He complains and groans, 'O wretched man that I am! who shall deliver me from this body of death?' But he comfortably cheers up his heart in the next verse, 'I thank God through Jesus Christ our Lord'; that through the power of the Spirit of Christ he should be able to subdue the body of sin, which otherwise would carry him headlong to death and destruction. And the same Paul, when buffeted with a messenger of Satan, he prayed three times; he would fain have been rid of the temptation (2 Cor. 12:9). He knocked one, and again, and a third time, as Christ prayed thrice [in Gethsemane]; but all the answer he could get was, 'My grace is sufficient for thee.' When this is our case, that we are dis-

couraged in our resistance of sin, because our endeavours at first succeed not, the promise should bear up our hearts.

2.2 The work of faith is to encourage us to wait in the use of means for our growth and improvement; for God, that fulfilleth promises, fulfils them in his own way. Faith is not a devout sloth [idleness] and idle expectation; we must up and be doing, praying, hearing, meditating, debating these promises with ourselves, that this work may go on and prosper, until we come to the full [good] of our hopes. God hath greater things to do for us and by us. All increase is by God's blessing upon our labour and diligence, and so is the increase of grace too: 'For to every one that hath shall be given' (Luke 19:26); that is, he that tradeth, and improveth his talent well, shall have more; that which God hath given him, he shall find a great increase of it, if he use well what he hath received. And therefore Christians, that have these promises, are to labour after a great increase of grace, and to improve Christ to a further use: 'I am come that they might have life, and that they might have it more abundantly' (John 10:10). We should not only be living, but lively Christians; not only make a hard shift to get to heaven, but labour that grace may abound yet more and more, that an abundant entrance may be given to them into Christ's kingdom: 'Furthermore, we beseech you, brethren, that as ye have received of us how ye ought to walk, and to please God, so ye would abound more and more' (1 Thess. 4:1).

2.3 The office of faith [the way faith works] is to increase our confidence and enlarge our expectations, according to the extent of the promises; for the more we expect from Christ, the more we receive from him: 'Open thy mouth wide, and I will fill it' (Ps. 81:10). The larger thoughts we have of Christ's fulness and excellency, the more do we experience it in ourselves; if we would increase in love, and zeal, and patience, we must increase in faith. It is a preposterous care [concern] in many [Christians] to seek the growth of other graces when they do not seek the growth of faith. This is as if we did water the branches of the tree, and not the root.

I come now to speak of sanctification more particularly; namely, the two parts of it: mortification and vivification. Faith hath a notable influence upon both these.

As to mortification – the mortifying of fleshy lusts

The flesh is our great enemy; so the apostle telleth us: 'Abstain from fleshy lusts, which war against the soul' (1 Pet. 2:11). And therefore, unless, we mean to run the hazard of the loss of our souls, the flesh must be subdued, which is our great clog and hindrance in our way to heaven. But how doth the flesh prevail against us? Answer: The flesh prevaileth two ways; both are specified in James 1:14: 'Every man is tempted, when he is drawn away of his own lust, and enticed.' There are two words, sometimes we are drawn away by our own lusts: at other times we are enticed.

1. Sometimes we are drawn away by the flesh; it hurries men into sin by its violent motions: 'Every one turned to his course as the horse rusheth into the battle' (Jer. 8:6); like a headstrong horse, hearing the noise of the trumpet, his rider hath no command of him; so fleshy lusts puts reason out of the throne, that his affections cannot be governed; checks of conscience, restraints of the word, profession, resolutions, all bonds and cords are too weak to hold us to our duty; the flesh moves, and then we are carried away to fulfil the lust thereof.

2. It enticeth us by the pleasure and satisfaction that we expect in gratifying carnal nature, or by hope of mercy and re-

THE LIFE OF FAITH AND SANCTIFICATION

pentance after it is committed; or by some other means it deceiveth the sinner into rebellion against God. Now faith is of great use to purge us from these lusts; for it is said in Acts 15:9, 'Purifying their hearts by faith.' What doth faith do to purify our hearts and weaken our fleshy lusts?

2.1 It applieth the blood of Christ: 'The blood of Jesus Christ his Son cleanseth us from all sin' (1 John 1:7). Christ's blood cleanseth us, but so as [when] faith applieth it to us. Look, as water cleanseth and soap cleanseth, but both are applied by the hand of the laundress that washeth, so the blood of Christ cleanseth as it is applied by faith. We may look upon the blood of Christ as the price by which the Spirit was purchased to cleanse us from sin: 'Through sanctification of the Spirit, unto obedience and sprinkling of the blood of Jesus Christ' (1 Pet. 1:2). The blood of Christ is applied and received by faith, and so the heart is cleansed.

2.2 Faith purifies the heart, as it excites the new nature to break the force of fleshy lusts, and puts a rub [restraint] in our way: 'The spirit lusteth against the flesh' (Gal. 5:17). It stirs up the new nature to draw the mind another way: 'Whosoever is born of God doth not commit sin, for his seed remaineth in him, and he cannot sin, because he is born of God' (1 John 3:9). There are dislikes and counter-buffs arising from the new nature, that sin shall not carry it [make headway] so freely.

But how doth faith excite the new nature? Partly as it *presents the threatenings of the word*, when lusts are sturdy and will not be broken: 'If ye live after the flesh, ye shall die' (Rom. 8:13); and 'He that sows to the flesh, shall of the flesh reap corruption' (Gal. 6:8). Now these things being represented and realised by faith, it stops the career of sin. And partly by *representing the promises*: 'I beseech you as strangers and pilgrims, abstain from fleshy lusts' (1 Pet. 2:1). We are for another country, and shall we trouble and pester ourselves with anything that should hinder us in our journey heavenward? We expect a room [place] among the angels, and shall we live as slaves in the world? Thou art in the way to Canaan, and why art thou in love with the flesh-pots of Egypt? 'Having these promises, let us cleanse ourselves from all filthiness of flesh and spirit, perfecting holiness in the fear of God' (2 Cor. 7:1); and 'He that hath this hope in him, purifieth himself as God is pure' (1 John 3:3). Faith excites the new nature by fear and hope, by terrors and promises. And then partly as it *sets love a-work*: 'Faith worketh by love' (Gal. 5:6) and so begets an hatred of sin: 'Ye that love the LORD, hate evil' (Ps. 97:10). Partly as it *represents the great things Christ hath done for us*: 'Christ hath loved me, and gave himself for me.' Now, shall I sin against this God that sent his Son to die for me? All this is to prevent the act, and break the force of sin.

2.3 It improveth all the means instituted by Christ for the weakening of sin and the abating the corruption of our natures. It is said, 'He gave himself, that he might sanctify us by the washing of water through the word' (Eph. 5:26). Christ did not only die to sanctify us, but to sanctify us in such a way that we might receive grace by the institutions of the gospel, that the word and sacraments and prayer might stir us up to mortify sin.

Faith maketh use of the word: 'Wherewith shall a young man cleanse his way? By taking heed thereto according to thy word' (Ps. 119:9); and verse 11: 'Thy word have I hid in my heart, that I might not sin against thee.' By the word we learn wisdom and spiritual counsel; that makes us discern the wiles of sin, that we may not be enticed nor enslaved by it: 'Now ye are clean, through the word which I have spoken unto you' (John 15:3). It is the work of the Spirit and faith to apply the efficacy of Christ's blood for the cleansing of sinners; but the word hath its use, as a glass [mirror] to discover [reveal] sin, and as it quickens [enlivens] us by new arguments to work it out. He that daily makes use of the word of God, and doth attend with conscience upon the ordinances, he hath some new consideration or other suggested to him to work out sin.

So for the sacraments. For baptism, 'Ye are dead'; therefore 'mortify your members' (Col. 3:2, compared with verse 5). You that are baptized have engaged yourselves to be mortifying sin, and to employ the strength of Christ for the subduing of it. So for the Lord's Supper: 'Purge out therefore the old leaven, that ye may be a new lump, as ye are unleavened; for even Christ our passover is sacrificed for us. Therefore let us keep the feast, not with the old leaven, neither with the leaven of malice and wickedness, but with the unleavened bread of sincerity and truth' (1 Cor. 5:7, 8). The remembering and applying Christ's death is a means to weaken sin yet more and more.

The word and sacraments are the means by which Christ applieth the virtue of his death. In the word we have the charter, the promise and grant of Christ and all his benefits from God unto every one that will receive him [Christ]; but in the sacraments there is a seal annexed to this grant, whereby we are confirmed in this grant; and by every new act we oblige ourselves to mortify sin more and more.

And then (lastly) prayer; for faith sets the soul a-praying that God would create in us 'a clean heart' (Ps. 51:10) and so makes good his promise of washing and cleansing us from all sin.

For vivification

By nature we are dead in trespasses and sins: 'You hath he quickened, who were dead in trespasses and sins' (Eph. 2:1). Christ came to help us out of this estate, and purchase grace and life for us, and to work it in us: 'I am come that they might have life' (John 10:10). And therefore he is called 'the Prince of life' (Acts 3:15), because he is the principal cause of it, and 'a quickening spirit' (1 Cor. 15:45). A spirit from his better part, his godhead, and a quickening or life-making spirit, because of the effects of his power on the hearts of believers; for we can never live to God till we are quickened by him.

And he is said to be our life: 'When Christ, who is our life, shall appear ...' (Col. 3:4). He is our life, not only *meritorie* [meritoriously], as he hath purchased life for us; but effective [effectually], as he works it in us. There is not only an everlasting merit, but a constant influence, for our life is a fruit of his: 'Because I live, ye shall live also' (John 14:19). Then we begin to live unto God, when by faith we are united to Christ: 'God hath given to us eternal life, and this life is in his Son' (1 John 5:11). It is in Christ, and we have it by virtue of our union with him.

And then faith doth continually derive vital influences from Christ for the supporting and maintaining and strengthening this spiritual life in us, as the branches have their sap and influence conveyed to them from the root: 'He that abideth in me, and I in him, the same bringeth forth much fruit; for without me ye can do nothing' (John 15:5). And as members of the body have strength and sensation by their union to the head: 'He is head over all things to the church, which is his body, the fulness of him that filleth all in all' (Eph. 1:22, 23). Here then is the use of faith, to look up to Christ, and depend upon him for the constant supplies of spiritual strength, to enable to the operations of the spiritual life: 'I can do all things through Christ that strengtheneth me' (Phil. 4:13). But the influence of faith on the particular operations of the spiritual life will be handled hereafter.

3

The Life of Faith and Glorification

Next, the life of faith, as it respects glorification, or the promises of eternal life; And here I shall show you:
  1. That this is a necessary part of the life of faith.
  2. What are the acts of faith with respect to this life.
  3. How we may bring our hearts so to live.

1. We cannot exclude this from being a branch of the life of faith; and that for these reasons:

1. Because eternal life is one of the principal objects of faith; and it is the first motive that inviteth us to hearken after the things of God. The apostle telleth us in Hebrews 11:6: 'He that cometh to God must believe that God is, and that he is a rewarder of them that diligently seek him.' He that would have anything to do with God musts be persuaded of his being and of his bounty. In the choosing of a religion, we look after a right object, whom to worship, and a fit reward; for that induceth us, and maketh up the match between our hearts and that object. Now God, that knoweth the heart of man, and what wards will fit the lock, doth accordingly deal with us; as he propounds himself as the first cause, and highest being, to be reverenced and worshipped by us, so also as the chiefest good, to be enjoyed by us in an everlasting state of blessedness. All the doctrines of the Christian faith tend to establish this hope in us; and therefore the salvation of our souls is called 'the end of our faith' (1 Pet. 1:9). This is the main blessing that faith waiteth for; all our believing, waiting, working, striving, is to this end: so John 20:31: 'These things are written, that ye might believe that Jesus is the Christ, the Son of God, and that believing, ye might have life through his name.' All this is written in the gospel is to establish faith in Christ the Messiah, and that in order to eternal life. This is the upshot of all, that we might have a true and well-grounded hope of eternal life.

2. Because this is always matter of faith, never of sense, in this world: 'For we walk by faith, and not by sight' (2 Cor. 5:7). Other privileges propounded in the promises are sometimes matter of sense; as sanctification and the comforts of this world; but this life and blessedness which is to come, and is hid with Christ in God, is always matter of faith, and never of sense, unless it be of spiritual sense, which is nothing but the result of faith, or some foretastes of blessedness to come, when we are firmly persuaded of the certainty of it.

3. This is that which indeed puts life and strength into us, and that which mainly constitutes the difference between us and others; and therefore, if there be such a thing as life spiritual, as certainly there is, it is fed and maintained by reflecting upon everlasting happiness, and the interests of the world to come:

> For which cause we faint not; but though our outward man perish, yet the inward man is renewed day by day. For our light affliction, which is but for a moment, worketh for us a far more exceeding and eternal weight of glory. While we look not at the things which are seen, but at the things which are not seen; for the things which are seen are temporal, but the things which are not seen are eternal (2 Cor. 4:16-18).

There is an outward man and an inward man, or the animal life and the spiritual and divine life. The animal life is that which is supported, cherished and maintained by the comforts and delights of the present world; as lands, honours and pleasures;

and when they are out of sight, they are in darkness that have nothing else to live upon, and are at a loss, and dead while they seem to live.

But now the spiritual and divine life is supported by the comforts and delights of the world to come, and they that live by faith live [as it were] in heaven, and have an anchor within the veil. And therefore, when we believe this, another spirit cometh upon us, and there is such a life and strength derived into our heart, that we bear up with joy and courage, when the outward and animal life is exposed to the greatest difficulties and decays; for we are for another world. And therefore we are said to live by faith, because it apprehends those great and glorious things which are kept for us in heaven. Yea, as soon as the spiritual life is begun in us, it presently worketh this way: 'Who hath begotten us to a lively hope' (1 Pet. 1:3). It is the immediate effect of the new life, which is given in regeneration; and by this the heart is kept up, till all that God hath promised be brought about. This is the staff and stay of the [believer's] spirit.

4. We need press this part of living by faith, because, whatever men pretend, eternal life is little believed in the world. The most part, even of those that live in the common light of Christianity, are purblind [totally blind], and 'cannot see afar off' (2 Pet. 1:9), or look beyond the grave. God's own children have many doubtful thoughts, not such a clear and firm persuasion of things to come, but that it needeth to be increased more and more. The apostle prayeth for the converted Ephesians: 'That the eyes of their understandings may be enlightened, that they may know what is the hope of their calling, and the riches of the glory of his inheritance in the saints' (Eph. 1:18); that is, that they might more clearly see and firmly believe those good things which they should enjoy in heaven. Alas!

We are so taken up with trifles and childish toys, that our faith is very weak about those excellent blessings. But I shall give you some evidences that these great and excellent blessings are little believed.

4.1 Because we are far more swayed with temporal advantages, than we are with the promise of eternal blessings. These blessings are more excellent and glorious in their natures, more certain in their duration: 'Whereby are given unto us exceeding great and precious promises, that by these we might be partakers of the divine nature' (2 Pet. 1:4). And yet they have less influence upon it than perishing vanities. What should be the reason? Who would prefer a cottage before a palace? A lease for a year before an inheritance? There is no compare [comparison] between the things themselves, but we are not equally persuaded of things to come, and things in hand, and of a present enjoyment. As in a pair of scales, though the weights be equal, yet, if the balances be not equal, a thing of less weight will weigh down a greater. Cyprian bringeth in the devil vaunting against Christ: 'I did not die and shed my blood for them; I had not heaven to bestow upon them, nor eternal happiness to reward them; I only propounded a carnal satisfaction in the pleasures of sin, that are but for a season, which, when they are gone, it is as nothing; and yet among all thy pensioners, O Christ! show me one that is so ready to follow thee as they are to follow me.' If we had faith, we would say with Paul, 'For I reckon that the sufferings of this present time are not worthy to be compared with the glory that shall be revealed in us' (Rom. 8:18); and as Moses, 'Esteeming the reproach of Christ greater riches than the treasures of Egypt; for he had respect to the recompense of reward' (Heb. 11:26). But alas! how many are there that pretend to believe as Christians, and yet a little profit or pleasure in the world is

THE LIFE OF FAITH AND GLORIFICATION 73

enough to sway with [influence] them, to run the hazard and forfeiture of all their hopes in the world to come.

4.2 Surely men do not believe [in] heaven, because they are so little affected with [have so little love for] it. If a beggar were adopted into the succession of a crown, he would please himself in thinking of the honour, and happiness and delights of the royal estate; or, to put a more likely supposition, if any poor man did understand that some great inheritance were bequeathed to him, he would often think of it, rejoice therein, long to go and see it, and take possession of it. But there is a promise of eternal life left us in the gospel of being heirs with God, and co-heirs with Christ; and who puts in for a share, thinketh of it, rejoiceth in the hopes of it, longs for it, taketh hold of this eternal life? Certainly if we were persuaded of these things, we would embrace them: 'These all died in faith, not having received the promises, but having seen them afar off, and were persuaded of them, and embraced them' (Heb. 11:13).

4.3 Because we do so little labour after it. For outward advantage, let it be certain or uncertain, men will endure great pains. If the things be certain, a man toileth hard all day for a small piece of money, for a shilling or two; do we seek heaven with the like earnestness? They that do believe will do so: 'Unto which promise our twelve tribes, instantly serving God night and day, hope to come' (Acts 26:7). Other do not. Or if the things be uncertain, as with merchants: how many hazards do they run? *Impiger extremos currit mercator ad Indos* [The eager merchants runs to the ends of the earth]. These are not uncertain; and why do *we* no more abound in the work of the Lord? 'Therefore, my beloved brethren, be ye steadfast and unmovable, always abounding in the work of the Lord, forasmuch as ye know that your labour is not in vain in the Lord' (1 Cor. 15:58).

4.4 Because we are contented with so slight assurance as to our title and interest: 'Give all diligence to make your calling and election sure' (2 Pet. 1:10). In matters of weight, men love great earnest [a firm guarantee], great assurance. Do we labour to make all so sure and clear as to heavenly things? 'Let us therefore fear, lest a promise being left us of entering into his rest, any of you should seem to come short of it' (Heb. 4:1). We should put it out of all question; as we should not come short, so we should not seem to give any appearance of coming short. Alas! Any fond presumption or slight hope serveth our turn [Many Christians, so called, take little trouble to make sure they really *are* saved].

4.5 The pretended strength of our faith about future recompenses doth in some measure show the weakness of it, and that it is but a slight and overly [exaggerated] apprehension. Most men will pretend to be able to trust God for their heavenly inheritance, and yet cannot trust God for their daily maintenance; they find it difficult to believe in temporals, and yet very easy in spirituals or eternals: what should be the reason? Heaven and things to come are greater mercies, and the way of bringing them about more difficult; and they are not so commonly dispensed by God as temporals are; and there lie more natural prejudices against these mercies when men are serious. What! Can you easily believe that you shall live, though you die? That your scattered dust shall be recollected and raised up into a beautiful and glorious body (John 11:25)? That a clod of earth shall shine as the stars?

What is more easily believed than this, that God will give you daily bread? The whole earth is full of his goodness, and

THE LIFE OF FAITH AND GLORIFICATION 75

God feedeth all his creatures, not a worm but is sustained by his providence; but he pardoneth but a few, saveth but a few, and blesseth but a few with spiritual blessings. But here is the mistake; bodily wants are more pressing, and faith is put there to a present exercise. Men are careless of their souls, and content themselves with some general desires of ease and hopes of eternal welfare; and therefore it is they say they find no difficulty in believing their salvation and eternal life. Eternal life is sought in jest, talked of as a plausible fancy; but worldly things are desired in good earnest.

4.6 Because we will venture so little upon our everlasting hopes. Where men have an expectation that will make adventures, for they know it will turn to a good account. God hath made many great and precious promises; he hath told us, 'Give alms, and you shall have treasure in heaven' (Luke 12:33). Leave anything for his sake, you shall have 'in the world to come eternal life' (Mark 10:30); 'Mortify the deeds of the body, and you shall live' (Rom. 8:13). Now, when we will not venture anything upon God's bond, it is a sign we do not count him a good paymaster, and so make him a liar in all his promises.

2. What is the work of faith with respect to this life of glory?

1. To assent firmly to the promises, that offer this eternal blessedness, and to convince the soul of the truth of what they offer. Assent needs to be strengthened, that we may believe more firmly. Foundation-stones can never be laid with care and exactness enough. Many hang between believing and unbelieving, neither assent to the truth of the promise, nor directly deny it. Though you do believe, believe it again, with more certainty and assurance of understanding. As when a picture waxeth old, we refresh the colours; so work up your hearts to a full assurance of the truth and certainty of these things. What is the great work of the gospel, but to establish our faith of eternal life? Here it is revealed to us: 'And hath brought life and immortality to light through the gospel' (2 Tim. 1:10). Here it is promised to us: 'This is the promise that he hath promised us, even eternal life' (1 John 2:25).

Why hath God made so many promises? What need had he to flatter and deceive us, to promise more than he will perform? He can strike us dead if we do not please him, and crush us easier than we can crush a moth or a worm. In all other parts of scripture God standeth to [is true to] his promises, even those of a present accomplishment, *et in ultimo non deficiet* [and he will not fail in the end]; surely he will not fail you at last, he is so faithful and punctual. The same God that gave the commands, which you find so powerful on your consciences, this same God gave the promises.

And God is willing to give us a pawn and pledge of these blessings promised in the joys of the Spirit: 'Who hath also sealed us, and given us the earnest of the Spirit in our hearts' (2 Cor. 1:22). It is not *donum*, a gift, but *pignus*, a pledge; and not only *pignus*, but *arrha*, an earnest: therefore work up faith to this assent. It is a notable assent that is described in Hebrews 11:1: 'Faith is the substance of things hoped for, and the evidence of things not seen'.

Faith is 'the substance of things hoped for'. Faith openeth a light into the other world; it is the perspective of the soul, by which we look within the veil. Faith hath an eagle-eye; it can see things at a distance, and pierce through all the mists and fogs that intercept the eyes of others. 'Abraham rejoiced to see Christ's day, and he saw it, and was glad' (John 8:56). And yet there were many successions of ages between Christ and Abraham, but he saw Christ with the eyes of faith. So the patriarchs saw things afar off by faith: 'These all died in faith,

THE LIFE OF FAITH AND GLORIFICATION

not having received the promises, but having seen them afar off' (Heb. 11:13). As the devil showed Christ the glory of the present world in a map and representation, so doth faith, which is the evidence of things not seen, represent to the soul the glory of the world to come in a map; they have a Pisgah-sight and view of heaven, so as they apprehend it as a real thing. Other men have but a general guess and tradition about heaven, a dream of Elysian field[2], or a surmise of happiness; but a believer has a sight of it by faith. As Stephen's eyes were opened, so are their eyes by the Spirit of wisdom and revelation. Others have an empty notion; they a real prospect.

The other expression is, that 'faith is the evidence of things not seen'; that is, it bringeth in the comfort of it to the soul. There is an intromission [entering in] of the object, as well as an extramission [going out] of thoughts.

How is it the substance? Things absent and to come, by the real persuasion and expectation of the believer, are made real and present with the soul, as if already enjoyed; and so faith defeateth sense, which prevaileth with us because of present temptation, dangers and delights. Faith is an anticipation of our blessedness, or a pre-occupation of our everlasting estate; as the air and winds carry the odours and sweet smells of Arabia into the neighbouring provinces, so faith, believing the promises causeth us to feel something of heaven in our own hearts. It is not a naked sight, but some foretaste and beginning of heaven.

2. There is need of faith to apply and make out your own interest; not only that there is such an estate, but such an estate reserved for you: 'Henceforth there is laid up for me a crown of righteousness' (2 Tim. 4:8); and 'And we know that if this earthly house of our tabernacle were dissolved, we have a building of God, an house not made with hands, eternal in the heavens' (2 Cor. 5:1); and 'That they may lay hold of eternal life' (1 Tim. 6:18). Faith hath an eye to see, and a hand to lay hold and claim it as your patrimony [inheritance]. It is comfortable with us when we can make out our own title and interest. Many catch [snatch] at it by a fond presumption, but they cannot hold it fast; it is an hope that will leave them ashamed. But upon clear and fair grounds we are enabled to apply and take home the promises, as so many conveyances of [titles to] our inheritance. There is a charter written with Christ's blood, sealed by the Spirit, and offered to us by God himself.

Now have you ever dealt with God about it, that you might make out your claim and title? I would not grate upon tender consciences, therefore, if you cannot apply it absolutely, because you have not assurance, yet the conditional offer should encourage you to work and wait, and deal with God about it: 'To them which, by patient continuing in well-doing, seek for glory, and honour, and immortality, eternal life' (Rom. 2:7). He will give it to all, as so to me; do God's work cheerfully, and continue with patience; be the more earnest to be such as may apply this general promise. And to help you to apply conditional promises, consider in whose disposal all this glory is, even in the disposal of a bounteous God, and a faithful and compassionate Saviour, who is ready to do good to thy poor soul: 'Looking for the mercy of our Lord Jesus Christ, to eternal life' (Jude 22).

3. There must be 'earnest expectation', that is the next work of faith, looking and longing for this blessed estate. I join both together, because the apostle speaks of the 'earnest expectation of the creature' (Rom. 8:18); the word signifieth the stretching out of the head of the creature, as Sisera's mother and her ladies looked through the lattice for the return of her son:

THE LIFE OF FAITH AND GLORIFICATION

'Looking for the blessed hope ...' (Tit. 2:13). Faith, having a promise looks to see the blessing a-coming in the midst of the labours and crosses of this world, not mounting up to heaven by fits [and starts]; but this is the posture of a gracious soul, to dwell upon the thoughts of God and the world to come, and to live in the constant expectation of it. The spiritual life is abated [declines] as this is abated:

> And not only they, but ourselves also, which have the first-fruits of the Spirit, even we ourselves groan within ourselves, waiting for the adoption, to wit, the redemption of our bodies (Rom. 8:23);

and

> If so be that being clothed, we shall not be found naked; for we that are in this tabernacle do groan, being burdened; not for that we would be unclothed, but clothed upon, that mortality may be swallowed up of life. Now he that hath wrought us for this selfsame thing is God, who also hath given to us the earnest of the Spirit (2 Cor. 5:3-5).

Can a man believe blessedness to come, and not long to enjoy it? No; the mind and heart will be set at work; a taste will make a man long for more. The little seeds in the earth will break through the clods to come to stalk and flower. As the clusters of Canaan put heart into the Israelites, and made them long to come to the possession of that good land; so the beginnings of the spiritual life will set you a-longing and groaning that you may be at home with God.

4. There is a waiting and tarrying the Lord's leisure with patience and perseverance, notwithstanding the distance of our hopes, and the difficulties of the present life: 'All the days of my appointed time I will wait till my change shall come' (Job 14:14). It is but a little while and we shall have full possession;

and the reason why we have not full possession sooner is, not because heaven is not ready for us, but we are not ready for it; for it was prepared by the decree and designation of God before the world was (Matt. 25:34); it was bought and purchased when Christ died (Heb. 4:15); and it is possessed by Christ in our name (John 14:2). Our nature is already in heaven, though not our bodies; we shall not sleep long in the dust; as soon as God's number is full. 'He that shall come, will come.'

Therefore tarry God's leisure. *Omne peccatum impatientiae est ascribendum*, saith Tertullian: 'Every sin is to be ascribed to impatience.' Men, like the prodigal, must have their portion presently: 'Father, give me the portion of goods that falleth to me' (Luke 15:12). They must have their good things in this life (Luke 16:25); they cannot be contented to wait for God: 'Ye have need of patience, that after ye have done the will of God ye may receive the promise' (Heb. 10:36). There is a time when God hath work for us to do in the world, to do and suffer his will. Whatever grace we can spare, we cannot spare patience: 'The good ground bringeth forth fruit with patience' (Luke 8:15). It endureth the plough, the harrow, the cold, the frost, that in due time the seed may spring up and flourish. So we, after a little patience, shall be received into an inheritance which our Father hath prepared, and Christ hath purchased for us.

5. The work of faith is to 'breed joy' in the hopes of this blessedness, and those tastes that we have of it. The apostle saith in Hebrews 3:6 that we are Christ's, 'if we hold fast the confidence, and the rejoicing of hope firm unto the end.' When we first believe in Christ, we do by hope take hold of the promised glory, and find a great deal of comfort and sweet encouragement therein. Now as this delight abateth in you, so doth the spiritual life. When in the outward life taste decayeth

THE LIFE OF FAITH AND GLORIFICATION

and is lost, so the animal life decays, and languishing and death come on. It was a comfortable thing to be working for heaven at first; it should be so still. Therefore keep up the rejoicing of your hope. It should do our hearts good, and make them leap within us for joy, every time we think what God hath provided for us in Christ. If worldly men cannot think of a little pelf [money], or any petty interest in the world without comfort, shall we think of the promises, and not be affected with them? To carnal men indeed, who have no spiritual appetite and savour, whose joy is intercepted and prepossessed by the vanities of the world, and delights of the flesh, the promises are as dry chips and withered flowers to them. But our hearts should leap for joy, because 'great is our reward in heaven' (Luke 6:23). What! Do we look for such great things, and no more rejoice in the Lord?

6. All this that faith doth is to be improved, to encourage us in a way of holiness, and to overcome the world.

6.1 To encourage and quicken us in the way of holiness. Hope sets all the wheels a-going; 'I press towards the mark for the prize of the high calling of God in Jesus Christ' (Phil. 3:14). We have no reason to begrudge God's service when we consider what wages he giveth. Certainly we do but talk of eternal life, we do not believe it, if we do no more in order thereunto. What labour and hazards do men expose themselves unto to be built one storey higher in the world. Now saith the apostle in 2 Corinthians 5:9: 'Wherefore we labour,' etc., we have an ambition to, – 'that whether present or absent, we may be accepted of him.' Surely did we believe things to come, our industry, and care, and thoughts, would be laid out more upon them. A man that spendeth all his time and care in repairing the house where he dwelleth for the present, but speaketh not of another house, nor sendeth any of his furniture thither, will you say such a man hath a mind or a thought to remove? A man that spendeth the strength of his cares on worldly things, surely he doth not believe [in] eternity! We work as we believe; if indeed we are persuaded of such an estate, why do we no more prepare for it?

6.2 To overcome the world. The world is the great let [restraint] and hindrance to the keeping of the commandments, and the victory that we have over the world is by faith (1 John 5:4); even that faith which doth counterbalance things temporal with things eternal.

(i) This giveth us victory over the afflictions and troubles that we meet with in the world; these are bitter to sense. Nature and grace teach us to have a feeling of our interests, and to be affected with God's providence when he maketh a breach upon them. We must neither slight the hand of God, nor faint under it: 'My son, despise not thou the chastening of the Lord, nor faint when thou art rebuked of him' (Heb. 12:5). There are extremes on both hands; when our Father is angry, we ought to lay it to heart, and to humble ourselves under his mighty hand; and yet we must not be like men without hope, altogether broken with difficulties.

Now what keepeth us from fainting, which is the other extreme? 'While we look, not to the things which are seen, but to the things which are not seen; for the things which are seen are temporal, but the things which are not seen are eternal' (2 Cor. 4:18). This must bear up our hearts against all sorrows: 'Ye took joyfully the spoiling of your goods, knowing in yourselves that you have in heaven a better and an enduring substance' (Heb. 10:34). Our happiness is not gone, and therefore we may bear it, not only patiently, but joyfully against all fears: 'Fear not, little flock, for it is your Father's pleasure to give you the kingdom' (Luke 12:32). We must look for hard-

THE LIFE OF FAITH AND GLORIFICATION

ships here in the world, but all will be made up when we get home to God. And therefore bear up with a generous confidence; if God will whip us forward, that we may mend [quicken] our pace to heaven, in the issue we shall have no cause to complain; if we have an anchor that 'entereth into that which is within the veil' (Heb. 6:19), this should keep us from being tossed and shaken, at least from being overwhelmed with the miseries of the present life. Nature will work, and have a feeling of these things, but grace must support us. The beauty and glory of the life of faith is never seen while all things succeed according to our heart's desire; we do not know whether we live upon God or the creature, the encouragements of earth or heaven, till we be reduced to some necessities. Paul said, 'None of these things move me, neither count I my life dear unto myself' (Acts 20:24).

(ii) That we may despise the pleasures, and profits, and honours of the world. Affectation [Desire for] of worldly greatness is the great expression of the animal life, but the spiritual life, or the life of faith, inclineth us to look after the happiness prepared for us by Christ. The great use and end of it is to keep us from aspiring after, and admiring great things here below; it quencheth the delights of the flesh, and begets [creates] a holy weanedness in us: 'They confessed themselves strangers and pilgrims here upon earth' (Heb. 11:13). To be carnally disposed argueth little faith. In a pipe, if there be a leak, the water gusheth out, and runneth not forward; our affections are diverted from things above, if they leak out to present comforts. They are the most active faculties; they cannot remain idle in the soul; either they leak out to present things, or they run forward to heaven and heavenly things; and if they do so, the esteem of the world is abated. And therefore this is the use of faith, to reject those fawning pleasures that would beguile us of those pleasures which are at God's right hand for evermore, those deceitful and vanishing honours that would bereave us of the glory, from whence we shall never be degraded.

3. How or what shall we do that faith may have its perfect work with respect to this life of glory?

1. Keep the eye of faith clear. When we are to see things at such a distance, and to see them with such affection, we had need of clear eyes. It is said in Hebrews 11:13: 'They saw them afar off.' The world is a very blinding thing: 'In whom the God of this world hath blinded the minds of them which believe not, lest the light of the glorious gospel of Christ, who is the image of God, should shine upon them' (2 Cor. 4:4). It is as dust cast into the eyes. A man may discourse of heaven, and talk at the same rate that other Christians do, but he hath not such a lively affective [affecting] sight of it. If we do not take heed of the suffusions [secret entrance] of lust and carnal affections, these brutify us insensibly, and make us judge of all things according to present interest, and as [make] mole-hills seem mountains.

2. Consider the harmoniousness of all the declarations that God hath made concerning eternal life, how they suit with the doctrine of God the Father, Son and Spirit.

2.1. As to God the Father, it suiteth his *decrees*; he hath determined to bestow everlasting happiness on some, to the praise of his glorious grace. 'Moreover whom he did predestinate, them he also called; and whom he called, them he also justified; and whom he justified, them he also glorified' (Rom. 8:30): 'God hath from the beginning chosen you to salvation, through sanctification of the Spirit and belief of the truth' (2 Thess. 2:13).

THE LIFE OF FAITH AND GLORIFICATION 85

And it suiteth to his *covenant*: God hath not only purposed out of his own love, but is under bonds [has promised] to give us eternal life. A covenant is God's solemn transaction with his subjects, and consists of precepts and laws invested with the sanction of promises and threatenings. His commands, all of them, imply such an estate, and some express it. All of them imply it; for they are work in order to wages, or a reward to be given, and it is not fit we should have our wages till our work be over. And some express it: 'Labour not for the meat which perisheth, but for that meat which endureth unto everlasting life, which the Son of Man shall give unto you' (John 6:27); and 'Lay not up for yourselves treasures upon earth, where moth and rust doth corrupt, and where thieves break through and steal. But lay up for yourselves treasures in heaven, where neither moth nor rust doth corrupt, and where thieves do not break through and steal' (Matt. 6:19, 20); and 'Strive to enter in at the strait gate' (Luke 13:24).

And so for his *promises*: 'He that believeth on me hath everlasting life' (John 6:47). If these [promises] were no such thing [did not have any reality], then all those commands and promises were given in vain, and would the wise and faithful God flatter us with lies?

And for his *threatenings*: 'He that believeth not, shall be damned' (Mark 16:16). And are all the threatenings of God a vain scarecrow?

2.2 Look upon the doctrines concerning Christ. Look upon Christ in his person, and states of humiliation and exaltation; his coming from heaven shows it; his going there again was to prepare a place for us; his sitting at the right hand of God is to promote our interest in heaven; his coming to judgment is to take us to himself.

Consider Christ in his *humiliation*: why was Christ

apparelled [clothed with] with our flesh, but that we might be clothed with his glory? If Christ were in the womb, and in the grave, why may not we be in heaven. It is more credible to believe a creature in heaven, than God in the grave.

And then for his *exaltation*: when he hath purchased a right and title, he went to heaven to prosecute and apply it. As the high priest went in to the holy of holies with the names of the twelve tribes upon his breast; so Jesus Christ is gone into heaven with the names of all the saints upon his breast.

And then consider his *benefits*: justification is our release from the curse, and sanctification is to fit us for God. All ordinances tend to this, to nourish in us hopes of everlasting life. The word [of scripture does so]: 'Hear, and your soul shall live' (Isa. 55:3). The Lord's supper [also] is food for our souls.

2.3 And then for the Spirit: his graces are life begun. Faith seeth it, love desireth it, hope looks for it: 'We, who have the first-fruits of the Spirit, groan within ourselves' (Rom. 8:23). The first-fruits show a harvest to come. And 2 Corinthians 1:22: 'Who hath sealed us, and given the earnest of the Spirit in our hearts.' Would God give us earnest, and not make good the whole bargain? Give us a taste to mock us, and no more? Is the whole scripture false, and a very [mere] fable? God's covenant a mockery? Christ's miracles a dream? And were the wisest men in the world fools?

3. Clear up [Make clear to yourself] your interest, otherwise your hope is but a fancy. The madman at Athens[3], was he ever the richer for saying all the ships were his that came into the harbour? 'The hope of the hypocrite shall perish' (Job 27:8). There must be an acceptance of the general covenant before there can be of particular promises. Did you ever choose God for yours, and give up yourselves to serve him? That you might be able to say, as David, 'I am thine, save me' (Ps. 119:94); and, 'Save thy servant, that putteth his trust in thee' (Ps. 86:2). A covenant supposeth both parties engaged; it doth not leave one bound [obliged] and the other at large [unobliged].

4. Exercise meditation, mind it more seriously, think of it oftener: 'Where your treasure is, there will your heart be also' (Matt. 6:21). Thoughts of heaven should be more familiar and sweet to us, and not lie [idly] by as neglected or forgotten. But alas! most are of the earth, and think of the earth and speak of the earth. Thoughts are the first-born of the soul, and if we did observe them, we should soon discover the temper of our souls. If they be set upon getting gain, carnal projects discover a carnal heart; as they in James 4:13: 'Go to now, ye that say, Today or tomorrow we will go into such a city, and continue there a year, and buy and sell, and get gain.' Or the rich fool in the gospel: 'This I will do, I will pull down my barns and build them bigger, and there will I bestow all my fruits and my goods' (Luke 12:18). These thoughts will engross all our time. But we should do as Abraham was bidden (Gen. 13:14), lift up our eyes, and take a view of the good land aforehand, and solace our souls with the contemplation of it.

5. Improve [Benefit from] the Lord's supper. When we are assembled there, and sit down at his table, it is a pledge of our 'sitting down with Abraham, Isaac, and Jacob, and drinking of the new wine in our Father's kingdom' (Matt. 26:29). When Christ instituted the Lord's supper, he discoursed to them of a kingdom: 'That ye may eat and drink at my table in my kingdom' (Luke 22:30). Here we come to think of that kingdom that cannot be moved, the purchase of Christ's blood, and to raise our affections to heaven and heavenly things, that we may be more confirmed in our hope. Here we come to taste of the cup of blessing which Christ hath prepared for us, even his own precious blood.

4

Living By Faith, as to the Promises and Blessings of the Present Life

Here I shall:

1. Show you the necessity of pressing this branch.

2. Give you some maxims and principles of faith, that have an influence upon this life.

3. Show what are the facts of faith, with reference hereunto.

4. How we shall bring our hearts thus to live.

1. There is a necessity of pressing [stressing] this part of the life of faith.

1. Because there are promises of [for] this kind of blessings, as well as of eternal blessings: 'Godliness is profitable to all things, having promise of the life that now is, and of that which is to come' (1 Tim. 4:8). It is not only profitable at the end of the journey, but by the way; when we come to die, it will be no grief of heart to us that we have been godly; for when we are about to set sail for eternity, then we shall receive the fruit of all our labours. Ay, but now where it seemeth to expose us to so many troubles, now when godliness is upon its trial and exercise, it is not left destitute and shiftless, it hath the promise of the life that now is, that is, of this life and the comforts of it, as health, wealth, favour, peace and safety.

Why hath God multiplied so many promises of this kind, but that we should trust him with our secular as well as our eternal concernments? 'First seek the kingdom of God, and the righteousness thereof, and all these things shall be added to you' (Matt. 6:33); that is, given in by way of overplus, cast into the bargain. He doth not say, Seek the world as hard as you can, and grace and glory shall be added unto you; but, Seek the kingdom of heaven, and then earthly things will not be stood upon [withheld], but cast in as paper and pack-thread [necessary accessories].

2. These are necessary for our maintainance during the time of our service: 'Your heavenly Father knoweth that you have need of these things' (Matt. 6:32). We consist of a body as well as a soul, and they have both their necessities. Now our heavenly Father knoweth our frame and make, and how serviceable these things are in our journey to heaven. Will he be so unkind as to deprive us of our necessary supports? Will any man send a message, and cut off the feet of them by whom he sendeth? Will God employ us in this world, and not give us a subsistence? Hezekiah took care that the Levites might have their portion, 'that they might be encouraged in the law of the Lord' (2 Chr. 31:4). Would God take care of our souls only, and as to the support of our bodies leave us to shift for ourselves? No, God is in covenant with the whole believer, his body as well as his soul; that is one ground and reason from which Christ proveth the resurrection of the body, because he is the God of Abraham: 'I am the God of Abraham, and the God of Isaac, and the God of Isaiah. God is not the God of the dead but of the living' (Matt. 22:32). And if he be Abraham's God, if he will be an infinite and eternal benefactor to Abraham, he must raise Abraham's body as well as his soul. And the mark of circumcision was in his flesh, as the water of baptism is sprinkled upon our bodies, therefore he will take care of the bodies of his saints.

And further, Christ purchased both body and soul. 'Ye are bought with a price, therefore glorify God in your body and in your spirit, which are God's' (1 Cor. 6:20). And this is not

LIVING BY FAITH

only an enforcement of our service, but doth also infer his care over us; for Christ will be tender of [protect] what he hath purchased. He did not only purchase us to service, but to a blessing. When God aimed at a new interest in us by redemption, it was such an interest as might be comfortable and beneficial to us; otherwise he had a full interest in us before, which we could not make void by sin; but it was such an interest as did oblige him to chastise us for our sins and rebellions. I speak this to show that Christ's purchase doth not only infer our duty to him, but his care of his people. And our bodies are united to Christ as well as our souls; as whole Christ is united to us in the mystical union, so whole we are united to Christ, bodies as well as souls. The outward man is a part of the mystical body as well as the soul, and accordingly the body is seized on by the Spirit, and used as his temple: 'He shall quicken our mortal bodies by his Spirit that dwelleth in us' (Rom. 8:11). It is true, these considerations are most concludant of [relevant as arguments to] the glorious estate of the body hereafter, but yet they do proportionably evidence God's care of the body for the present, as long as he will use us for his glory.

3. Without this part of the life of faith we should be encumbered with a world of destructive and distracting cares and troubles, which would much infringe the happiness of the spiritual life, and weaken the duty of it so that we could not attend the service of God with any freedom and cheerfulness. Therefore to ease us of this burden and clog, God would have us depend upon his care and all-sufficiency, and take no thought what we shall eat, and what we shall drink, and wherewithal we shall be clothed: 'Commit thy works unto the Lord, and thy thoughts shall be established' (Prov. 16:3). As the spiritual life is the most noble kind of life, so it is the most comfortable;

for God taketh all our cares upon himself, and easeth us of those anxious and tormenting thoughts which otherwise would eat out all our comfort and vigour. So 1 Peter 5:7: 'Casting all your care upon the Lord, who careth for you.' The care of duty, that is ours; but the care of events, that is God's work. Do your work, and as for success, and support, and maintenance, commit it to God's faithfulness and all-sufficiency, and submit it to his sovereign will. God would not have us overburdened and discouraged, and therefore he hath undertaken to do what is necessary for us.

4. There is a necessity of this part of the life of faith, because we are trained up to believe in God for eternal things, by waiting upon him for temporal. As we try how to swim in the shallow brooks before we venture into the deep waters, so before we trust Christ with our eternal estate we must try how we can trust him for temporal mercies. Experience confirms us in waiting upon God; his word is now put to a present proof and trial: 'The word of the Lord is tried' (Ps. 18:30). When you put it in suit [use it in prayer], you see God standeth to [is faithful to] his promises, and certainly he will not fail you in greater things. Faith would be but a notion, and we should never know the strength and comfort of it till we die, if there were not some present proof as to the intermediate promises [those which refer to this life], before we come to receive our final and consummate happiness. So that if we cleave not to the promises of God concerning temporal things, we shall adhere to the promises of eternal life with less certainty and assurance. Both promises flow from the same fountain of God's everlasting love, and are established in the same mediator, and received by the same faith. Yea, the promises of everlasting life are more spiritual, and farthest removed from sense, and are more difficult to be believed, and therefore first we must begin with easier things. And the Lord, by giving us outward things, would nourish our faith in things spiritual and heavenly; for when we see his care over us in these lesser things, we may be sure he will not neglect us in things of a greater moment. They are pledges to the soul that if God be so punctual in the lesser things, he will not fail in the greater.

5. This part of the life of faith is necessary, not only for the supplies of the outward man, but for the sanctifying of our outward condition, that it may not be a snare to us. If we have outward blessings, we should see them coming from the covenant; and so they are sweeter, and turn to a better use, when we receive them from the promise by faith. For it is said in 1 Timothy 1:4-5 that 'all creatures are sanctified by the word of God and prayer to them that believe and know the truth'. There is but a sour taste in these outward comforts, meat, apparel, riches, honour, favour of men; if they be not received and improved by faith, they soon taint and pervert the heart, and withdraw it from God and heavenly things. But when we see his love in them, and they come from our heavenly Father, they are much sweeter and better. To be carved to by a great person is counted as great a favour as affording the meal itself. To take these things out of [as from] God's hand, to see that he remembereth us, and sendeth in our provisions at every turn, this endeareth the mercy, and raiseth our thankfulness. So on the other hand, if we want [lack] these blessings, it keepeth us from a snare to find them in the covenant. Distrust in temporal promises hath driven the faithful servants of the Lord to many hard and dangerous shifts, and hath occasioned their falls more than other things. Abraham thought to save his life by a lie, and David by dissembling, when he could not trust God. And daily experience shows it, what a shrewd [powerful] temptation this is, even to the godly.

2. Let me give you some maxims, grounds, and principles of faith, which, being well digested, will help us to depend upon God for this kind of blessings.

1. That God hath the sole disposing of this life, and the interests thereof. It is by his providence that everything is ordered, when, where, and how we shall live: 'He hath determined aforehand the times, and the bounds of our habitation' (Acts 17:26). The land of Canaan was divided by lot, and the partage [division] thereof was merely by God's decision, and his governing the chance of the lot. So it is true of all other countries; a man hath not a foot of land more than God hath set out for him by his all-wise providence; so all the wealth that we enjoy: 'Thou shalt remember the Lord, who giveth thee power to get wealth' (Deut. 8:18). It is God that appointeth who shall be wise, and who shall be rich; who shall have great gifts of the mind, and who shall have great and ample revenues by the year. The world is not governed by blind chance, but by his wisdom.

However wealth cometh to us, it is from God as the First Cause, whether it come by donation, purchase, labour or inheritance. If it come by gift, the hearts of all men are in God's hand. He that sendeth the present is the giver, not the servant that bringeth it to us. It was God that made them able and willing. If it come by inheritance, it is by the providence of God that a man is born of rich parents, and not of beggars. He hath cast the world into hills and valleys, put some in a high and some in a low condition. If by our own labour and purchase, it is God [who] gives the ability, the skill to use it, and the success in our callings; the faculty, the use, the success, are all from God. He doth not leave second causes to their own work, as an idle spectator, but interposeth in all the affairs of the world.

So for favour and respect in the eyes of enemies, or people averse from us: 'When a man's ways please the Lord, he maketh his enemies to be at peace with him' (Prov. 16:7). There is a great deal of difference between pleasing God and pleasing men. Please men, and yet God may be angry with you, and blast all your happiness; but please the Lord, and that is the way to be at peace with men too. So for favour in the eyes of princes: 'Many seek the ruler's favour, but every man's judgment is from the Lord' (Prov. 29:26). Among the multitude of suitors and expectants, the event is as God casts it, who is the great judge and umpire in human affairs. And humble prayer doth more than ambitious affectation. Notwithstanding all our blowing, the fire will not burn without the Lord.

2. Another principle that hath an influence upon our faith is this, that God is ready and willing to distribute and dispense the blessings of this life to his people; for his fatherly providence is ever watching over them for good. He is liberal and open-handed to all his creatures, but much more to his saints. There is not a poor worm but feeleth the benefit of his providence; all the beasts of the field are provided for by him; he sendeth showers of rain and fruitful seasons, and filleth the lap of the earth with blessings, that they may have food; the fishes of the sea, that multiply in such fries and shoals, yet they are fed; the fishes, that are but mute creatures, that cannot so much as make a sound, yet have a voice to proclaim a bountiful God: 'Ask the beasts, and they shall tell thee; the fowls of the air, and they shall teach thee' (Job 12:7). God sends us to school to the beasts of the field. Go and ask them if God be not liberal and open-handed.

St. Luke instanceth in the ravens: 'Consider the ravens, that they neither sow nor reap, that have neither storehouse nor barns; yet God feedeth them. How much better are you than fowls?' (Luke 12:24). Shall a kite be more dear to him than a child? But why is the raven mentioned? Some say it is *animal cibi rapacissimum*, the most ravenous fowl; yet they are supplied. But there seems to be some other reason, for they are elsewhere instanced, in Job 38:41, 'Who provideth for the raven his food? When his young ones cry unto God, they wander for lack of meat; so Psalm 141:9, 'He giveth to the beast his food, and to the young ravens which cry.' Why should the raven be propounded as the great instance of providence? The naturalists tell us that the ravens expose their young ones as soon as they are hatched, but they are fed either by the dew of heaven, or by a worm that breeds in the nest, one way or other they are provided for.

Surely the Lord of hosts never overstocks his common; where he sends mouths, he will send supplies, but especially to his people: 'He taketh pleasure in the prosperity of his servants' (Ps. 35:27). The Lord delights to see his servants do well in the world; and it is no pleasing spectacle to him to see his people in a suffering, afflicted, ruinous condition. Oh then! Why do we not rouse up our faith? If God hath said he takes pleasure in the prosperity of his people, shall we not rouse up ourselves, and wait upon him for these outward things?

3. When God withholdeth any degree or measure of earthly blessings from us, it is for our good: 'O fear the Lord, ye his saints, for there is no want to them that fear him! They that fear the Lord shall not want any good thing' (Ps. 34:9). They may lack many things which others enjoy, but no good thing; so Psalm 84:11: 'The Lord will be a sun and shield, he will give grace and glory, and no good thing will he withhold from them that walk uprightly.' Good is not to be determined by our fancies and distempered appetites, but God's wisdom. We say this and that is good for us, as children desire green [unripe] fruit, but our Father saith not so. Every distemper [illness] affecteth the diet that feedeth it, but we must be contented with God's allowance, who is faithful to our souls, and taketh away those comforts that would hurt us, and eclipse our graces, and hinder us in serving him in the way he requireth. Every man's present portion given him by providence is best; not what we would have, but what God thinks good to give us. That is best which is fittest for us, not that which is largest. If you were to choose a shoe for your child's foot, you would not choose the largest, but the fittest. A garment too short will not cover our nakedness, and a garment too long will soon become a dangling dirty rag. Goliath's armour may be too big for little David.

4. The best way to get and keep worldly blessings is to get and keep in with God. This is a paradox to the world; a strict, severe holding to the truth is the ready way to expose us to dangers, and doth often bring great loss and inconveniency upon those that do so; and yet it is a truth for all that; for sin bringeth a curse, and righteousness a blessing: 'You shall walk in all the ways which the Lord your God has commanded you, that ye may live, and that it may be well with you, and that ye may prolong your days in the land which ye shall possess' (Deut. 5:33). Our reward lieth not in this world, and yet here God is not altogether wanting to [does not fail] his people.

5. There are certain qualifications wherein if we do excel we shall not want, as to instance in three, justice, mercy and honouring of parents. God, that is the patron of human societies, is so well pleased with the respects of inferiors to superiors, and with equity and justice between man and man, and relieving the indigent [needy], by which the world is kept in order and harmony, that if these things be in you, and abound, you shall not want the comforts of this life: 'He that followeth after righteousness and mercy findeth life, righteousness and honour' (Prov. 21:21). So Psalm 34:12-13: 'What man is he that desireth life, and loveth many days, that he may see good? Keep thy tongue from evil, and thy lips from speaking guile.'

But more particularly, see how the Lord doth reward justice: 'He that walketh righteously, and speaketh uprightly; he that despiseth the gain of oppression, and shaketh his hands from holding of bribes, that stoppeth his ears from hearing of blood, and shutteth his eyes from seeing of evil, he shall dwell on high, his place of defence shall be the munitions of rocks; bread shall be given him, his water shall be pure' (Isa. 33:15-16); and Proverbs 10:6: 'Blessings are upon the head of the just, but violence covereth the mouth of the wicked'; and Deuteronomy 15:15: 'But thou shalt have a perfect and just weight; a perfect and just measure shalt thou have, that thy days may be lengthened in the land which the Lord thy God giveth thee.'

So for mercy: he that watereth shall be watered himself: 'Cast thy bread upon the waters, and after many days thou shalt find it' (Ecc. 11:1); and Psalm 112:3: 'Wealth and riches are in his house, and his righteousness endureth for ever.' And this is spoken of the merciful man, for so the apostle doth apply it: 'And God is able to make all grace abound towards you, that ye, always having all-sufficiency in all things, may abound to every good work. As it is written, He hath dispersed abroad, he has given to the poor, his righteousness remains for ever' (2 Cor. 9:8-9). And so for honouring of parents: 'Honour thy father and mother, that thy days may be long in the land which the Lord the God giveth thee' (Exod. 20:12). This is the way to live well and long in the world. God having such a love to human society hath made these promises here specified.

LIVING BY FAITH

6. The more we trust God, and look to him in all things, the more we have; for trust is a very endearing, engaging thing: 'Because thou hast made the Lord which is my refuge, even the Most High thy habitation, there shall no evil befall thee, neither shall any plague come nigh thy dwelling' (Ps. 91:9-10). There shall no evil befall the man that always liveth upon God; so 2 Chronicles 20:20: 'Believe in the Lord your God, so shall you be established; believe his prophets, so shall you prosper'; and 1 Chronicles 5:20: 'They cried unto the Lord in the battle, and he was entreated of them, because they put their trust in him.' How did they trust? What! had they particular confidence in God? No, they committed the affair to him with submission to his will. Or had they a particular revelation? No, but they sought to God, and put the case into his hands.

7. That temporal promises, if they are not made good to our persons, are sometimes made good to our posterity. The blessing lieth asleep for a while, and then it riseth up to their seed, in great abundance: 'The just man walketh in his integrity, and his children are blessed, after him' (Prov. 20:7). It may be he is afflicted and greatly oppressed in the world, and maketh a hard shift to run through it; but then his children are provided for, and have a strange blessing of providence accompanying them; so Isaiah 44:3-4: 'I will pour water upon him that is thirsty, and floods upon the dry ground; I will pour my Spirit upon thy seed, and my blessing upon thy offspring; and they shall spring up as among the grass, as the willow by the watercourses.' David was a great student in [of] providence, and observed God up and down in the traverses [ups and downs] of his [God's] dispensations, and gives this as the result of his inquiry and observation: 'I have been young, and now am old, yet I never saw the righteous forsaken, nor his seed begging bread. He is ever merciful and lendeth, and his seed is blessed'

(Ps. 37:25-26). God hath a blessing for them and theirs, so as to bestow necessaries [necessities] upon them.

And 'A good man leaves an inheritance to his children's children, and the wealth of the sinner is laid up for the just' (Prov. 13:22). They that thrive by the oppression of others, and seek to grow great in the world, lay up for the heir of a poor, godly man.

8. God will provide many times when we are at an utter loss; as Abraham answered his son Isaac, when he asked his father, 'Where is the lamb for a burnt-offering?' 'God will provide himself a lamb for a burnt-offering' (Gen. 2:7-8). So we may quiet our hearts in God's promises for our supplies.

God hath means that come not within our ken [view] and perceivance: 'And the passover, a feast of the Jews, was nigh at hand. When Jesus lifted up his eyes, and saw a great multitude coming unto him, he saith unto Philip, Whence shall we have bread, that all these may eat? And this he said to prove him, for he himself knew what he would do' (John 6:4-6). Such straits many times befall poor believers. There are many mouths, and little meat; trading dead, and means of supplies cut off; but this he doth to try us what we will do in such a case of straits and great necessities. But God will find out means of supplies that we could never think of; and when we have it out of the hands of God's providence immediately [directly], it is the sweeter, and doth more evidence God's love and care of us: so Zechariah 8:6: 'If it be marvellous in your eyes, should it therefore be marvellous in mine eyes? saith the Lord of hosts.'

'Yea they turned back and tempted God, and limited the Holy One of Israel' (Ps. 78:41). This was the fault the Israelites were taxed with [rebuked for], they limited the Holy One of Israel within the circle of human probabilities. Thus we

LIVING BY FAITH

should not be: 'The Lord knoweth how to deliver the godly' (2 Pet. 2:9). This should answer all our doubts; we know not and cannot see. When all lawful means have been tried unprosperously, then is the time for the Lord to show forth his skill and power.

9. Our faith must be tried in these things as well as in others. Look, as in all other promises, God tries our faith before he gives us the blessing. How shall we know that we believe, and depend upon God for outward supplies, unless we be reduced to some straits, and have but from hand to mouth, and be cut short in our temporal conveniences? There are times of trial in which God will try all his children: 'The Lord tries the righteous' (Ps. 11:5). Thus he tried them (Heb. 11:36-37). God tried them whether they would live by faith upon him when they were 'destitute, afflicted and tormented, when they were stoned, and sawn asunder, slain with the sword, and wandered about in sheep-skins, and goat-skins.' And thus he tried Israel in the wilderness, before he had them into a land flowing with milk and honey: 'And thou shalt remember all the way which the Lord thy God led thee these forty years in the wilderness, to humble thee, and to prove thee, to know what was in thine heart, whether thou wouldst keep his commandments or no' (Deut. 8:2). God will try us whether we serve him for love or wages; whether we live merely upon the creature or the promises, and can depend upon his all-sufficiency.

10. We cannot be absolutely confident of success as to temporal things. This is not the faith required of us, for they are not absolutely promised; but with exception [taking up] of the cross, and as God shall see them good for us. God hath reserved a liberty of showing his justice in punishing a sinning people: 'He will visit their iniquity with the rod, and their transgression with stripes' (Ps. 89:32). The world shall know that he doth not allow sin in his own people and children. It is as odious to God in them as in others, yea more, and therefore they feel the smart of it. When we go out of the way in which the blessing falls, it is no marvel it falls beside [at a distance from] us.

But here is a doubt that might be largely discoursed upon, *Why then are temporal blessings so often expressed in the covenant?*

I answer:

1. Partly because it is the ordinary practice of the Lord's free-grace to supply his people with things comfortable and necessary. While he hath work for them to do, he will give them protection and maintenance. I observe two different speeches of Paul whilst he was in the middle of his work. He saith in 2 Corinthians 1:10: 'Who hast delivered us from so great a death, and doth deliver, and in whom I trust that he will yet deliver'; but when his work began to draw to an end, he speaketh at another rate in 2 Timothy 4:6-8: 'For I am now ready to be offered, and the time of my departure is at hand. I have fought a good fight, I have finished my course, I have kept the faith; henceforth is laid up for me a crown of righteousness.' God by a secret instinct begat a confidence in him. But when [God] he began to call him off [home], and the time of his departure was drawing nigh, he speaks more faintly, as one that was sensible that God was calling him off from his service in the world.

2. Partly, because these blessings are adopted into the covenant that they may be a ground of prayer and praise.

2.1 It is a ground of prayer. We go the more confidently to God when we have a particular promise of the blessing we

LIVING BY FAITH

ask; as Psalm 119:49: 'Remember thy word unto thy servant, wherein thou hast caused me to hope.' When God hath given out a promise, and enables us to apply it, and then to challenge him upon his word, then we are the more borne up to prayer. A general intimation is not so clear a ground to trust as an express and particular promise. Our necessities lead us to the promise, and the promise to God, that we may put his bonds in suit [plead his promises]. We have somewhat to urge and plead, and have a greater holdfast upon God; it is a sweet argument that increaseth out earnestness in prayer.

2.2 It is a ground of praise. It is a greater comfort when we can see our mercies coming out of the womb of the covenant. What others have by common providence, that [believers] have by special mercy; others have by simple donation and indulgence, they have everything by promise; others receive from a creator, they from a loving Father; though for substance the gift is the same, yet the cause and end differ. 'God blesseth them out of Zion' (Ps. 128:5). Mercies wrapt up in the bowels of Christ, and dipped in his blood, are a ground of praise indeed.

3. We now come to the third thing: What faith is required? or what are the acts of faith about these promises? In general, to depend upon God's all-sufficiency, that he is able, and his promises, that he is willing to provide for us; for if God were not willing, why hath he multiplied so many promises concerning temporal things? Now this dependence is to be manifested several ways.

1. By recommending our case to God in prayer. We may lawfully pray for temporal things; for Christ hath made it one of the petitions in his perfect form; 'Give us this day our daily bread,' next to 'Thy will be done.' Such things are to be asked as are necessary to the being of the subjects [those who pray for them]. Prayers to God for spiritual things are most acceptable, but these [prayers for outward things] are not despised. A child pleaseth his father most when he desireth him to teach him his book [school work] rather than give him an apple. Yet he is not refused when he desireth food; both requests are allowed, though one be preferred. Well then, pray we must, and in prayer we act faith: 'Trust in him at all times, ye people; pour out your hearts before him' (Ps. 62:8); and 1 Samuel 22:3, 4: 'God is my rock, in whom I trust; I will call upon the name of the Lord, so shall I be saved.' If we trust God we will be often with him at the throne of grace, for there we act our trust, and encourage ourselves in our belief of God's hearing. Whenever we feel ourselves pinched with any earthly necessity, we run to God, and spread his promises before him. This is trust, for it always keepeth up an acknowledgement of God as the giver of corn, and wine, and oil and the comforts of this life: 'She did not know that I gave her corn, and wine, and oil and multiplied her silver and gold' (Hos. 2:8). It easeth the heart of the burden of distracting cares: 'Be careful for nothing, but in everything let your requests be made known unto God' (Phil. 4:6). When the wind is gotten into the bowels and caverns of the earth, it shaketh, and heaves, and causeth terrible earthquakes,[4] till it get a vent, then all is quiet. So we are full of unquiet tossings in our minds till we go and pour out our hearts before the Lord.

2. This dependence is manifested by keeping us from the use of unlawful means, and base shifts [compromises]. Faith can rather trust God though we have nothing, than step out of the way for a supply: 'Better is a little with righteousness, than great revenues without right' (Prov. 16:8). That proverb expresseth the disposition of a gracious heart: though a man might easily help himself out of his straits by bending a little to some sinful way, yet he rather waiteth upon God, and looks for his blessing in his own way. They that use ill [sinful] means, and do not tarry God's leisure, they live upon the creature, not God. The protection of the law is only for them that travel in the day, and upon the road; a man never gets anything by going aside out of God's way. Therefore faith looketh upon unjust gain as a certain loss, like the flesh stolen from the altar with a coal in it, that fireth the bird's nest. Besides peace of conscience which we lose, faith seeth a ruin in the estate: 'Bread of deceit is sweet to a man, but afterwards the mouth is filled with gravel' (Prov. 20:17). They think to find a great deal of comfort in that bread [which] they have gotten by deceit, but it proveth gravel in the belly. To make haste to be rich is to make haste to be poor, to bring a curse upon ourselves and families.

3. By doing our duty without distraction, and referring the event, issue, and success of every business to the Lord.

Because this is the sum of the whole duty of trusting upon God for temporal things, I shall show you: (1) That duty must be done by us without distraction, with quietness and a contented mind; (2) That events must be left to God.

3.1 Duty must be done. God would not put the trouble of the event upon us, but only requireth us to perform the subservient duty: 'Be careful for nothing' (Phil. 4:6); and 1 Peter 5:7, 'Cast all your care upon the Lord'; he is willing to take the burden upon him, all of it. What! must we leave all things to sixes and sevens, and let wife and children shift for themselves? There is anxious solicitude and holy diligence. As in a pair of compasses one foot is fixed in the centre, whilst the other wandereth about the circumference. The work of faith is not to abate industry, but to fix the heart. The dependence of faith is not an idle and devout sloth [inactivity], but an industrious waiting. Not to labour is to tempt providence, and to cark [worry] is to distrust it. Miracles are not to be multiplied without necessity. When we neglect means, we discharge God of the obligation of his promise. If we starve for want of industry, you can blame none. God hath not undertaken that sin shall not be your ruin, rather the contrary. By a quiet use of means you enter into God's protection; do your duty, and then take no thought what you shall eat and drink, or wherewith you shall be clothed, nor how sustained. That is to take God's work out of his hands.

3.2 Events must be left to God. There are two acts of faith, committing and submitting all our affairs to God.

First, committing all your affairs, persons, and conditions, and all events that concern you, to the will, wisdom, power and goodness of God. Put them into his hands, and see what he will do for you. We are directed to do so in two places, each of which hath a distinct promise, the one of ease, the other of success. The one is in Proverbs 16:3: 'Commit thy works unto the Lord, and thy thoughts shall be established'; the other place is Psalm 37:5: 'Commit thy way unto the Lord, and he shall bring it to pass.' This will bring success, or else ease us of a great deal of unnecessary trouble. Some do not understand the weight and burden of their affairs, because they are retchless, and foolish, and have slight spirits. Other that have a sense of their business and difficulties, take all the burden upon themselves, and so through their own distrust are eaten out with piercing cares. But the believer that is sensible of his own weakness, and acknowledgeth the wise and faithful conduct of God's providence, after he hath done his duty leaveth the event of all things to God. Into how many inconveniences, temporal and spiritual, do we plunge ourselves, till we do so! Let God alone, for he will guide all to his own

LIVING BY FAITH

glory and our comfort, for he is a faithful God. This is the true depending upon his providence, when we put all our comforts into his hands.

Secondly, submit your thoughts and affections to God in the disposal of your condition. As Jesus Christ our Lord said: 'Not my will be done, but thine' (Luke 22:42). Lord, if thou wilt bring about this comfort, I will bless thee; if not, here I am, let the Lord do to me as he will. 'If I find favour in the eyes of the Lord, he will bring me again, and show me both it and his habitation: but if he say thus, I have no delight in thee, behold here am I, let him do as seemeth good unto him' (2 Sam. 15:25-26). Such a man puts himself and all his interests as a die into the hands of God's providence, to be cast high or low, as he pleaseth; as those in Acts 21:14: 'When they saw he would not be persuaded, they ceased, saying, The will of the Lord be done.' When we cannot by lawful means avert evil, let us acquiesce in his providence. He knows what way is best to bring us to heaven. Whether is it most equal [which is more proper] for us to desire that the will of God should be subject to our affections, or our wills and affections [to be] subject to God's providence? If things fall out contrary to our inclinations, they are agreeable to his wisdom; and though they are against our wills, yet not against our salvation. For God in all the ways of his providence aimeth at his own glory and the salvation of his people. Therefore what is against our will, is not against our profit, and it is not fit [that] the wheels of providence should move according to our fancies, as if we could guide things better than God. It is man's duty to submit, admire, not quarrel at providence. If things are not as we would have them, they are as God would have them. We all condemn the blasphemy of Alphonsus, who said, *Si Deo a consiliis adfuisset in creatione mundi, se consultius multa ordinaturum* ('If he had been by when God made the world, he would have ordered things a great deal better than now they are'). Yet we are guilty of the same blasphemy in our murmurings; we think if we had the reins of government in our own hands, we would order the affairs of the world in a better way. Foolish creatures! thus are we offended, because we know not God, and do not consider the end and meaning of his dispensations.

But you will say, There may be obedience in this submission, but how is it an act of dependence?

I answer, thus: When we believe that God is so good and faithful that he will do what is best, though we see not how. Certainly murmuring is the effect of unbelief: 'They believed not, but murmured in their tents' (Ps. 106:24-25). So submission is an act of faith. Could we believe that the wise and faithful God is carrying on all things for our good, that would make us in quietness and silence to possess our souls, till we see the end of the Lord, and what he purposeth by all the straits he reduceth us unto.

This dependence is manifested by using all comforts vouchsafed [granted] with reverence and thankfulness. There is a living by faith in prosperity as well as adversity; and it is a part of the divine and spiritual life 'to learn how to abound' as well as 'how to be abased,' (Phil. 4:12). Faith must be exercised when we have comforts as well as when we want [lack] them. In 1 Timothy 4:3, it is said: 'the creature is to be received with thanksgiving of them that believe'; and verse 5: 'Every creature is sanctified by the word and prayer.' We are to take all our comforts out of the promise, and to seek God's blessing upon them, giving thanks for the use. Alas, otherwise when we have earthly things, we have them not with God's blessing; and then the creatures will be like a deaf [empty] nut, when we come to crack it there is no kernel in it. Compare Proverbs 10:4 with Proverbs 10:22; in one place it is said, 'The diligent hand maketh rich'; and in the other place it is said, 'The bless-

LIVING BY FAITH

ing of the Lord maketh rich, and he addeth no sorrow with it.'

Well then, it will not be amiss to treat of living by faith when we have these outward supplies, and the comforts of this life. Now the acts of faith when we have these blessings, are these:

1. To look up and acknowledge God, the donor of all that we have: 'Charge them that are rich in this world that they be not high-minded, nor trust in uncertain riches, but in the living God, who giveth us richly all things to enjoy' (1 Tim. 6:17). These blessings do not come by chance, but from the God of heaven. You shall find your betters [Christ and all his eminent followers] made conscience of this duty.

Jesus Christ ever gave thanks, when he made use of the creatures (John 6:11); though he were Heir and Lord of all things, and thought it no robbery to be equal with God, he gave thanks to God; and that not for the choicest dainties which we enjoy, but for sober and coarse fare, five barley loaves and two small fishes (verse 9). And it seemeth Christ had expressed himself very affectionately, for mark, it is said in verse 23: 'When they came nigh unto the place where they had eaten bread, after the Lord had given thanks.' He doth not say, where the Lord wrought the miracle, but where the Lord had given thanks; he characteriseth the place, not by the miracle, but the thanksgiving. Christ's way of expressing himself made some deep impression upon them, therefore it is repeated.

Well then, so much faith we should express, as to acknowledge the donor of all our comforts, and have our minds raised thereby; and therefore the spouse's eyes are compared to 'dove's eyes' (Cant. 5:12). Doves sip and look upward, so should we; not like swine that raven upon the acorns, and never look up to the oak from whence they drop; especially at your full and well-furnished tables, where such clusters of mercies crowd in before your eyes and observations: 'When thou hast eaten and art full, then thou shalt bless the Lord' (Deut. 8:10). They are great mercies, and sweetened and sanctified to you when you acknowledge them to come down from heaven; though the matter of the provision be fetched from the field or the sea, yet it comes from God as the first cause.

2. This piece of living by faith is necessary too, not only to take them out of the hands of [receive them gratefully from] God as a creator, but to take them out of the promise. It is said they are 'to be received with thanksgiving of them that believe and know the truth' (1 Tim. 4:3). It is good to see by what right and title you have your mercies, comforts and supplies. There is a two-fold right: a providential right, and a covenant right – *Dominium politicum fundatur in providentia, et doninium evangelicum fundatur in gratia* ['Political power is founded on providence, and gospel power is founded on grace'].

By a providential right, wicked men as well as the godly possess outward things as the fruits and gifts of God's common bounty; it is their portion (Ps. 17:14). They are not usurpers of what falleth to their share in the course of God's providence, and are not responsible merely for possessing what they have, but abusing what they have. They have not only a civil right by the laws of men to prevent the encroachment of others, but a providential right before God, and must give an account to him for the use of them.

But then there is a covenant-right from God's special love; so believers have a right to their creature-comforts. And that little which the righteous have is better than the treasures of many wicked. As the mean fare [allowance] of a poor subject is better than the large allowance of a condemned traitor. This we have by Christ who is the heir of all things, and we by him, in his claim: 'All are yours, for you are Christ's, and Christ is God's' (1 Cor. 3:23). This covenant-right, then, is that which we should look after [to], that we may enjoy all things as the gifts of God's fatherly love and compassion to us, and take all out of the promise, as a part of our portion in Christ, which doth very much better the relish [improve the taste] of our comforts.

3. That we may have the comfortable use of them, with God's leave and blessing. The natural, comfortable use is the fruit of faith; for 'Man liveth not by bread only, but by every word that proceedeth out of the mouth of God' (Matt. 4:4). The power of sustaining life is not in the means, but in God's word of blessing. As God hath a creating word by which he made all things, so a providential word by which he preserveth and upholdeth them from falling into nothing. He may give the means, when he doth withdraw the blessing. When that happens they do not prosper [have no power] to continue us in health, and strength, and vigour, and blessing, and fitting us for the service of God: 'He gave them their requests, but sent leanness into their souls' (Ps. 106:15). That is, no comfort in that which they obtained. Therefore the apostle maketh it an argument of [for] God's bounty to the heathens that he gave them not only food, but 'gladness of heart' (Acts 14:7), and cheerfulness. And in scripture there is a distinction between bread, and 'the staff of bread' (Lev. 26). We may have bread, and yet not 'the staff of bread'; we may have worldly comforts, but not with a blessing.

4. We must act faith in the promises, that we may have a sanctified use of them, that our hearts may be raised the more to love God for every taste of mercy: 'They did not know that I gave them corn, and wine and oil' (Hos. 2:8). The [lower] creatures live upon God, but they are not capable of knowing the First Cause; man only is capable, and God giveth him an heart to love him as the strength of our lives and 'the length of our days' (Deut. 30:20); and to serve him cheerfully and 'with gladness of heart for the abundance of all things' (Deut. 28:47).

Alas! when people live by sense, all their meals are but a sacrifice, a meat or a drink-offering, to their own lusts; but when we live by faith, we use all these comforts for God. 'Holiness to the Lord' was written in all the pots of Jerusalem (Zech. 14:20); not only upon the vessels and utensils of the temple, but upon the very pots and horse-bells. All blessings that come from God must return to God again; as all rivers come from the sea, and in all countries discharge themselves into the sea again. The most part of the world abuse these gifts of God, as occasions of sinning against the Giver, and so we fight against him with his own weapons: 'Their table is their snare' (Ps. 69:22), and that is a heavy judgment. We think the want of worldly comforts is a great judgment, but the abuse of worldly comforts is a greater, for that is a spiritual judgment; and this not only when they are grossly abused to surfeiting and drunkenness, and open contempt of God, but when they are abused to security, hardness of heart, forgetfulness and neglect of God, which is the more secret and common evil.

Christ giveth a caution to his own disciples: 'Take heed, lest at any time your hearts be overcharged with surfeiting and drunkenness, and the cares of this life' (Luke 21:34). Take these words in the vulgar and gross notion of them, they are not unseasonable. We had two common parents, Adam, the father of all mankind, and Noah, the preserver of all mankind, and both miscarried by appetite, the one by eating, the other by drinking. The throat is a slippery place, and had need be well guarded. But I suppose the words are to be taken in a more spiritual notion; the heart may be overcharged, when the

LIVING BY FAITH 113

stomach is not, when we are less apt to praise God, or when we settle into a worldly, sensual, careless frame of spirit, and from an inordinate delight in our present portion are taken off from minding better things, and are fully satisfied with these things.

4. How shall we bring our hearts thus to live by faith?

1. We must empty our hearts of covetous desires: 'Let your conversation be without covetousness, and be contented with such things as ye have; for he hath said, I will never leave thee, nor forsake thee' (Heb. 13:5). This implies that he will depend upon God, and receive the comfort of the promise, that God will not leave him nor forsake him, [indeed, he] must so do. He that would cast himself upon God's providence, must be content with God's allowance. We do but ensnare and perplex our thoughts while we would go about to reconcile the promises with our lusts, and crave more than God ever meaneth to bestow. Many men set God a task, to provide meat for their lusts: 'They tempted God in their hearts by asking meat for their lusts: yea, they spake against God, they said, Can God furnish a table in the wilderness?' (Ps. 78:18-19). And what was the issue? The carnal affections and hopes did but made trouble to themselves. Though it be the ordinary practice of God's free grace and fatherly care to provide things comfortable and necessary for his children, whilst he hath work for them to do, yet he never undertook to maintain us at such a rate, to give us so much by the year, such portions for our children, and supplies for our families. We must leave it to the great Shepherd of the sheep to choose our pastures, bare or large. This is the way to breed faith: 'Take heed, and beware of covetousness; for man's life consisteth not in the abundance of the things which he possesseth' (Luke 12:15). That is faith's principle: I shall never be the more safe, happier, or the better provided for, in a spiritual sense, or the more comfortable because I have abundance. Faith looketh to heaven, and a little serveth turn to keep us by the way. He is not poor that hath little, but he that desireth more. Enlarged affections make want [that is, lead us to be covetous].

2. Secure your great interest, and then it will be easy to wait upon God for temporal supplies: 'First seek the kingdom of God and his righteousness, and these things shall be added' (Matt. 6:33). That once sought after, and well secured, draweth other things along with it; and then you need not be anxious about food, and raiment, and protection, and maintenance, and such like things. When this is our care, to live eternally, our desires of other things are abated [relaxed], and so are our fears about them. Yea, this will assure us that in some measure we shall have them. Provide for the soul, and the body shall not want its allowance; provide for the body, and we cannot have assurance for our souls. Men carry it so, as if it were their work to provide for their bodies, and leave their soul at all adventures. If God take care of it, well; if not, they are not troubled. Indeed it is quite contrary. It is true, we are to serve God's providence for both, but first for our souls. A man may have a little provision in the world without so much ado; these things are cast into the bargain, and by way of overplus. He that giveth a jewel will not stand upon a trifle. God that blessed the house of Obed-edom for the ark's sake (2 Sam. 6:11-12), will bless you, and keep you, because Christ is received into your hearts. Remember 1 Kings 3:11-13: 'Because thou hast asked this thing, and hast not asked for thyself long life...; lo, I have done according to thy words, ... And also I have given thee that which thou hast not asked, both riches and honour ....'

LIVING BY FAITH

3. Be persuaded of the particularity of God's providence, that he doth not only mind the greater affairs of the world, but is conscious to [of] everything and every person that liveth here. Christ knew when virtue passed out from him in a throng (Luke 8:45), 'Somebody hath touched me,' saith he. It is a notable passage which we have in Acts 9:11: 'Arise, go into the street, which is called Straight, and inquire in the house of Judas for one called Saul of Tarsus; for behold he prayeth.' God knoweth where we are, what we do, what we think, and what we speak; as where Saul was, in what street, in what house, and what he was doing. God seeth all in what posture [state of mind] we are, whether we fear or rejoice, whether we are sad or merry, whether angry or pleased, whether we are toying, fooling or praying.

God doth not only look after the preservation of the species, or kinds of things, but after every individual, and careth for them, as if he had none to care for besides them.

Every child that is born into the world God taketh notice, and therefore Paul is said to be 'separated from his mother's womb' (Gal. 1:15). As soon as a child is born, God is making way by particular acts of providence, for some hidden purpose and design of his about that child, fitting the temper, etc. But you will say, Paul was a notable instrument of God's glory; but he takes care, not only for great and notable instruments of his glory, but poor and despicable persons: 'This poor man cried, and the Lord heard him' (Ps. 34:6). This is one of no account and reckoning in the world, such a one as was forgotten, or never thought of in his neighbourhood.

Yea, the beast and fowls are known of God: 'I know all the fowls of the air, and the wild beasts in the field are mine' (Ps. 1:11). Though there be such innumerable flocks, yet God knoweth them particularly, yea, all their motions [movements]: 'Are not two sparrows sold for a farthing? and one of them shall not fall to the ground without your Father' (Matt. 10:29). And if God be at leisure to look after all the beasts of the field, and the fowls of heaven, and the fishes of the sea, will he not look after his saints and servants? Yes, they and everything about them is cared for: 'The hairs of your head are numbered' (Matt. 10:30); not only the head itself, or hands and feet, which are *partes integrantes* [essential parts], but the hairs of your head: excrementitious [less vital] parts, rather for conveniency and ornament, than necessity. Well then, be settled in the belief of this truth of God's particular providence.

There is not only a common providence to be ascribed to God, that he doth in general furnish the world, and store it with sufficiency, and so leaving us to our own industry, catch that catch can, and so make it our own. No, but he hath a personal eye upon every one of us. He doth not leave us scattered upon the face of the earth to forage for ourselves, but we all live upon his findings, and he appoints to every one their lot and portion. In common plenty he can punish with personal scarcity, as he did the prince of Samaria. And in general scarcity he can furnish with personal plenty, as Elijah did the Sareptan widow. Many will allow God a general inspection, that he upholdeth the pillars of the earth, but believe not that he taketh care of particulars, and so resolve to shift for themselves. But be once persuaded of his particular notice and care, and that will help you to live by faith.

4. Feed trust with arguments, and reason sometimes from the greater to the less. He hath given us his Christ and his Spirit: 'How shall he not with him give us all things else?' (Rom. 8:32). Sometimes from the less to the greater: 'If he clothe the lilies and feed the ravens, how much more will be provide for you, O ye of little faith' (Matt. 6:26, 30).

Reason from things past to things present: as David in 1

Samuel 17:37: 'The Lord hath delivered me from the paw of the lion and the mouth of the bear, and he will deliver me out of the hands of this uncircumcised Philistine.'

And then reason from things past and present to things future: 'Who hath delivered us from so great a death, and doth deliver, in whom we trust that he will yet deliver us' (2 Cor. 1:10). God hath provided for me hitherto, even when I lay in my mother's womb. It was he who prepared thy swaddling-clothes when thou was not able to shift for [look after] thyself. He provided two bottles of milk for thee before thou wast born; and he provided for thee when thou hadst no reason, no grace, no interest in him; certainly he will provide for thee now.

And on the other side, reason from things to come to things present: 'Fear not, little flock, it is your Father's good pleasure to give you the kingdom' (Luke 12:32). If he will give heaven, why not daily bread?

Thus may we help faith by reasoning. Christ hath taught us this skill.

5. Consider your relations to God, and improve them to increase your confidence. The apostle saith in 1 Timothy 5:8: 'He that provideth not for his own is worse than an infidel.' God is your creator, and you are his creatures; and God is bountiful to everything that he hath made: 'The eyes of all things wait upon thee, and thou givest them their meat in due season; thou openest thine hand, and satisfiest the desire of every living creature' (Ps. 145:15-16). He that is so tender of all his works, will he forget you and forsake you? The apostle saith in 1 Peter 4:19: 'Commit your souls unto him, as unto a faithful creator.' They were in a great deal of danger, they carried their lives in their hands from day to day, and therefore the apostle gives them this advice And then he is a shepherd, that is his relation to the visible church, and you may draw conclusions from it: 'The Lord is my shepherd, I shall want no good thing' (Ps. 23:1). And then he is your father: 'Your heavenly Father knoweth that ye have need of these things' (Matt. 6:32). And will a father be unmindful of his children? Yea, he is your God, in covenant with you: 'I trusted in thee, O God; I said, Thou art my God' (Ps. 31:14). A man must make sure [of] his personal interest [in Christ], and then it will be more easy to live by faith, and draw comfortable conclusion[s] from thence.

6. Consider the vanity of carking [anxiety]: 'Which of you by taking thought can add one cubit to his stature?' (Matt. 6:27). We cannot change the colour of a hair, nor make ourselves a jot taller or stronger. A man is pierced through with worldly cares, and yet the world frowneth upon him.

'Except the Lord build the house, they labour in vain that build it. It is in vain to rise early, and go to bed late, to eat the bread of sorrows; for so he giveth his beloved sleep' (Ps. 127:1-2). There is a general and a particular meaning in this psalm. The general sense is this: there are many that follow their business close [attentively], with great wisdom and dexterity; they labour and toil, live sparingly, do this and that, and yet are destitute of these outward things. It is the Lord [who] must give the blessing.

But then there is a more particular meaning in this psalm, concerning Solomon, who was called Jedidiah, the beloved of the Lord (2 Sam. 12:25), who was a builder (1 Chr. 22:9). Adonijah and Absalom thought to have stepped into the throne, but it is in vain. The Lord giveth his beloved rest. The kingdom is for Solomon, do what you can, so it is in vain for us to cark [worry] and care, and trouble ourselves. The Lord giveth these things to whom he pleaseth. In Luke 5:5, our Saviour

Christ bids his disciples 'cast out the net'. They had toiled all night and wearied themselves, and caught nothing; but at his command they cast out the net, and enclosed a multitude of fishes. Our diligence and toiling cometh to nothing without God's blessing. Thus do, and usually God prevents [goes before] us with the blessings of his goodness; or if we be pinched [in want], and feel want, it is to make our supplies the more glorious. 'How many loaves have ye? and they said, Seven, and a few little fishes' (Matt. 15:34-35). Here Christ, to supply the wants of the multitude, wrought a miracle; he will have it seen what he will do, though he hath never so little to work upon.

5

The Life of Faith and the Temptations of Satan

Here I shall: (1) Prove that this is a considerable part of the life of faith; (2) I shall show you what props and supports faith hath, that we may overcome the temptations of the devil; (3) What are the acts of faith, with respect to these temptations.

That this is a considerable branch of the life of faith
Two considerations will evidence that: (1) the necessity of temptations; (2) the necessity of faith to grapple with those temptations.

1. This must be considered in the life of faith, because of the necessity of temptations. And without this part of the life of faith, the spiritual life would not be guarded against all inconveniences, and the molestations of it; for whosoever doth unfeignedly dedicate himself to the service of God must expect to be assaulted by Satan. We took an oath in our infancy to fight under Christ's banner. Baptism is *sacramentum militare*, an engagement to the spiritual warfare; and the grace that is infused into us is not only called clothing, but 'armour of light' (Rom. 13:12), and 'armour of righteousness' (2 Cor. 6:7), because Christ arrayeth us *non ad pompam, sed ad pugnam*; not to set us out in a vain show, but to furnish us and secure us for the spiritual combat. A Christian's life is a warfare, and we cannot discharge the duties of it without a battle or conflict. We do evil easily, but we must fight for the good that we do; they that think this unnecessary, scare know what Christianity meaneth.

LIFE OF FAITH AND TEMPTATIONS OF SATAN

Many are never acquainted with any such thing as temptations, because they know not what Christianity meaneth. When wind and tide go together, the sea must needs be smooth and calm. 'The strong man keepeth the house, and all the goods are in peace' (Luke 11:21). Satan and they are agreed. They that are least troubled may be most hurt; they are quiet and secure, because Satan hath gotten them into the snare, and hath a quiet dominion in their souls. Many there are that are contented to bear his image, being conformed to him in infidelity and love of temporal good, in pride and malice, and the like; they embrace his principles, are guided by his counsels, do his will and works; they strive for the establishing of his kingdom, hating those that oppose it. It is in vain to comfort those against temptations.

But whosoever doth seriously purpose to live to God will be molested with the devil; and they cannot serve God cheerfully, unless there be provision made against it, which Christ hath abundantly done: 'That being delivered out of the hands of our enemies, we might serve him without fear, in holiness and righteousness before him all our days' (Luke 1:74-75). Such encounters are to be expected. Certainly there must be temptations; for God in wisdom permits it, and Satan in malice and policy effects it.

2. God seeth it fit that we should be tempted

2.1 Partly, that we may be the oftener with him. We keep off from the throne of grace, till temptations drive us thither. When the sheep are apt to wander from the fold, the shepherd lets loose the dog upon them; so doth God let loose Satan to drive us to himself for mercy and grace to help.

2.2 And partly, because such a dispensation is necessary, to prove and humble us, that we may not be proud of what we have, or conceited of more than we have. Paul was buffeted with a messenger of Satan, 'lest he should be exalted above measure' (2 Cor. 12:7). A ship laden with precious wares needs to be balanced with wood or stones. Spiritual evils needs a spiritual cure; outward afflictions are not so conducible [do not lead] to humble a gracious heart as temptations to sin. And:

2.3 Partly to conform us to Christ, that we may pledge him in his own cup. For he himself was tempted: 'Then was Jesus led up of the Spirit into the wilderness to be tempted of the devil' (Matt. 4:1). Now the disciple is not above his Lord. The devil that did once set upon Christ will not be afraid of us.

2.4 And partly, that we may be pitiful to others: 'Considering thyself, lest thou also be tempted' (Gal. 6:1). We are fierce and severe upon the failings of others; now when we are tempted ourselves, we learn more pity and compassion. When we know the heart of a tempted man, we are more compassionate to others.

3. Satin in malice effects it, out of envy to mankind who enjoy the happiness which he hath lost; and out of hatred to God, the devil is always vexing the saints, and sending abroad the sparks of temptations, either with hopes to recover the prey taken out of his hands, as Pharaoh made pursuit after the Israelites, thinking to have brought them back again, or else to discourage and weary and vex the children of God and make their lives uncomfortable. The enemy will be tempting, either to draw us to sin or to trouble. Now two ways doth Satan assault us: (1) either by his *wiles*: 'Put on the whole armour of God, that ye may be able to stand against the wiles of the devil' (Eph. 6:11); (2) or by his *fiery darts*: 'Take the shield of faith, that you may be able to quench the fiery darts of Satan' (Eph. 6:16), those poisoned and envenomed arrows. These are their lusts, and their consciences are sometimes set a-raging. He seeketh to stir up despairing fears; or he inflames their lusts and corruptions, that he may draw them to dishonour God, or lose their own peace.

3.1 He that wiles; and if we descry [see] them not, we are soon surprised and taken. The immoderate use of carnal pleasures is accounted Christian cheerfulness. The apostle tells us that Satan 'turneth himself into an angel of light' (2 Cor. 11:10). Would Peter ever have made a motion [done service] for Satan to our Saviour, if he had seen his hand in it? (Matt. 16:22) He covereth his foul designs with plausible pretences. Carnal counsel shall be [called] pity and natural affection; revenge shall be zeal: 'Wilt thou that we command fire to come down from heaven and consume them, as Elias did?' (Luke 9:53-54) Immoderate use of pleasure shall go for cheerfulness, and covetousness for frugality, and licentiousness for Christian liberty. The devil observeth our humours and inclinations and suits his bait accordingly. He can preach up the gospel to beat down the price of it; as he came crying after Christ: 'I know thee who thou art, the Holy One of God' (Mark 1:24); to render the person of Christ odious, and his doctrine suspected. He urgeth the comforts of Christianity, to exclude the duties thereof, and to rock us asleep in ease and carnal pleasure, till conscience be benumbed. At other times he urgeth duties to exclude comforts, and so to keep us in a dejected frame and under bondage and fear: 'Lest Satan should get an advantage of us, for we are not ignorant of his devices' (2 Cor. 2:11). He doth not only abuse the inclinations of our concupiscible [tendency to lust] faculty, but the inclinations of our irascible [anger] faculty: 'They that are Christ's have crucified the flesh, with the affections and lusts thereof' (Gal. 5:24). By lusts he meaneth vexing, troublesome passions; and by affections, sorrow, grief, fear. He observeth us in our duties, and 'catcheth the word out of our hearts' (Luke 8:12). As soon as we begin to be serious, and to have any good motions within us, he diverts us by one business or delight or other.

3.2 He hath 'fiery darts', either setting-a-work in us despairing fears, as he did in Cain: 'My sin is greater than I can bear' (Gen. 4:13); and Judas: 'I have sinned in that I have betrayed innocent blood. And he departed and hanged himself' (Matt. 27:4-5); or casting in blasphemous thoughts against God and Christ, and the truths of the gospel and world to come. David[5] was sorely shaken: 'Verily, I have cleansed my heart in vain, and washed my hands in innocency, for all the day long have I been plagued, and chastened every morning' (Ps. 73:13-14). Even good David[5] thought that all religion was in vain. The envious one will be flinging his darts into our souls, and casting over the seeds of many noisome [harmful] plants into the heart, that is new ploughed up and broken, or inflaming our lusts and corruptions; he sees our looks, affections, speeches, gestures and behaviours, observes our humours [moods], when we are inclined to wrath, or lust, or any other transport of soul; he knoweth what use to make of a frown, or an angry look, or a wanton glance: 'That Satan tempt you not for your incontinency' (1 Cor. 7:5); 'Give not place to the devil' (Eph. 4:27). He sets some lust or other a-boiling. Or to draw us to some gross sin, thereby to dishonour God: 'Because by this deed thou hast given great occasion to the enemies of the Lord to blaspheme' (2 Sam. 12:14). Or to disturb their peace: 'When I kept silence, my bones waxed old through my roaring all the day long; for day and night thy hand was heavy upon me, my moisture is turned into the drought of summer'

(Ps. 32:3-4). Or by some extreme grief, to stir up murmurings, repinings [complaints], and distrust of God. Well then, you see a necessity of some remedy for this great annoyance of the spiritual life.

Now the great remedy is faith, without which we are at an utter loss; yea, a great part of the work and life of faith is to resist Satan: 'Whom resist, steadfast in the faith' (1 Pet. 5:9).

That is the way of resisting Satan, to keep up our courage against him. Bernard hath a saying, *Increduli timent diabolum quasi leonem, qui fide fortes despiciunt quasi vermiculum*; that unbelief feareth Satan as a lion, but faith treadeth on him as a worm. And that is a good step to victory when we have courage to stand to it [resist the devil]. Stand your ground, and Satan falleth. In assaulting us he hath only weapons offensive, he hath none defensive; but a Christian hath defensive and offensive weapons, a sword and a shield; therefore our security lieth in resisting with assurance of help and victory.

In the next place observe that [word] of the apostle Paul in Ephesians 6:16: 'Above all, take the shield of faith, wherewith ye shall be able to quench all the fiery darts of Satan.' We are bidden to 'put on the whole armour of God' (verse 11). No faculty of the soul or sense of the body must be left naked and without a guard. There must be not one saving grace wanting. The spiritual soldier is armed cap-a-pie. The poets feign of their Achilles that he was vulnerable only in his heel, and there he got his death's-wound. A Christian, though never so well furnished in other parts, yet if any part be left naked, he is in danger. Our first parents, and Solomon, who had the upper part of the soul so well guarded, were wounded in the heel, miscarried by sensual appetite. Many have great sufficiencies of knowledge, yet are intemperate and unmortified. Well then, a Christian must be completely armed. The apostle there reckoneth up 'the helmet of salvation', which is hope; 'the breastplate of righteousness, the girdle of truth, the feet shod with the preparation of the gospel of peace, the sword of the Spirit' and lastly, 'the shield of faith'. There is no piece or armour for the back-parts, because there is no flight in this spiritual warfare. We must stand to it: 'Resist the devil and he will flee from you' (James 4:7). Now, which is the choicest piece of this armour? 'Above all, take the shield of faith.' Why? Because it giveth life, and being, and vigour to other graces; it preserveth all the rest, and therefore is fitly compared to a shield which covereth the whole body.

The apostle beginneth with 'the girdle of truth', or sincerity; or an honest intention to live according to the will of God: when a man endeavoureth to be, both to God and man, what he seemeth to be. Satan useth wiles, but we must be sincere. It is dangerous to fight against him with his own weapons; we cannot match our adversary for craft and policy; our strength lieth in truth and plain-dealing. A girdle strengtheneth the loins, so this giveth courage and boldness.

Then there is 'the breastplate of righteousness', or that grace that puts us upon a holy conversation suitable to God's will revealed in the word, whereby we endeavour to give God and man their due. This secureth the breast, or the vital parts; that seed of inherent grace, or an honest, fixed purpose to obey God in all things.

And then 'the feet must be shod with the preparation of the gospel of peace'. We shall meet with rough ways as we are advancing towards heaven. And what is the 'preparation of the gospel of peace?' It is a sense of the peace and friendship made up between God and us by Christ. Without this we shall never follow God in ways of duty, when we meet with difficulties and hardships.

Then 'the helmet of salvation', which is the hope of eternal life: 'And for a helmet the hope of salvation' (1 Thess. 5:8), which maketh us hold up our heads in the midst of all blows and sore assaults, and is our great motive and encouragement in the Christian course.

Then 'the sword of the Spirit, which is the word of God', dwelling in us richly, furnishing us with arguments against every particular temptation. These do all worthily [These parts of our armour are all good].

But 'above all, take the shield of faith', which covereth [protects] all the other armour. Who would care for the girdle of truth, if he did not believe there was a God to see and reward all that he doeth? The breastplate of righteousness would lie by neglected if faith did not persuade us this is the way to please God, and attain our own happiness. We should never learn to put on the shoes of the gospel of peace if we were not justified by faith in Christ's death; for so we come to have peace with God: 'Being justified by faith, we have peace with God' (Rom. 5:1). Hope would languish did not faith give us a real and an effective sight of the world to come. And 'the sword of the Spirit', or word of God, is only managed by faith persuading us of the truth of the threatenings, and promises, and precepts, that these are of God. So that it is faith, or a constant adhering to the truth of the gospel, that quickeneth, and covereth, and enableth us to make use of all the other parts of the spiritual armour.

And therefore in another place it is said, 'Fight the good fight of faith, lay hold of eternal life' (1 Tim. 6:12). The whole spiritual combat is a fight between faith and sense, faith and Satan. The great thing for which we fight is faith: 'I have fought a good fight, I have finished my course, I have kept the faith' (2 Tim. 4:7). And the great thing by which we fight is faith; this is evident in those words of Christ to Peter: 'Satan hath desired to winnow you as wheat, but I have prayed that they faith fail not' (Luke 22:31-32); implying that we shall be able to abide the encounter while faith holdeth out. Why?

(i) Because by faith we set God before us as the spectator and helper in the conflict: 'He endured, as seeing him that is invisible' (Heb. 11:27). And so we see more for us than against us: 'Fear not, for they that be with us are more than they that be with them' (2 Kgs. 6:16).

(ii) By faith we believe that God is true in all the promises of the gospel; and so temptations are defeated, whether they tend to atheism, blasphemy, unbelief, despair, or any sensual practice. Man fell at first by believing the devil rather than God (Gen. 3:3), and we stand now by believing God rather than the devil. When we are tempted to any unworthy thoughts of God, or unseemly practices against him, while we keep close to his word, because God cannot lie, this giveth us victory.

(iii) And by faith we set the merit and power of Christ a-work for us, and so are encouraged to make resistance. Satan is not only called the enemy, that assaults by strength and force, but *antidikos*, our adversary (1 Pet. 5:8), in point of law and right, he is both a tempter and an accuser. Now in point of law Satan would carry it against all that come of Adam, were it not that Christ hath freed us from the curse of the law. Now without faith we are destitute of Christ's imputed righteousness; for that is 'unto all, and upon all them that believe' (Rom. 3:22). And only received by faith: 'And be found in him, not having our own righteousness, which is of the law, but that which is through the faith of Christ, the righteousness which is of God by faith' (Phil. 3:9). And so we are not only exposed to the dint of sin-pursuing justice, or the wrath of God: 'He that believeth not the Son, hath not life, but the wrath of God abideth on him' (John 3:36), but to all the bitter accusations and challenges of the devil our adversary. But when we are possessed of it by faith, then, 'Who shall lay anything to the charge of God's elect? it is God that justifieth' (Rom. 8:33). We may silence Satan by the righteousness of Christ.

Again, as he opposeth by strength and power, faith engageth the power of God on our behalf: 'Be strong in the Lord, and in the power of his might' (Eph. 6:10). Without this, if we stand by our single [own] strength, we are exposed as a prey to every temptation; but when we set Christ against the tempter, we are not so weak in the hands of Satan as Satan is in the hands of Christ. He that sideth with us against Satan hath an absolute command over him. If he will be our second [supporter], why should we fear? Satan hath no more power in him than any other creature, which may be taken away at God's pleasure, and is in the meantime limited by him. The unclean spirits obeyed Christ in his lifetime upon earth (Mark 1:27). If Christ do but say the word, at his rebuke they vanish.

Well then, you see temptations from Satan must be, will be; and the means to resist him is not by spells, but by faith, or confidence in the death, intercession and power of Christ. This evil spirit is not driven away with crosses, and holy water, and charms, and relics, but by a steadfast faith in Christ, according to the promises of the gospel.

2. Having showed the necessity of living by faith in an hour of temptation, I now come to show what are the grounds, props and supports of faith against Satan's temptations.

1. Christ's victory over Satan. Christ hath obtained a fourfold victory over Satan, all which doth encourage our faith:

1.1 By his personal conflict with him in his own temptations. Jesus Christ himself was tempted (Matt. 4); and therefore we should not be dismayed when we are tempted. It becomes good soldiers to follow the captain of their salvation. He is the more likely to pity and succour us: 'For that himself hath suffered, being tempted, he is able to succour them that are tempted' (Heb. 2:18); as a man troubled with the [gall] stone, or gout, his heart is entendered to pity others, labouring under the same exquisite and racking pains; as Israel was to pity strangers, because they themselves were once in the same condition. *Non ignara mali, miseris succurrere disco* [Knowing trouble as I do, I have learned to help the wretched]. He hath pulled out the sting of temptations by submitting to be tempted in his own person. He sanctified every condition that he passed through. His dying hath pulled out the sting of death; so his being tempted hath made that condition the more comfortable. He hath directed us how to stand out, and by what kind of weapons we are to foil Satan. He that is a pattern in doing and suffering is also a pattern in resisting; and not only so, but he hath overcome Satan. Our general in whose quarrel we are engaged, hath already vanquished Satan; he got his victory over Satan for us. *Christus diabolum vicit*, saith Austin[7], *et pro te vicit, et tibi vicit, et in te vicit.* [Christ conquered for you, to you and in 'you'.] Christ hath beaten Satan to our hands. Christ's victory over Satan, though it be by himself, yet it is not for himself, but for his members, that we may have the victory over him, and comfort in all our temptations; as he hath shown us the way to fight, so he hath assured us of victory, that we shall overcome.

1.2 Another victory he obtained over him was by his death: 'Through death he destroyed him that had the power of death, that is the devil' (Heb. 2:14). Never was such a blow given to the kingdom of darkness as then; not to take away his immortal life and being, but his power and strength to hurt. Then was Satan disarmed, and afterwards by his Spirit Christ cometh and dispossesseth him; so Colossians 2:15: 'And having spoiled principalities and powers, he made a show of them openly, triumphing over them in it; and Ephesians 4:8: 'He hath led captivity captive.' Upon the cross he overcame his and our enemies, and triumphed over them; satisfying his Father's justice, he spoiled the devil of that power which he once had over the souls of men through the law's curse; so that, though the devil doth tempt believers, yet he cannot overcome them – *Non pugnâ sublatâ sed victoriâ*. The devil may molest us, not totally vanquish us: Christ will not exempt us from a battle, yet it is a spoiled adversary we fight with, he hath secured us the victory. He may hold us in exercise, but he cannot break our head. The wounds we receive from Satan may be painful, but not mortal so as to quench the life of grace. Though he foil us sometimes, yet we are kept by the power of God to salvation. A man may be bruised in the heel by divers temptations, and slip into sins thereby; but is it but in the heel, far enough from any vital part.

1.3 He prevailed over the devil by his gospel, when he first sent abroad his disciples to the lost sheep of Israel: 'And he said unto them, I beheld Satan as lightning fall from heaven' (Luke 10:18); but especially after his ascension, and the pouring out of the Spirit, when he sent abroad his disciples into the world, casting down the idols of the gentiles, under which the devil was adored: 'What say I then? that the idol is anything? or that which is offered in sacrifice to idols is anything? but I say, The things which the gentiles sacrifice, they sacrifice to devils, and not to God' (1 Cor. 10:19-20). And he still goeth on conquering and prevailing, putting Satan out of possession: 'When a strong man armed keepeth the house, his goods are in peace; but when a stronger than he shall come upon him, and overcome him, he taketh from him all his armour wherein he trusted, and divideth his spoils' (Luke 11:21-22); as he doth enlighten, reclaim, and sanctify all the elect, and subdue those lusts by which Satan ruleth in the hearts of men. If Christ conquereth Satan by his word, and by the preaching of the gospel establishing his kingdom, his word shall dwell richly and abundantly in our hearts, that we may oppose the commandments of God and his counsels to the counsels and solicitations of the devil, and look that this word that prevaileth over all the world should prevail with us also: 'This word is come into all the world, and bringeth forth fruit, as it doth also in you' (Col. 1:6).

1.4 The last victory that Christ shall have is at the day of judgment: 'That at the name of Jesus every knee should bow, of things in heaven, and things in earth, and things under the earth' (Phil. 2:10). Compare this with Romans 14:10-11: 'We must all stand before the judgement-seat of Christ; for it is written, as I live, saith the Lord, every knee shall bow to me.' Then 'the devil shall be cast into the lake of fire and brimstone' (Rev. 20:10), and all the saints, together with Christ, shall triumph over him: 'The God of peace shall bruise Satan under your feet shortly' (Rom. 16:20); as Joshua and his followers set their feet on the necks of the Canaanitish kings in the cave. So that our absolute and final victory is near and sure. God will do it, and shortly. Then we shall never be troubled [any] more with a busy devil. All his power shall be broken in pieces. This will be a glorious conquest indeed and a mighty comfort and relief to us in the sharp conflicts we now have.

2. There are many promises that concern this warfare: promises of strength, of victory, and of the reward of victory.

2.1 Of strength, or such supplies of grace as we may be enabled to stand out against the powers of darkness. Paul was buffeted with a messenger of Satan, and he knocked at the door of grace thrice, all the answer he could get was, 'My grace is sufficient for thee, for my strength is made perfect in weakness' (2 Cor. 12:7). This promise was particularly made to Paul, but the reason is general; God's power is perfected, that is, manifested to be perfect, in the weakness of the creature. It is his glory to give 'power to the faint; and to them that have no might he giveth strength' (Isa. 40:29), that they may rejoice in the Lord their strength. Jesus Christ, who is the head of the church, will also be the Saviour of the body, that the glory may rebound to him alone. He hath a tender sense of our danger, and is never more at work for his people than when they are more assaulted by Satan. He doth in effect say, They are undone if I help them not; 'And he showed me Joshua the high-priest, standing before the angel of the Lord, and Satan standing at his right hand to resist him. And the Lord said unto Satan, The Lord rebuke thee, O Satan, even the God that hath chosen Jerusalem, rebuke thee. Is not this a brand plucked out of the fire?' (Zech. 3:1-2). And thereupon he puts forth the strength and efficacy of his mediation. Our friend in heaven, and advocate, is pleading for new grace for us. When a town is besieged, they are not left to their standing provisions, but relief is sent to them. Christ will engage and fight for us.

2.2 Promises of victory; there are many in scripture: 'The seed of the woman shall break the serpent's head' (Gen. 3:15). It is not only true of Christ, but of his seed; they shall prevail at length and conquer, together with Christ: so Matthew 16:18: 'Upon this rock I will build my church, and the gates of hell shall not prevail against it.' In the gates was their munition and defence, and there they sat in council and judicature; so that the expression intimateth that all the power and policy of hell shall not prevail against the church of God, nor any member thereof, to destroy utterly the work of God's grace in their hearts; so 1 John 5:18: 'He that is begotten of God keepeth himself, and that wicked one toucheth him not'; that is *tactu qualitativa* [with a qualitative (touch)], as Cajetan[8] speaks, with a deadly, mortal touch; and James 4:7: 'Resist the devil, and he will flee from you.' Though he cometh ramping and roaring, and seeking to devour us yet if we seriously resist, Satan will depart; whereas, the more we yield, he tyranniseth the more (Matt. 12:44). These and many other promises there are made, to assure us that if we will but stand to it, Satan shall not prevail.

2.3 Of reward upon victory: 'Be faithful unto death, and I will give thee a crown of life' (Rev. 2:10), that is, a garland of immortality, if we will be faithful, seriously own God's cause, and make a stout and peremptory resistance, without thinking of flying from him, or yielding to him in the least. So in many other places: 'He that overcometh, shall not be hurt of the second death' (Rev. 2:11); and 'To him that overcometh I will grant to sit with me upon my throne, as I also overcame, and am sat down with my Father upon his throne' (Rev. 3:21). Stay but a while, and there will a time of triumph come, and you shall be able to say, 'Henceforth there is laid up for me a crown of righteousness, which the Lord the righteous Judge shall give me that day' (2 Tim. 4:8). He that is now a soldier, shall then be a conqueror, and the danger of the battle will increase the joy of victory. Travellers, when they come into their inn, can sweetly remember the troubles and dangers of the road.

3.1 To cause us to renounce our own strength, and to look up to the Lord for help: 'We have no might against this great company that cometh against us, neither know we what to do,

LIFE OF FAITH AND TEMPTATIONS OF SATAN

but our eyes are unto thee' (2 Chr. 20:12). It is a good address in spiritual cases as well as temporal. There must be a renouncing of our own strength before we can expect help from the Lord; for 'God giveth grace to the humble' (Jas. 4:6). And you shall see in the next verse, it is that whereby we resist, not only natural corruption, but the devil's temptations: 'Submit yourselves therefore unto God, resist the devil, and he will flee from you' (verse 7). Here he explains who are the humble, they 'that submit themselves to God'. It is not to be understood morally of those that are of a lowly carriage towards men, but spiritually of those that in the brokenness of their hearts do acknowledge their own nothingness and weakness. God withholdeth and withdraweth his influences when we do not acknowledge the daily and hourly necessity of grace, when we do not desire it with such earnestness, nor receive it with such joyfulness as we were wont. In the Lord's prayer, the word *daily*, though it be only mentioned in the fourth petition, yet it concerneth all the rest, especially the two following petitions, 'daily bread', and 'daily pardon', and 'daily strength' against temptations, they are all alike necessary: 'I have set the Lord always before me, because he is at my right hand, I shall not be moved' (Ps. 16:8); we must set God before us in point of reverence, and in point of dependence. As a glass without a bottom falleth to the ground, and is broken as soon as it is set out of hand; so doth a sensible Christian apprehend himself to be in such a condition out of God's hand that he falleth, and is broken to pieces. If the new creature could live of itself, God would seldom hear from us; therefore every day we must come for new supplies [of grace].

3.2 To keep us from discouragement and fainting under temptations. Wherefore have we armour, but to use it when we are called to fight? For what use serveth Jesus Christ, but 'to destroy the works of the devil'? (1 John 3:8) He came into the world to grapple with our enemy, that by the fall had gotten an hand and power over us. If he hath conquered the devil, and that for our sakes, why should we be afraid? Satan cannot tempt us one jot further than the Lord will permit him; his malice is limited and restrained. If you be in Satan's hands, Satan is in God's hands. He could not enter into the herd of swine without leave (Mark 5:12); and will God suffer him to worry and destroy the sheep of his flock without any regard or pity? God gave him a commission to afflict Job (chapters 1 and 2). Hath he not engaged his faithfulness that we shall not be tempted more than we are able to bear? He will give strength (2 Cor. 10:13). If he lets Satan loose upon you, look to Jesus Christ, with all his merits, value, virtue and power. Is he not able to defend thee? It is true in general, Christ as mediator hath done nothing apart [but what benefits Christians]. All his members have an interest with him [in all that he has done] Did he overcome Satan for himself? No, he hath overcome, and his people overcome with him: 'I write to you, young ones, because ye have overcome the wicked one' (1 John 3:13). Christ needed no such combat with Satan, nor victory over him, for anything that concerned himself, seeing he had in the beginning cast him down to hell, where he holdeth him still in chains of darkness.

3.3 But this is not all the work of faith, to keep us from fainting; it should also fill us with courage, and assurance of victory:

> 'Nay, in all these things we are more than conquerors, through him that loved us. For I am persuaded that neither death, nor life, nor angels, nor principalities, nor powers, nor things present, nor things to come, nor height, nor depth, nor any other creature, shall be able to separate us from the love of God which is in Jesus Christ our Lord' (Rom. 8:37-39).

LIFE OF FAITH AND TEMPTATIONS OF SATAN

Before the battle a believer is sure of victory. In other fights the event is uncertain: *Non aeque glorietur accinctus, ac discinctus*; but a believer, when he goeth to fight, is sure to have the best of the war, because the Father and Christ are stronger than all their enemies, and they cannot pluck him out of their hands:

> 'And I give unto them eternal life, and they shall never perish, neither shall any man pluck them out of my hand. My Father which gave them me is greater than all, and no man is able to pluck them out of my Father's hand' (John 10:28-29).

They may have many shakings and tossings in their condition, yet their final perseverance is certain. Christ is so unchangeable in his purpose, so invincible in his power, that when once he taketh a man into his custody and charge, who can destroy him? We do overcome, are sure of victory before we fight. Believe and prosper: 'Believe in the Lord your God, so shall ye be established; believe his prophets, so shall ye prosper' (2 Chr. 20:20). In temporal cases a man doth not presently conquer those he shall fight with; though he doth believe he shall conquer them, yet a particular impression doth much. But here is a promise made by God; there is a covenant passed between us and him; to what end? We have his bond for it, that if we fight against Satan, we shall overcome; resist and he will fly. You will say, Is it no more but [than to] believe the promise, and Satan is gone?

Answer: Yes; if it be with a right faith, such as quickeneth us to a serious and thorough resistance, then thou hast nothing to do but to remember that thou fightest God's battle, in God's sight, and he will crown thee.

4. To engage us to use all the means God hath appointed for the vanquishing [of] temptations, namely, watching and striving.

4.1 Watching: 'Be sober and watchful; for your adversary the devil goeth about seeking whom he may devour' (1 Pet. 5:7). Watch, that you may not give Satan an advantage (2 Cor. 2:11), or an occasion (1 Cor. 7:5); and 'Use not your liberty as an occasion to the flesh' (Gal. 5:13). They cannot stand long that lay themselves open to Satan's snares, and ride into the devil quarters [territory]. Therefore we must guard the senses and take off [avoid] occasions leading to sin.

4.2 Striving and resistance: 'Whom resist, steadfast in the faith' (1 Pet. 5:9); 'Resist the devil, and he will flee from you' (Jas. 4:7). We make but a faint and cold resistance. Some kind of resistance may be made by common grace; but it must be earnest and vehement as against the enemy of our souls: 'Get thee behind me, Satan' (Matt. 4:10). A merchant that hath a precious commodity, and one biddeth a base price, he foldeth up his wares with indignation. As the olive-tree said in Jotham's parable, 'Shall I leave my fatness to rule over the trees?' so [must you] say, 'Shall I leave my soul open, without a guard, for every temptation to make a prey of me? A thorough resistance there must be; yielding a little bringeth on more mischief.

6

The Life of Faith and the Temptations of the World

That faith hath a great use and influence upon our victory over this kind of temptations appeareth by that scripture which we have in 1 John 5:4: 'Whosoever is born of God overcometh the world; and this is the victory that overcomes the world, even our faith.'

First, I shall explain this maxim; secondly, I will show the necessity of this part of the life of faith; thirdly, I will show what are the acts of faith; fourthly, how we may bring our hearts to such a frame [attitude].

1. What is meant by 'the world?'

All worldly things whatsoever, so far as they lessen our esteem of Christ and heavenly things, or hinder the cheerful performance of our duty to God, namely, honour, riches, pomp, pleasure, the favour or fear of men, their wrath, praise or dispraise; as these prevail and find entertainment [a welcome] in our hearts, so far they hinder the life of faith: 'How can ye believe which receive honour one of another, and seek not the honour that cometh from God only?' (John 5:44) and 'Nevertheless, among the chief rulers also many believed on him; but because of the Pharisees they did not confess him, lest they should be put out of the synagogue, for they loved the praise of men more than the praise of God' (John 12:42). We read in 1 John 2:15: 'Love not the world, nor the things that are in the world. If any man love the world, the love of the Father is not in him.' Another text is 2 Timothy 4:10: 'For Demas hath forsaken me, having embraced the present world'; and so far as faith prevaileth, the heart groweth dead to these things; in short, to the delights and terrors of the world, the fears and snares of it. A Christian should have on the 'armour of righteousness, on the right hand and on the left' (2 Cor. 6:7).

Man is apt to be wrought upon both ways, by the fears of evil, and hopes of good. Accordingly, in the world to come, where lie the great objects propounded to faith, there is something to outweigh the fears of this life:

> 'Then Peter began to say unto him, Lo, we have left all, and have followed thee. And Jesus answered and said, Verily I say unto you, There is no man that hath left house, or brethren, or sisters, or father, or mother, or wife, or children, or lands, for my sake, and the gospel's. But he shall receive a hundredfold now in this time, houses, and brethren, and sisters, and mothers, and children, and lands, with persecutions; and in the world to come eternal life' (Mark 10:28-30).

Here is something to outweigh the pleasures of this world and to set the recompense of reward against the pleasures of sin. Luther said: *Contemptus a me est Romanus, et favor et furor* ['I despise both the pope's favour and fury]. But chiefly that scriptural instance of Moses is remarkable. Moses had temptations of all kinds (Heb. 11:24-27). There were temptations on the right hand and on the left; if honour would have tempted him, he might have had it; but 'by faith he refused to be called the son of Pharaoh's daughter' (verse 24). If pleasures would have tempted him, he might have enjoyed them; but 'he chose rather to suffer afflictions with the people of God, than to enjoy the pleasures of sin for a season' (verse 25). If the riches and treasures of this world would have enticed him, he might have flowed in them [had them to the full]. But 'he esteemed the reproaches of Christ greater riches than the treasures of Egypt' (verse 26), than 'left-handed' tempta-

LIFE OF FAITH AND TEMPTATIONS OF THE WORLD 141

tions, or the terrors of the world. 'By faith he forsook Egypt, not fearing the wrath of the king; for he endured, as seeing him who is invisible.' Thus we must stand out against all temptations: 'Add to temperance, patience' (2 Pet. 1:6).

A Christian that would hold out with God must have a command over all his passions of anger, fear and grief, and over his affections of love and delight, that he may not be corrupted with sensual delights, nor discouraged with the crosses and trials that he meeteth with in the world. We must observe both, lest we be, like Ephraim, a 'cake not turned', that we do not forfeit our integrity, as Joab did, who turned not after Absalom, but turned after Adonijah (1 Kgs. 1:19). On the other side, some may bear up against boisterous temptations out of stubbornness, humour, and interest [gain], and the pre-engagement of credit, the expectation of applause, or to carry a name, yet are lost in the lusts of the flesh and vanities of the world. Again, all are not called to the afflictions of the gospel, and so are not tempted to apostasy. In the parable of the sower there is the stony ground that withered in persecution (Luke 8:13), and the thorny ground that brought forth no fruit to perfection, being choked with the cares, riches and pleasures of the world (Luke 8:14). Here is our daily conflict. The holding on of profession is an external thing; the victory is less over outward inconveniences than inward lusts. It is the sharpest martyrdom for a man to tear his own flesh, more than to give his body to be burned (1 Cor. 13:3). The secret and sly victory of the world is over our will and affections, and if we do not prevent this, our profession is as good as nothing. Though we should keep on a profession, whilst we secretly gratify our lusts, all our sufferings are but like swine's blood offered in sacrifice, which was an abomination to the Lord.

2. In what sense are we said to have victory over the world?

Faith is said to be the victory over these things by a metonomy of the effect for the instrumental cause. It is the means whereby we overcome. However the force of the expression is to be noted: faith is not only said to be the means of overcoming, but the victory itself. But when may it be called a victory?

2.1 We are said to overcome the world when we stand our ground and are not overcome by it. It lieth not in being free from troubles and temptations, but in a courageous and resolute resistance. Though the temptation cease not, yet if we keep what we fight for all is won. See 2 Timothy 4:8: 'I have fought a good fight, I have kept the faith'; Romans 8:37: 'We are more than conquerors'; and Revelation 12:11: 'They overcame him by the blood of the Lamb, and by the word of their testimony, and they loved not their lives unto the death.' So it is when a man abideth constant with God, notwithstanding the flatteries or threatenings of the world, and is not drawn to apostasy, as the Levites left their possessions for the sake of God's pure worship (2 Chr. 11:14).

2.2 We overcome the world when we get ground by the temptation, and this either externally or internally.

(i) Externally, when our profession is glorified and commended to the consciences of men by our resolved defence and avowing of it: 'They overcame by the word of their testimony, not loving their lives to the death' (Rev. 12:11). *Sanguis martyrum semen ecclesiae* ['The blood of the martyrs is the seed of the church]; by their steadfast profession and adhering to the truth they defeated the devil and propagated the gospel. So Paul in Philippians 1:12: 'The things that have happened unto me have fallen out rather for the furtherance of the gospel.' His suffering for the truth conduced as much to the propagation of it as his preaching.

(ii) Internally, when we are more confirmed in the truth of the gospel and the pursuit of heavenly things, and gain strength by every conflict; as the apostle telleth us in Romans 5:3-5 that 'tribulation worketh patience; and patience experience, and experience hope, and hope maketh not ashamed, because the love of God is shed abroad in our hearts.' The more we are assaulted, the more the habit of grace is perfected; as David when scoffed at by Michal: 'I will yet be more vile' (2 Sam. 6:22). It often falleth out that our courage groweth by sufferings, and those that were ready to faint are at least more rooted by being shaken; and so Christians are 'more than conquerors' (Rom. 8:37), as they thrive by opposition. A staff is held the faster [firmer] by how much it is sought the more to be wrested [wrenched] out of our hands.

What faith is this that overcometh the world?
Answer: It is not a naked assent, or a cold opinion, or that which the scripture calleth a 'dead faith' (Jas. 2:17), but such as is lively and operative. It is described in 1 John 5:5: 'And who is he that overcometh the world, but he that believeth that Jesus is the Son of God.' That is the great vital or enlivening truth, that Christ is God; therefore when Peter made his confession ('Thou art Christ, the Son of the living God') Christ telleth him that 'flesh and blood hath not revealed it unto thee, but my Father which is in heaven. And I say also unto thee, that thou art Peter, and upon this rock will I build my church' (Matt. 16:16-18). This truth, that Jesus is the promised Messiah, very God and man in one person, and the anointed Saviour of the world, is a truth that cannot be attained by any human means, and is the cornerstone upon which the faith of

all believers is founded; and whosoever doth indeed build his hope upon it, the gates of hell shall not prevail against him. Many take up this opinion upon human credulity, or as the current and avowed truth of the age and country in which they live; the universal consent of the Christian world hath taken up such a principle. But those that do indeed receive it, and put all their hopes of salvation upon it, these overcome the world. More particularly:

1 It is such a faith as receiveth a whole Christ, as king, priest and prophet: 'To as many as receive him' (John 1:12); that doth so believe Jesus to be the Messiah and Saviour of the world, as to believe his promises, and fear his threats, and obey his precepts. For such a one hath far stronger allectives [enticements] and encouragements to piety that the world can afford to the contrary. Christ hath promises of life and immortality with which this world with all its emoluments is not to be compared, or brought into reckoning the same day (Rom. 8:18). Christ hath threatenings (Mark 9:44), in comparison of [with] which all the punishments and tortures in the world are but a flea-biting, or a thing not to be mentioned. His commands of bearing the cross and denying ourselves may be well digested, and will outweigh all the allurements and terrors of the world, if we indeed cordially believe them. But when men stick at [hesitate to obey] these poor inconsiderable vanities, surely they do not take Christ to be the Messiah or Son of God. There are no comforts, no terrors like his and no commands like his, because they are his commands: 'My hands also will I lift up unto thy commandments, which I have loved, and I will meditate in thy statutes' (Ps. 119:48).

2 It is such a faith as receiveth Christ with the whole heart, a cordial assent: 'If thou believest with all thy heart' (Acts 8:37).

A naked opinion is easily begotten in us. But we must so believe Christ as to profess his name, to hope for the things promised by him, and under that hope to follow his precepts and directions. Such an effectual faith overcometh the world.

3 Such a faith as 'worketh by love' (Gal. 5:6); as draweth us to love God above all, and to make the enjoyment of him our chief scope and happiness. This will excite us to observe what conduceth to this enjoyment of God, and eschew [avoid] the contrary. Our first sin was a turning from God to the creature, and our conversion is a turning from the creature to God, to love him above all, as our reconciled God and Father in Christ. He that hath such a faith may with ease overcome the world, and the terrors and temptations thereof; and he that is carried captive to the world hath not such a faith and is not a cordial believer.

The necessity and profit of this part of the life of faith.
1. It is by the world that our spiritual enemies have advantage against us. Satan lieth in ambush in the creature, and seeketh to work us off from God by the terrors and allurements of the world; therefore it is said in 1 John 4:4: 'Ye are of God, and have overcome him, because greater is he that is in you than he that is in the world.' Conquer the world, and the tempter is disarmed, and disabled from doing that hurt to you which otherwise he would. He blindeth as 'the god of this world' (2 Cor. 4:4). He troubleth us 'as the prince of this world'; 'The prince of this world cometh, and hath nothing in me' (John 14:30). He findeth it no hard matter to entice a sensual worldly mind to almost anything that is evil. He may do what he lists with them; but when once these inclinations are mortified and broken, the cord is broken by which he was wont to bind and lead you. The strength of temptations lieth in the bent [bias] of

our affections. Let a man be in love with wealth, or honours and pleasures, and how soon will the devil draw him to betray, and cast away his soul for any of these things! The world is the bait and provision for the flesh: 'Whatever is in the world' is in 'the lust of the flesh, the lust of the eyes, and pride of life' (1 John 2:16). The lust is put for the object, either riches, pleasures or honours. It is the world that fits us with a diet for every distemper, and a bait agreeable to every appetite. A proud corrupted mind must have honour and high place, and be supplied with pomp of living. An inordinate, sensual appetite must have pleasures and meats and drinks. So the covetous must have wealth and bags of gold. So that if you conquer the world, you may pluck up temptations by the root. Lusts will wither and come to nothing. The flesh is furnished with its prey from hence.

2. It is the great let [restraint] and hindrance from keeping the commandments, and keeping them cheerfully. Worldly lust and allurements soon tempt us to transgress, till faith gets the upper hand: 'That denying ungodliness and worldly lusts, we should live righteously sober, and godly in this present world' (Titus 2:12). The world soon maketh a breach upon sobriety, or justice or godliness. Denying worldly lusts must first be done, and as a means to the other, or else your hearts will never be free for God and his service. It is the world that hindereth you from duty, and from walking sweetly and comfortable with God in your whole course. While these fetter and clogs [handicaps] are upon you, you cannot run the race that is set before you:

> 'Wherefore seeing we also are compassed about with so great a cloud of witnesses, let us let aside every weight, and the sin which do so easily beset us, and let us run with patience the race that is set before us' (Heb. 12:1).

You have no heart, no life for holy things, because your affections are diverted: 'Turn away mine eyes from beholding vanity' (Ps. 119:36). Inordinate desire of, and delight in worldly things, diverts our minds from the pursuit of heavenly things.

3. This constituteth the great difference between the animal life and the spiritual life. The rational soul, being void of grace, accommodateth itself to the interests of the body, and the difference lieth in being addicted to the world or vanquishing the world. A mere animal man is one that merely looketh after the concernments of this life, and is swayed by the interests of this life, as power and pomp, and greatness of rank and place in the world. But a spiritual man is one that looketh after the world to come: 'For we have not received the spirit of this world' (1 Cor. 2:12). And these two lives are distinguished again:

> For they that are after the flesh do mind the things of the flesh; but they that are after the Spirit, the things of the Spirit. For to be carnally-minded is death; but to be spiritually-minded is life and peace. Because the carnal mind is enmity against God, for it is not subject to the law of God, neither indeed can be (Rom. 8:5-7).

A mere animal life is the same with the carnal life; for those that do not live the life of grace are sometimes described by their worse, and sometimes their better part. So John 3:6: 'That which is born of the flesh is flesh, and that which is born of the Spirit is spirit.' Christ showeth the necessity of being born again before a man can enter into the kingdom of God; they can never else be spiritual in their disposition, motions and inclinations. The merely animal life is wholly bent to please the flesh, and to seek the interests and concernments thereof, as riches, honours and pleasures. For reason is either brutified and debased by sense, or elevated and refined by faith.

4. We have a daily conflict with the world. If we are not daily put upon dangers and difficulties (in which respect the apostle saith, 'I die daily' (1 Cor. 15:31), yet we are daily put upon snares and temptations, and the pleasant baits of the flesh. These things are suitable to our natures, and comfortable to our senses, and necessary to our uses. We have a fleshy part as well as a spiritual; so that if we do not continually watch and guard our hearts, we are overcome, and that to our utter ruin. This is the case with many men; the good word is choked in them by the pleasures and cares of the world (Matt. 13:22-23; Luke 8:14), so that they are never thorough Christians, whatever proficiency they have attained unto, or whatever profession that make of the name of Christ. Multitudes are thus deceived that make a profession of religion, whilst their worldly lusts remain in full strength, as thorns draw away the strength of the earth from good seed, and overtop [overgrow] it, and keep it down. Many have a form of godliness, but are lovers of pleasures, lovers of riches and honours, more than God. God hath but the flesh's leavings.

3. The acts of faith in this victory over the world

3.1 It overcometh the world, as it digesteth and applieth the word of God. The word of God is the sword of the Spirit, the great weapon against the world, the devil and the flesh; and the more richly we are furnished with the knowledge of it, the more we are prepared for a victory over Satan and the world: 'I have written unto you, young men, because ye are strong, and the word of God abideth in you, and ye have overcome the wicked one' (1 John 2:14). There are notable counsels, pure precepts, rich promises, powerful directions and sundry considerations to draw us off the world, that we may look after [forward to] the world to come; that is the drift of the whole scripture. Now all must be digested and applied by

LIFE OF FAITH AND TEMPTATIONS OF THE WORLD 149

faith, or it worketh not: 'Let us therefore fear, lest, a promise being left us of entering into his rest, any of you should seem to come short of it. For unto us was the gospel preached, as well as unto them; but the word preached did not profit them, not being mixed with faith in them that heard it' (Heb. 4:1-2). In the word of God there are 'precious promises, that we may escape the corruption that is in the world through lust' (2 Pet. 1:4); promises that contain spiritual and eternal riches. If we can believe the pardon, grace and blessedness that are offered in them, then these things will keep us from being ensnared by the world. Among all these promises, the chiefest is the promise of entering into his rest. Meat will nourish us if it be eaten, and water will quench thirst if we drink it, and receive it into our bodies. So will these promises where they are applied.

3.2 As it receiveth the Spirit, or strength from Christ, whereby to overcome the world. He died to purchase this grace for us: 'He gave himself for us, to deliver us from the present evil world' (Gal. 1:4); that is, to purchase the Spirit to dwell in our hearts. For this end and purpose, see 1 John 4:4: 'Greater is he that is in you than he that is in the world.' We must not rest upon our own strength in our war against the world, but by faith lean upon Christ, who worketh is us by his Spirit, and beateth down Satan under our feet.

3.3 It prepossesseth [occupies] the mind with the glory of the world to come. Moses had an eye to 'the recompense of reward' (Heb. 11:26); and 2 Corinthians 4:18: 'While we look not to the things which are seen, but to the things which are not seen; for the things which are seen are temporal, but the things which are not seen are eternal.' The more sight we have of the worth and excellency of spiritual things, the more is our esteem of the world abated (weakened), and consequently the force of the temptation. Diversion is the cure of the soul. While the mind is kept intent upon the greater matters of everlasting life, the heart and affections are drawn off from present things. The world will not be cast out of our affections but by the real sight of something better than itself. Till faith hath opened heaven to you, and evidenced things invisible and showed you that they are not shadows but substances, which the promise revealeth and believers expect, you will still be catching at present things [of this present time] as your portion. No eye can pierce so far as heaven, but only faith: 'Faith is the evidence of things not seen' (Heb. 11:1).

3.4 It improveth Christ's victory over the world, and applieth it for our comfort and encouragement: 'In the world ye shall have tribulation: but be of good cheer, I have overcome the world' (John 16:33). He overcame the world in his personal conflict, and by his death. Now the victory of Christ our head concerneth his members. For he did not overcome the world for himself, but for us: 'But thanks be to God, who giveth us the victory through our Lord Jesus Christ' (1 Cor. 15:57). He overcame the world in our name, and when we are interested [have an interest] in him, he maketh us conquerors together with himself, and in all our conflicts and sufferings assureth us of a certain victory. So that his suffering people need not be dismayed with the power and policy, the threats and terrors of the world. For though Christ will not exempt them from a battle and exercise, yet they are partakers of his victory by faith, and shall, abiding in him, find they have to do with enemies already vanquished. He would have us so certain, that yet we should not be secure; and doth so exhort us to fight, that first he promiseth the victory before we go to the battle. *Non aeque glorietur accinctus, ac discinctus* ['Let not him who putteth on his armour as he who putteth it off'].

LIFE OF FAITH AND TEMPTATIONS OF THE WORLD

3.5 Faith enlighteneth the mind to see things in another manner than the world seeth them, and maketh that evident to a Christian which the world seeth not; not only things to come, or the riches of the glory of the inheritance of the saints, but things present – the vanity of earthly things, that 'man in his best estate is altogether vanity' (Ps. 34:5). To see it so as it begets a weanedness from the world, and maketh us 'use the world as if we used it not' (1 Cor. 7:29-30). Others have empty notions, so as to be able to discourse of the vanity of the creature, but not an affective sight; eyes to see, but not a heart to see. But in faith there is not only notional apprehension, but spiritual wisdom and prudence (Eph. 1:17). It is opposed not only to ignorance, but folly: 'O fools, and slow of heart to believe?' (Luke 24:25). It affects us suitably to the things we know. Carnal men know all things after the flesh, and are affected with them according to their present interest. They have false practical conceits of the world, and so are enamoured upon a dream. They do not consider and therefore admire flesh-pleasing vanities; they do not weight things in the balance of reason, nor improve those general notions that they have. The sight that faith hath of the world is as the apprehensions of a dying man, serious and piercing; those that worldly men have are like the notions of a disputant [one who simply talks].

3.6 It enableth us with patience to wait upon God for his salvation: 'It is good that a man should both hope and quietly wait for the salvation of the Lord' (Lam. 3:26). Sense is all for present satisfaction, and so it undoeth the soul; but faith can tarry God's leisure till those better things which we do expect do come in hand; and though they are opposed with afflictions for a while, yet it is but a little while, and all shall be made up to our full content: 'He that believeth shall not make haste' (Isa. 28:16). Where there is a certain expectation, we can bear a little inconveniency for the present. We are but tarrying in the place where God hath set us for the present, till be brings us unto his kingdom: 'That which we hope for, we do with patience wait for' (Rom. 8:25). Impatience and precipitation [haste] is the cause of all mischief. What moved the Israelites to make the golden calf, but impatience in not waiting for Moses, who remained too long, according to their fancy and mind, in the mount with God? What made the bad servant in Matthew 14:48 to 'smite his fellow-servants, and to eat and drink with the drunken', but this, 'My lord delayeth his coming'? Hasty men are loath to be kept in doubtful suspense. David said in his haste, 'I am cut off' (Ps. 31:2), and 'I said in my haste, All men are liars' (Ps. 116:1). Samuel and all the prophets that had told him he should enjoy the kingdom. Carnal men cannot wait for the time when they shall have pleasures at God's right hand for evermore, and therefore take up with present delights; like those that cannot tarry till the grapes be ripe, but eat them sour and green. Solid and everlasting pleasures they cannot wait for; therefore choose the pleasures of sin that are but for a season. A covetous man would wax [grow] rich in a day, and cannot tarry the leisure of God's providence: 'An inheritance may be gotten hastily at the beginning, but the end thereof shall not be blessed' (Prov. 20:21). The covetous man will not stay till God doth give crowns, and honours, and glory in his kingdom. Revolts and apostasies from God proceed hence; they cannot wait for God's time, or tarry for the fulfilling of the promises. Finding themselves pressed and destitute, the flesh, which is tender and delicate, groweth impatient. It is tedious to suffer for evermore. Thence come murmurings, and unlawful attempts, stepping out of God's way, as if troublous waters would only heal them. As an impetuous river is always troubled and thick, so is a precipitate, impatient spirit always out of order, and ready for a snare.

4. How shall we bring our hearts into such a frame?

4.1 Engage in no business but what you have Christ's warrant for, for truth and duty to him: 'Ye have not yet resisted unto blood, striving against sin' (Heb. 12:4). We must be sure it is sin [that] we strive against, for we cannot expect God's blessing upon our private quarrels, or that he should be the patron of our faction, and lacquey upon [serve] our humours [moods]. When conscience is clear, we may comfort ourselves in all the opposition we meet with. When there is no medium [middle way] between sin and suffering, then we ought to bear up with courage and cheerfulness, as the only and best course for us, and that which God calleth us to: 'For it is better, if the will of God be so, that ye suffer for well-doing, than for ill-doing' (1 Pet. 3:17); again, 'Let none of you suffer as a murderer, or as a thief, or as an evil-doer, or as a busybody in other men's matters' (1 Pet. 4:15). Conflicts with the world, and sufferings, are not to be taken up lightly or rashly. We are accountable to God for our temporal interests and opportunities of service. But when the cause is clear, then cheerfully lay down all at Christ's feet, not upon other men's humours and fancies, nor pre-engagements of our own: 'For this is thankworthy, if a man for conscience towards God, endure grief, suffering wrongfully. For what glory is it, when ye are buffeted for your faults, ye shall take it patiently? but if, when ye do well, and suffer for it, ye take it patiently, this is acceptable with God' (1 Pet. 2:19-20).

4.2 Consider God is able to bear you out, and will do so, whilst he hath a mind to use you for his glory. For what cannot the Son of God do? Fears in Christ's company argue little faith. When they embarked with him in the same vessel: 'Why are ye so fearful, O ye of little faith?' (Matt. 8:23-26). So when engaged with Christ in the same cause, why should we perplex ourselves with vain fears? It is said in Hebrews 11:27: 'By faith Moses forsook Egypt, not fearing the wrath of the king, for he endured as seeing him who is invisible.' Pharaoh was incensed against him, a potentate of mighty power, yet Moses had his call, his supplies and helps, though invisible to others. All the power in the world is nothing to this, and it was by faith, and you see there how his faith wrought. Therefore we should fortify ourselves against the greatest and most enraged adversaries.

4.3 You can suffer no loss by Christ. Why hath he made such great promises to you? We think much of our petty interests: 'Behold we have forsaken all, and followed thee; what shall we have therefore?' (Matt. 19:27). A great 'all'! What had Peter to forsake? A small cottage, a net, a fishing boat; and yet: 'What shall we have?' You need not seek another paymaster – in the great regeneration, you shall receive an hundred-fold (Mark 10:29-30). You shall be recompensed abundantly in kind or in value.

4.4 Temptations from the world should the less prevail with us, because it is the whole drift of religion to call us off from the world. So that if we be baptized into the spirit of our religion, we should be quite of another temper, not apt to be wrought upon by temptations of this kind. Do we profess to believe in our crucified Lord? and what is the great effect his death hath upon us? 'He gave himself, that he might deliver us from the present evil world' (Gal. 1:4). Who have interest in him? 'They that are Christ's have crucified the flesh with the affections and lusts thereof' (Gal. 5:24). He doth not say that they are Christ's who believe that he was crucified or that he died for sinners, but they who feel the power and efficacy of his death in mortifying their sins. What! a Christian, and so worldly? A Christian, and so vain and frothy [superficial]? It is a contradiction. You that are carried out after the pomp and vanities of the world, do you believe in Christ, whose kingdom is not of this world? False Christians are branded. They are engulfed in the world, and they would fain draw others to be as bad as themselves.

4.5 Consider Christ's example: 'Consider him that endured such contradictions of sinners against himself, lest ye be wearied, and faint in your minds' (Heb. 12:3). Christ himself was exercised. His religion was counted an imposture, his doctrine blasphemy, his miracles questioned as a cheat, and yet he endured this without fainting; so should we. Weariness is a less, and fainting an higher, degree of deficiency. The devil's design [plan] is to weary and tire us out in God's service. But let me persuade you to be dead to the world and the delights of the world. To the world: have you lost your credit for Christ in the world? Remember that Christ made himself of no reputation. Are you driven from your habitations? Christ had not a place where to lay his head. Are you reduced to great straits in the world? Christ was hungry and thirsty. Are you forced to live upon ordinary fare? Christ was contented, and blessed God for a few barley loaves, and two fishes. And then, to the delights of the world: whatsoever this world affordeth, must be left [behind] on this side of the grave: pomp, honour, pleasure, estates, must be left behind us. 'Naked came I out of my mother's womb, and naked must I return again' (Job 1:22). Here we bustle for rank and greatness, and death endeth the quarrel. Open the grave, and thou canst not discern between the rich and the poor, the king and the peasant. Skulls wear no wreaths and marks of honour in the grave. All are alike obnoxious to stench and rottenness.

7

The Life of Faith and Afflictions

I am treating of the life of faith with respect to the opposites of it, and have handled it with relation to temptations from the devil and from the world. Now I come to speak of the life of faith as to afflictions. And here I shall show you: (1) That there is need of faith; (2) the grounds, or principles of faith; (3) what are the acts of faith as to this branch [division].

1. The need of faith will be seen if we consider

1.1 The troubles and afflictions of the people of God: 'Man is born to trouble as the sparks fly upward.' All have their crosses and sorrows, much more God's own people: 'Many are the afflictions of the righteous' (Ps. 34:19); though it be those whom God dearly loveth, their afflictions may be many, great and long. This is often the lot of God's children, and heavy to be borne: 'Thou settest me up as a mark, so that I am a burden to myself' (Job 7:20); and Job 16:14: 'He breaketh me with breach upon breach.' The expression (chapter 7:20), as it implieth some comfort, that affliction doth not hit the saints by chance, but by aim and direction. We are 'appointed thereunto' (1 Thess. 3:3); also it expresseth much terror. A mark is set up on purpose to receive the darts, arrows and bullets that are shot at it. Now what shall relieve us in such a case but faith? Sense seeth no good in all this, because it judgeth by the outside and present feeling: 'Now no chastening for the present seemeth joyous but grievous' (Heb. 12:11). When we feel nothing but pain, and smart, and blows, how can God love us? Sense telleth us of nothing but wrath and anger, and is not able to unfold the riddles of providence. Will natural courage bear us out? 'The spirit of a man will bear his infirmity' (Prov. 18:14). For a while this will hold out; but when God redoubleth his blows, many and great troubles will quite break it. The stoutness of the creature is soon borne down by a few trembling thoughts, or a spark of God's wrath falling upon the conscience; therefore only faith will help us to bear crosses in the right manner: 'I had fainted, unless I had believed to see the goodness of the Lord in the land of the living' (Ps. 27:13). It is believing that keepeth us from being overcome by our troubles, whilst it helpeth us to wait for gracious experiences in them, or a comfortable issue [deliverance] out of them.

1.2 The many sins that are incident [common] to this condition show the need of faith:

(i) Impatience when our will is crossed: 'Give me children, or I die' (Gen. 30:1). To be sick of the 'fret' is a disease incident to us: 'Fret not' (Ps. 37:1). We murmur and repine [complain] against God, and that even for small matters; as Jonah for a gourd: 'I do well to be angry' (Jon. 4:9). So strangely are we transported [affected].

(ii) A spirit of revenge against [human] instruments. Christianity establisheth a universal and diffusive charity, even to enemies; to pray for them, and seek their good. Now we are vindictive and transported into uncomely passions when wronged by men: 'Why should this dead dog curse my lord the king? let me go and cut off his head.' No, saith David, 'let him alone, God hath bid him curse' (2 Sam. 16:9). No man is troubled at a shower of rain that falleth; but if any cast a bucket, or a basin of water upon us, we are presently all in a rage against them.

(iii) Waxing weary of our duty, and being quite tired and discouraged in our service: 'For consider him that endured such contradictions of sinners, lest you be weary, and faint in your minds' (Heb. 12:3). Weariness and fainting belong to the body properly, and they differ gradually [by degree]; weariness is a lesser, and fainting a higher degree of deficiency; as when labour, or hunger, or travail [work] abateth [weakens] the strength, weakens the active power, or dulleth the spirits and principles of motion; and from the body, it is translated to the mind. When troubles are many and long-continued, then we faint and begin to be weary of the faith and service of Christ, and sink under the burden. It is the devil's design to tire and weary us out.

(iv) Closing with [using] sinful means for an escape: 'Look me out a woman that hath a familiar spirit' (1 Sam. 28:7). Carnal shifts are very natural to us, and if we cannot trust God and wait upon him, we are apt to take indirect courses. Afflictions are often compared to a prison, and the sorrows that accompany it to fetter and chains. Now God that puts us in can only help us out, for he is the judge and governor of the world. But now we attempt to break prison; we are not able to hold out till God sends a happy issue [outcome], but take some carnal course of our own. The devil will make an advantage of our afflictions. He tempted Christ when he was hungry: 'When he had fasted forty days, he was an hungry; then came the tempter to him' (Matt. 4:3).

(v) Despairing and distrustful thoughts of God. David, after all his experiences, said in 1 Samuel 27:1: 'I shall one day perish by the hand of Saul.' He had a particular promise and assurance of a kingdom, and had seen much of God's care over him; yet after all this, David doubteth of the word of God. So Psalm 31:2: 'For I said in my haste, I am cut off from before thine eyes'; God hath no more care and thought of me; and this at that very time when deliverance was coming: 'Nevertheless thou heardest the voice of my supplications when I cried unto thee'; so Psalm 77:7: 'Will the Lord cast off for

THE LIFE OF FAITH AND AFFLICTIONS 159

ever? and will he be favourable no more? Is his mercy clean gone for ever? Doth his promise fail for evermore?' These are questions, as to their appearance, full of despair. Yet there is some faith couched under them. *Will the Lord cast off?* It implieth that the soul cannot endure to be thrust from God. *Will God be favourable no more?* It implieth some former experience, and desire of new proof. *'Is his mercy clean gone for ever? Doth his promise fail for evermore?'* Faith maketh some defence. He hath a conscience of sin. I have deserved all this but God is merciful; will not mercy help? But to [outward] appearance despair carried it from faith.

(vi) Not only despairing thoughts do arise, but atheistical thoughts, as if there were no God, no providence, no distinction, between good and evil: 'Verily, I have cleansed my heart in vain, and washed my hands in innocence' (Ps. 73:13). When there is so little enjoyed, and the flesh is so importunate [eager] to be pleased, we question all things.

(vii) Questioning our interest in God by reason of the cross. Our Lord hath taught us to say, 'My God,' in the bitterest agonies; but few learn this lesson: 'If God be with us, why is all this befallen us?' (Judg. 6:13). Sometimes we question the love of God because we have no afflictions, and anon [at other times], because we have nothing but afflictions, as if God were not the God of the valleys, as well as of the mountains. Well then, if all these distempers [evils] be incident to the afflicted, there is great need of faith, which is the proper cure and remedy for them. If we had faith, we would be more submissive to God and meek to men, constant in waiting without using ill [sinful] means, or yielding to distrustful, despairing thoughts and atheistic debates.

1.3 There is need of faith because of our duty under troubles, and that equal temper of heart that is necessary for the right bearing of [putting up with] them. There are two extremes, slighting and fainting, and they are both prevented by that exhortation in Hebrews 12:5: 'My son, despise not thou the chastening of the Lord, nor faint when thou art rebuked of him.' To despise them is to think them fortuitous [accidental], and to bear them with a stupid and a senseless mind, not considering and understanding that they come from God, that their end is repentance, and their cause is sin. Or if we understand these things, we do not lay them to heart, or regard God's chastising hand, so as to make a right use of our sufferings. A sense we must have of our Father's displeasure. We owe reverence to God's anger and should humble ourselves; as Miriam in Number 12:14: 'If her father had spit in her face, should not she be ashamed seven days?'

Men cannot endure to have two things despised, their love and their anger. Their *love*: when David thought his kindness despised by Nabal, he in his fury resolved to cut off all the men that pissed against the wall (1 Sam. 25:36); and Nebuchadnezzar, when his anger was despised, was in a rage and said, 'Heat the furnace seven times hotter.' Now faith keepeth us from slighting the hand of God. It seeth the hand of God in the affliction. The world ascribeth things to blind chance, but faith seeth God in it; for an invisible hand can only be seen by faith: 'Affliction doth not come out of the dust, nor trouble spring out of the ground' (Job 5:6). It doth not come by chance, nor by the stated course of nature, as all things grow in their season, but it hath a cause from above. A wise God hath the ordering of it.

The other extreme is that of *fainting*. To faint under these is to be weary of our profession, and to incline to apostasy because our sufferings are numerous, and of long continuance. Therefore faith and patience are necessary for us (Heb. 6:12), that we may hold out [endure] with God, and keep up a holy confidence. The former principle is of use here too; God hath the whole guiding and ordering of the affliction, and though the rod is in his hands, there is no anger in his heart. He is a wise God, and cannot of overseen. He afflicteth no more than is needful: 'For the Lord is a God of knowledge; by him actions are weighed' (1 Sam. 2:3). He weighs every ounce of the cross. He is a just God, and afflicteth us no more than is deserved: 'He will not lay upon man more than is right, that he should enter into judgment with God' (Job 34:23). Man can never commence a suit or have a just pretension to except against [complain of] his providence. He is a good God – 'He doth not afflict willingly, nor grieve the children of men' (Lam. 3:33), but as a tender father, hath tears in his eyes when the rod is in his hand. It is only what our need and profit requireth; therefore faint not. So then, there is need of faith.

2. I shall show you what are the grounds and principles for [of] faith, that will bear it up under afflictions.

2.1 That God hath a hand in all afflictions that do befall us: 'Is there evil in the city, and I have not done it?' (Amos 3:8). God is not the author of the evil of sin, but there is no evil of punishment but he hath a hand in it: 'The Lord hath given, and the Lord hath taken' (Job 1:23). It is Chrysostom's gloss upon the place: he doth not say that the Chaldean hath taken or the Sabean hath taken, but the Lord hath taken. Job doth not look to the instruments, but to God.

2.2 He chasteneth us only as our need and profit requireth. There is a vain conceit that possesseth the minds of men, as if the godhead were envious, and had no pleasure in the happiness of men, and therefore did delight to cross [frustrate] and thwart them. Job alludeth to this conceit when he saith in

Job 10:3: 'Is it good unto thee that thou shouldst oppress and despise the work of thine hands, and shine upon the counsels of the wicked?' Doth God take delight to torment his creature? Doth it do him good to grieve and afflict his own children? We have hard thoughts of God. The devil seeketh much to weaken the opinion of God's goodness in our hearts; for if God be not good, he is no longer to be regarded and trusted; he seeketh to insinuate into our first parents a distaste of God, and so still he doth in us. Therefore it concerneth us to cherish good thoughts of God, that when he correcteth it is but as our need and profit requireth.

Our *need*: 'Ye are for a season, if need be, in heaviness' (1 Pet. 1:6). All the afflictions that come upon us are needful for us, to reclaim us from our wanderings, and to cut off the provisions of our lusts, and restrain us from doing evil or growing evil. It is a sad and woeful thing for a child to be left to himself, and to give him the reins upon his own neck; but more sad for a man to be suffered to go on in sin without any chastisement or correction. Those whom God does not correct he casts off and delivers to their own lusts; and then they must needs perish.

He correcteth us as our *profit* requireth: 'They verily for a few days chastened us after their own pleasure, but he for our profit, that we may be partakers of his holiness' (Heb. 12:10). Our earthly parents many times act out of passion, rashly, not considering what is meet [fitting] for their children. Their chastenings may be arbitrary and irregular. They for a few days chastened us, for fancy; God for the whole term, till he hath made us perfect and done his whole work upon us. His corrections are regulated by his perfect wisdom, issue from the purest love, tend to and end in our highest happiness. It is no ways arbitrary, for he never chasteneth us but when he seeth cause, and knoweth certainly that it will be good for us:

'He for our profit,' not that we may increase in the world; no, no, but in some better things, some spiritual and divine benefit. It is that we may be more like God, capable of communion with him. That is *true* profit.

2.3 That the afflictions he bringeth on his people come from love: 'For whom the Lord loveth he chasteneth, and scourgeth every son whom he receiveth' (Heb. 12:6); and 'As many as I love I rebuke and chasten' (Revel 3:19). It is good to see whence our evil cometh. Afflictions upon God's own children mostly come from God's paternal love, out of *mere* love, for the increase and trial of grace. God may punish others, but he chasteneth none but sons. That is an effect of his fatherly love, or else from mere anger 'an evil, an only evil' (Ezek. 7:5). In a design of vengeance God does not fan or purge, but destroys. So upon the reprobate, all their troubles are the beginnings of sorrow, the suburbs of hell. Or else from anger mixed with love, or fatherly displeasure; as the corrections that follow sin. David's child was taken away (2 Sam. 12:10-12). Anger beginneth, but love tempereth the dispensation. Or else from love mixed with anger; as Job out of love was put upon trial, that his patience and faith might be manifested. But Job mingleth his own corruption, and his murmurings, and then God puts in a measure of anger, and speaketh to him out of the whirlwind.

2.4 Then he corrects in much measure. His love sets him a-work, and then his wisdom directeth and tempereth all the circumstances of the cross, that they may suit the effect which God aimeth at. We read in Isaiah 27:8: 'In measure when it shooteth forth thou wilt debate with it. He stayeth his rough wind in the day of the east wind.' God meteth out [measures] their sufferings in due proportion, in weight and measure; as physicians [doctors] in prescribing pills and potions to their patients have a respect to the ability of the patient, as well as the nature and quality of the disease: 'I will correct thee in measure' (Jer. 30:11).

This moderation and mitigation of evils is seen, either in proportioning the burden according to our strength, or in proportioning the strength according to the burden. God sometimes does the one and sometimes the other.

By mitigating the temptation according to our strength: 'But God is faithful, who will not suffer you to be tempted above what you are able' (1 Cor. 10:13). A merciful man will not overburden his beast; so God will not lay a man's burden upon a child's back.

Sometimes in proportioning the strength to the temptation; if he layeth on a heavy burden, he will give strength to bear it. He is ready to help us and support us: 'The Spirit also helpeth our infirmities' (Rom. 8:26). When we begin to sink, the Spirit beareth a part of the burden with us: 'Thou he fall he shall not utterly be cast down; for the Lord upholdeth him with his hand' (Ps. 37:24). He may seem to be pressed down, but not quite lost: 'I can do all things through Christ that strengthened me' (Phil. 4:3). Upholding strength is there spoken of. So Colossians 1:11: 'Strengthened with all might, according to his glorious power, unto all patience, with long-suffering and joyfulness.' There is a graduation. The power of God doth not only strengthen us to patience, but to *all* patience. We may have patience in some afflictions, and not in others. Some people may bear loss, perhaps, who cannot bear affront [insult] or disgrace. Long-suffering is patience extended. Not only the weight of afflictions is considerable, but the length. We may tire under a long affliction. He goeth on to joyfulness. We may endure a heavy affliction, and endure it long, but yet go drooping and heavily under it. But God will give strength to bear it cheerfully.

THE LIFE OF FAITH AND AFFLICTIONS

2.5 The affliction shall not always last; yea, it shall be very short. God's wrath on the church abideth but for a little moment: 'Come, my people, enter into thy chambers, and shut thy doors about thee; hide thyself, as it were, for a little moment, until the indignation be overpast' (Isa. 26:20). A moment is the smallest part of time. That point of time which is indivisible we call a moment. Now the time by which misery is set forth is called a moment, yea, a small moment. This is a great comfort to us. Our afflictions are bitter but short.

If it be distress of conscience; God 'will not always chide'; 'The Lord is merciful and gracious, slow to anger, and plenteous in mercy; he will not always chide, neither will he keep his anger for ever' (Ps. 103:8-9). He will not pursue the dry stubble.

If it be Satan's rage, 'he hath great wrath, because he knoweth he hath but a short time' (Rev. 12:12); dying beasts bite shrewdly.

Pains of body cannot last long: 'Who shall change our vile body, that it may be fashioned like unto his glorious body' (Phil. 3:21).

Church distresses will at length be over. All our toil and labour is but till dust return to the dust.

During the pre-eminence of enemies, or when rules are unfriendly: 'For the rod of the wicked shall not rest upon the lot of the righteous, lest the righteous put forth their hands unto iniquity' (Ps. 125:3). The rod is the ensign of power. Do not murmuringly cry, 'How long?' Within a little while we shall be as well as our heart can wish.

Let us therefore humble ourselves under the mighty hand of God: 'Come and let us return unto the Lord, for he hath torn and he will heal us; he hath smitten and he will bind us up' (Hos. 6:1-2). The afflictions of the church are from God, and his hand; and so the healing must come alone from him. But when? 'After two days he will revive us; in the third day he will raise us up.' It may seem long to sense, but it is short to faith. As Christ's death lasted but for a while, the church hath her resurrection as well as Christ. Nay, but one day; 'Weeping may endure for a night, but joy cometh in the morning' (Ps. 30:5). If we make a right reckoning, our sufferings are very short. So we read in Isaiah 17:14: 'And behold at evening-tide trouble, and before the morning he is not; that is the portion of them that spoil us, and the lot of them that rob us.' A tempest whirleth and roareth in the night; but when the sun ariseth in its strength, it is gone.

Objection: But common sense and experience [feeling] against this.

Answer: It contradicts sense in a way. I shall explain the point and show in what ways suffering is long and short.

How is it long?
1. It is long because of the pain we feel at the time. It is irksome to sense. Men in a fever reckon hours, and quarters, and minutes. Winter nights, to one who sleepeth not, seem tedious in the passing, though when they are past, they are as a thing of nothing: 'A thousand years in thy sight are but as yesterday when it is past, and as a watch in the night' (Ps. 90:4). A child would fain pass [like to] over his hard lesson.

2. It is long, because of our earnest desire of the blessings hoped for. To an hungry stomach the meat seemeth long a-dressing [before it is ready to eat]: 'As vinegar to the teeth and smoke to the eyes, so is the sluggard to them that send him' (Prov. 10:26). The least delay to earnest expectation is tedious: 'Hope deferred maketh the heart sick' (Prov. 13:12).

3. We measure things by a wrong rule, not by the standard of scripture computation. The longest time [in comparison to] to eternity is nothing: 'A thousand years in thy sight are but as yesterday' (Ps. 90:4). What the point at the centre [of a circle] is to the circumference, that time is to eternity. *Sapienti nihil magnum est, cui nota est aeternitatis magnitudo* ('He that is acquainted with the vastness of eternity accounts nothing great').

How is it short?
1. It is not so long as it might be in regard of the enemy's rage: 'And I am very sore displeased with the heathen that are at ease; for I was but a little displeased, and they helped forward the affliction' (Zech. 1:15). Satan and wicked men know no bounds when God set them a-work to correct his people; they go about it with cruel minds, and destructive intentions. God intended to correct and purge them; they intend to root out and destroy them.

2. Not so long as it may seem to be in the course of second causes. In a natural way no end can be seen, when those that hate them seem to be fortified with a strong back [backing] of secular interests, and stand upon an immutable foundation: 'And except those days shall be shortened, there shall no flesh be saved; but for the elect's sake those days shall be shortened' (Matt. 24:22) Though they shall run out to the full length of the prophecies, yet as to the course of second causes they are nothing so long as they appear.

3. Not so long as the merits of our sins would seem to call for: 'And after all that is come upon us for our evil deeds, and for our great trespass, seeing that thou our God hast punished us less than our iniquities deserve' (Ezra 9:13). In justice it might be for ever. Like the punishments of the wicked in hell, these flames might never be quenched. The evil of one sin cannot be expiated in thousands of years; but yet though our suffering be sharp and bitter, yet it is but short and not so long as sin would make it. God relents presently [by and by]: 'Comfort ye, comfort ye my people, saith your God. Speak ye comfortably to Jerusalem, and cry unto her, that her warfare is accomplished, that her iniquity is pardoned; for she hath received of the Lord's hand double for all her sins' (Isa. 40:1-2). It is not as if they had suffered more at God's hand than they have deserved, but they had endured so mush as God deemed fit to be inflicted.

4. Love to God doth not count them long: 'Jacob served seven years for Rachel, and they seemed to him but a few days, for the love he had to her' (Gen. 29:20). All our afflictions and troubles are nothing to those who love God. Shall not we endure a few years afflictions for our Christ, who lived a life of sorrows, and died a cursed death for our sakes? Surely if we have any love to him, it would not be so tedious.

5. Not long with respect to our reward in heaven: 'For I reckon that the sufferings of this present time are not worthy to be compared with the glory that shall be revealed in us' (Rom. 8:18). It is no more than a feather to a talent. See 2 Corinthians 4:17: 'For our light affliction, which is but for a moment, worketh for us a far more exceeding and eternal weight of glory.' It is but as a drop of vinegar to an ocean of sweetness, a rainy day to an everlasting sunshine. As the forty martyrs in Basil, that were put out naked on a cold winter's night, and to be burned the next day, comforted themselves thus, saying, 'Sharp is the cold, but sweet is paradise; it is but a night's enduring, and tomorrow we shall be in the bosom of God.'

6. It shall turn to good. This is the comfort of the people of God, that all that befalleth them is either good or shall turn to

THE LIFE OF FAITH AND AFFLICTIONS

good: 'All things shall work together for good to them that love God' (Rom. 8:28). If we have but a little faith, we may know it for the present, and be assured of it before we see it; and if we have but a little patience, we shall know it and find it by experience. All things work together, for good. Singly and apart they may be against us but *omnia simul adjumento sunt* ['All taken together are helpful']. Poisonous ingredients in a medicine, taken singly, are destructive; but when they are tempered with other things by the hands of a skilful physician, they prove wholesome and useful. So all things that befall us are tempered and ordered by God for good. There is no beauty in a building till all the pieces be set together. If we view God's work by halves, his providence seemeth to be against us. But all together it worketh for our good. How for our good? Sometimes for good temporal, usually for good spiritual, but certainly for good eternal.

(i) Sometimes for our *good temporal*, or for our greatest preservation: 'Ye thought evil against me, but God meant it unto good, to bring it to pass, as it is this day, to save much people alive' (Gen. 50:20). The Egyptians and Israel would have had no preserver if Joseph had not been sold and sent into Egypt. If a man were to go to sea, in a voyage upon which his heart is much set, but finds the ship is gone before he cometh and then afterwards heareth that all that were in the ship were drowned – this disappointment is for his good. Crasses' rival in the Parthian war, when he heard how that army was intercepted and cut off by the craft of the barbarians, had no reason to stomach his having been refused the command of it. Many of us have cause to say *Periissem, nisi periissem* ('We had suffered more if we had suffered less'). In the story of Joseph there is a notable scheme and draught of providence. He is cast into a pit; thence drawn forth, and sold to the Ishmaelites; by them brought into Egypt, and sold again. What doth God mean to do with poor Joseph? He is tempted to adultery by his mistress; refusing the temptation he is falsely accused, sent to prison, kept for a long time in ward [prison] and duress [hardship]. All this is against him. Who would have thought that in the issue [outcome] all this should have turned for his good or that the prison had been the way to preferment [promotion]? By the pit he came to the palace of the king of Egypt, and exchanged his party-coloured [many-coloured] coat for a royal robe. Thus in temporal things we gain by our losses, and God chooses better for us than we could have chosen for ourselves.

(ii) For our *spiritual good*. All affliction is made up and recompensed to the soul. It afflicts the body, but bettereth the heart: 'It is good for me that I have been afflicted, that I might learn thy statutes' (Ps. 119:71). There is more to be learned in the school of affliction than in the vastest libraries. Bodley and the Vatican[9] cannot furnish us with a book that will teach us as much as a little experience under God's discipline. Madmen are cast into prison, kept in the dark, and under all hardships, to bring them to their mind [senses] again. So, to cure us of our spiritual frenzy and dementation [madness] in a course of sinning, God is forced to use us a little hardly [roughly]. Thou darest not pray, Lord, let me have worldly comforts, though they damn me; let me not be afflicted, though it do me good. And if thou darest not pray so, wilt thou murmur when it falleth out to be so? If a man break an arm or leg in pulling us out of the water wherein we shall certainly be drowned, would we be angry with him? and shall we fret against the Lord when he taketh away the fuel of our lusts? Is it not a good exchange, to part with outward comforts for inward holiness? Certainly that will be of more gain to us than all the affliction, pain, and loss which we suffer will do us hurt.

Learning God's statutes by heart is a good lesson though it cost us trouble in learning. We lose nothing but our rust by scouring. If God will take away our outward peace, and give us peace of conscience; our worldly goods, and give us true riches, have we any cause to complain if our outward wants be recompensed by an abundance of inward grace? 'But though our outward man perish, yet the inward man is renewed day by day' (2 Cor. 4:16); and we have the less of the world that we may have more of God and are kept poor that we may be 'rich in faith' (Jas. 2:5). Who is the loser, if we have a healthy soul in a sickly body, as Gaius had (3 John 2)? And an aching head maketh way for a better heart; doth not God deal graciously and lovingly with us? Afflictions are compared to fire that purgeth away the dross (1 Pet. 1:7); to the fan that driveth away the chaff (Matt. 3:12); to a pruning-hook that cuts off the luxuriant branches, and maketh the others that remain more fruitful (John 15:2); to physic [medicine] that purgeth away the sick matter (Isa. 27:9); to ploughing and harrowing the ground, that fitteth it to receive the good seed (Jer. 4:3). Wilt thou be troubled when God cometh to make use of this fire to purge out thy dross, this fan to winnow away thy chaff, this pruning-hook to lop off the luxuriancies of thy soul, this physic to purge out thy corruption and filth, this plough to break up thy fallow ground, and destroy the weeds that grow in thy heart? Should we not rather rejoice that he will not let us alone in our corruptions, but refine us as metal is by the fire; and fan and winnow us, that we may be pure grain; and prune us, that we may be fruitful in holiness. So too if he uses a medicine to cure those distempers, which otherwise would destroy us; and suffers the ploughers to make long furrows upon our backs, that we may enjoy the richer crop? Thus it is for our spiritual good.

(iii) For our *eternal good*. Heaven will make a complete

amends: 'For our light affliction, which is but for a moment, worketh for us a far more exceeding and eternal weight of glory' (2 Cor. 4:17). The affliction worketh it as a means which God useth. It shall either hasten or secure our glorious estate. This mainly is intended in Romans 8:28-30:

> For we know that all things shall work together for good to them that love God, to them who are called according to his purpose. For whom he did foreknow, he also did predestinate to be conformed to the image of his Son, that he might be the first-born among many brethren. Moreover, whom he did predestinate, them he also called; and whom he called, them he also justified; and whom he justified, them he also glorified.

Well then, as a bee sucketh honey from a bitter herb, so there is a great deal of good which faith can extract out of afflictions. There is no water, but it can turn into wine; no stones out of which faith cannot make bread.

2.7 Then, we shall have comfort, and support and direction, and many intervening blessings, before the deliverance cometh.

(i) *Comfort*; we shall have it: 'For as the sufferings of Christ abound in us, so our consolation also aboundeth by Christ' (2 Cor. 1:5). God will refresh and relieve our troubles with many comfortable experiences of his grace; comforts proportionable to our afflictions. Should we have great sufferings and small comforts, we should not be well enough provided for. Such a degree of heat will not warm cold water unless it be made more intense; a little boat that would serve well enough in fresh water, will not serve at sea, where we are to conflict with boisterous waves and mighty billows. Therefore as our sufferings abound, so our consolations by Christ abound also. God suits his dispensations to the need and want of the creature. The disciples, when they had lost the bodily presence of Christ, received the Spirit. God will not give comforts upon

THE LIFE OF FAITH AND AFFLICTIONS

conflicts till the affections be purged from the dross and feculency of outward delights. Till then we cannot relish spiritual delights. Troubles usually enlarge the capacity of the soul, for they humble us, and an humble soul is a vessel fit to receive grace. They put us upon the exercise of grace. Then men pray most, and have most communion with God; and the more grace is exercised, the more comfort is increased; for the comforts of the Spirit follow the graces of the Spirit, as heat doth the fire. After the sharpest winter there is the sweetest spring, and the more fruitful summer and autumn.

(ii) For *support*. Although deliverance cometh not yet, if God giveth support, we have no reason to complain; as he that is well clad is not much annoyed with the cold. David prayed, and counted support an answer: 'In the day when I cried thou answeredst me, and strengthenedst me with strength in my soul' (Ps. 138:3). It is a real answer to have strength to bear out in our troubles, though deliverance be not yet come. Sustentation [support] is a degree and beginning of deliverance, though God doth not remove the trouble: 'But they that wait upon the Lord shall renew their strength; they shall mount up with wings as eagles, they shall run and not be weary, they shall walk and not faint' (Isa. 40:31). God enables them to bear up and hold out when they seem to be quite spent.

(ii) So for *direction*. This is another of those intervening mercies. David was in great danger, and beggeth for deliverance; or if not that, yet for instruction: 'Teach me to do thy will, for thou art my God' (Ps. 143:10). The danger of sin is a greater inconvenience than the danger of troubles. Now he beggeth wisdom of God to carry it well under his trouble; for in our troubles we are very apt to miscarry [go astray], unless God guides us continually. Necessity is an ill [unwelcome] counsellor, and will soon tempt us to some indirect course; and therefore it is a great mercy to have our guide: 'And the

Lord shall guide thee continually, and satisfy thy soul in drought' (Isa. 58:11). In our gloomy and dark condition, God will lead us by the hand and help us over our stumbling-blocks.

3. What is the work of faith under afflictions?
3.1 To enlighten the mind, that we may judge aright of afflictions. Sense maketh lies of God, and causeth us to judge amiss of his dispensations. Why? because it judgeth of them by the outside and present feeling: 'No affliction for the present seemeth to be joyous, but grievous' (Heb. 12:11). Alas! if we judge of all God's care and love by our sense of his present dealing, we shall conclude that he hath no respect to his people. Therefore faith, that is the evidence of things not seen, is needful, that we may interpret God's providence, and rightly understand his dealings with us. Faith remedieth this double evil of sense, because it interpreteth things not according to their outside and visible appearance, but according to the promise. Again, it looketh not upon providence by pieces, but in their whole draught [taken as a whole], to the end of things.

(i) Faith is necessary, that we may not dwell in the dark [on the fringe] and outside of God's dispensations. Sense judgeth by outward appearances, and so informs you of nothing but expressions of God's anger; but faith can see love in his anger, and unfold the riddles and mysteries of providence, and showeth you how God can extract honey and sweetness out of gall and wormwood, and that his heart is full of love when his hands are smart and heavy upon us; as when he had a mind to bless Jacob he breaketh his thigh, and maketh him halt and go lame. So the bucket goeth down into the well the deeper, that it may come up the fuller. So that whatsoever appeareth, faith concludeth that God is a good God. Faith, ploughing with God's heifer, cometh to know his design: 'And that he would show thee the secrets of wisdom, that they are double

THE LIFE OF FAITH AND AFFLICTIONS

to that which is' (Job 11:6). By the secrets of wisdom is meant the hidden ways of his providence. Divine providence hath two faces, the one of rigour, the other of clemency sweetly tempered therewith; like a plaited picture, that one way representeth the face of a virgin, another way the face of a serpent. We look upon it but of one side, and think that he dealeth harshly with us, and that all is wrath and severity. His love is hidden from us when we feel nothing but pain, and smart, and blows; but faith showeth it to us.

(ii) Faith is necessary, that we may not judge by present [troubles], not looking to what is to come. He that looketh upon the first rude draught of any notable work seeth no beauty in it. 'For I said in my haste, I am cut off from before thine eyes' (Ps. 31:22); and 'I said in my haste, All men are liars' (Ps. 116:11). David was fain [ready to] to eat his words spoken in haste. The fumes of passion and carnal affection blind the mind, that we look only to what is present. David[10] was quieted when he saw their end (Ps. 73:17). This settled him and satisfied him, to consider what this will be in the issue [outcome]. The end puts [make all] the difference.

3.2 To teach us to carry ourselves heroically [bravely], above our present conditions, not as overcome and dejected by it to have an uncomely sorrow: 'For this cause we faint not; for though our outward man perish, our inward man is renewed day by day' (2 Cor. 4:16). He was happy in the increase of comfort and grace by the decrease of worldly felicity, by his outward pressures being the more incited, and made the more towards the performance of his duty:

> 'By honour and dishonour, by evil report and good report, as deceivers, and yet true, as unknown, and yet well known; as dying, and behold we live; as chastened, and not killed; as sorrowful, yet always rejoicing; as poor, yet making many rich; as having nothing, and yet possessing all things' (2 Cor. 6:8-10).

Thus doth a Christian live above his outward estate by faith. If contumeliously [he is insultingly treated] used by some, yet reverently respected by others; though vilified by some, yet commended by others; 'deceivers, yet true,' that is, though he was represented as an imposter, yet those that had eyes to see might easily see and find him to be a faithful dispenser of the truths of God. Good Christians are persuaded of it, and the wicked are convinced of it, however they seem to dissemble [conceal] it. We are looked upon by some as if they knew us not, yet by others we are owned and valued; in danger, but yet sustained; exercised with a little affliction, yet we have a being and an opportunity of service; looked upon as miserable, and in a sinking condition, yet always cheerful, rejoicing in the testimony of a good conscience; as poor, and having little of worldly substance, yet enriching others with grace and the gifts of the Spirit; as having nothing, yet we are so provided for by God's providence as to want nothing that is necessary and useful for us; not having the wealth of the world in our hands, yet having enough for necessary use with contentment.

Thus should a Christian live above, yea, contrary to his worldly condition. Once more, hear Paul again expressing his condition: 'We are troubled on every side, but not distressed; we are perplexed, but not in despair; persecuted, but not forsaken; cast down, but not destroyed' (2 Cor. 4:8-9); wrestling with all difficulties, yet sustained by an invisible assistance; brought to extremity as to any secular and human means, yet carried through. This should be the temper of a gracious heart, never more exalted than in his low degree, never more humble than when most exalted. Still there is work for faith, but no ground for discouragement.

3.3 To see made up in God what is wanting [lacking] in the creature. A Christian's life is made up of riddles and mysteries; he wanteth all things, and yet he hath all things, and can see fulness of supplies in the midst of want, and an all-sufficiency in God, when there is no means of outward help. As a wicked man in the midst of his sufficiency is in straits: 'In the fulness of his sufficiency he shall be in straits' (Job 20:22). So a godly man in the midst of his wants can satisfy himself in God. It is the happiness of heaven to have all things in God, without the intervention of means, for there 'God is all in all' (1 Cor. 15:28). The life of faith is but heaven anticipated and begun: 'Yet I will rejoice in the Lord, I will joy in the God of my salvation' (Hab. 3:18). 'Yet,' that is, 'though the fig-tree do not blossom, and the labour of the olive fail, and the fields shall yield no meat, the flock shall be cut off from the fold, and there shall be no herds in the stall' (verse 17). When all outward supplies are cut off, to rejoice in such a low condition, *that* is faith indeed. As David, when all was lost at Ziklag: 'David encouraged himself in the Lord his God' (1 Sam. 30:6). That is living by faith indeed, when God's all-sufficiency is enough to [for] us.

3.4 To wait on the Lord for a final and sanctified issue out of all our afflictions: 'Rest in the Lord, and wait patiently for him' (Ps. 37:7). This waiting is an act of *dependence* on God as the fountain of our life and happiness, though he seem to turn away from us: 'I will look unto the Lord, I will wait for the God of my salvation' (Mic. 7:7).

And an act of *patience*, or tarrying the Lord's leisure. He that waiteth, must be content to stay [stand still]: 'He that believeth shall not make haste' (Isa. 28:16). Faith doth patiently attend upon God: 'I waited patiently for the Lord, and he inclined his ear unto me, and heard my cry' (Ps. 40:1). It is not enough to wait for a while, but to wait till the blessing cometh. And it is an act of hope, or an expectation of a comfortable issue: 'I will wait upon the Lord that hideth his face from the house of Jacob, and I will look for him' (Isa. 8:17); notwithstanding the present tokens of his wrath and displeasure. He that waiteth is in expectation to receive. Now if we could bring our hearts thus to wait upon God patiently, a blessed end would surely follow; for none ever waited but they found the deliverance [to] come in due time: 'Lo, this is our God, we have waited for him, and he will save us; this is the Lord, we have waited for him, we will be glad and rejoice in his salvation' (Isa. 25:9).

Or else the promises are not for our turn; our dependence is loose, our patience is quickly tire, and our hope soon lost. When the people saw that Moses stayed too long in the mount, then presently they must have an idol. Samuel directed Saul to go to Gilgal, and there to tarry for him seven days (1 Sam. 10:8). Saul tarried till the seventh day was come, but could not tarry till the seventh day was over and past; therefore he himself offered sacrifice (1 Sam. 13:12), which cost him the loss of his kingdom. So many bear out a while, but cannot tarry till our Lord cometh to take his work into his own hands, and so miscarry in the very haven, just when God is about to right the wrongs done to his people.

3.5 Obstinately [Tenaciously] to cleave to God when he seemeth to thrust us from him by many disappointments: 'Though he slay me, yet I will trust in him' (Job 13:15). This is a holy obstinacy that is very acceptable to God: such as blind Bartimaeus showed: 'Many charged him that he should hold his peace, but he cried the more, Thou son of David, have mercy on me!' (Mark 10:48); or as the woman of Canaan, that standeth fending and proving with Christ till he giveth her satisfaction, and telleth her, 'O woman! great is thy faith; be it unto thee, as thou wilt' (Matt. 15:28). When we turn discourage-

THE LIFE OF FAITH AND AFFLICTIONS

ments into motives of believing and draw so much the nearer to Christ as he seemeth to drive us away from him, it will be well with such in the issue. For however God seemeth to wrestle with such for a while, yet it is with a purpose to give faith the victory, and to yield up himself to do for us what our souls desire of him. This holy obstinacy of faith we should get.

Lukewarm dealing, however it may please us in a calm day, yet when we are to conflict with great difficulties, and delays of deliverance, nothing but such a kind of faith will make us hold out. You pray, and God keepeth silence, and will not seem to take notice for a time; as the woman of Canaan called to Christ, and he 'answered her not a word' (Matt. 15:23). It is not said he heard her not a word, but he answered her not a word. These two differ. Christ often heareth when he doth not answer. His not answering is indeed an answer, and speaketh this, 'Pray on, continue your crying still, the door is kept bolted that you may knock again.' Afterwards he gives her a rebuke: 'It is not meet to take the children's bread, and cast it to the dogs' (verse 26). Observe, first 'he answers her not a word'; and then he gave an answer to the disciples, not to the woman, and the answer is sad, 'She is not within my commission' ('I am not sent but to the lost sheep of the house of Israel' verse 24). He saith, 'It is not meet to take the children's bread, and give it to the dogs.' But she fastens upon him, and turns discouragements into arguments: 'Truth, Lord, but the dogs eat of the crumbs that fall from their master's table' (verse 27). Then Christ saith unto her, 'O woman! great is thy faith' (verse 28). Thus when Christ seemeth to look away from you, and to rebuke you, you should cleave to him the more by a holy obstinacy of faith.

3.6 To look for the recompense of reward: 'While we look not at the things which are seen, but at the things which are not seen; for the things which are seen are temporal, but the things which are not seen are eternal' (2 Cor. 4:18). Faith sees the eternal glorious things that are to be enjoyed after this life. Certainly an object, though never so glorious, cannot be seen without eyes; if there be looking, there must be an eye wherewith to look and see. Faith is the eye of the soul, without which there can be no prospect of the other world. Therefore faith is said to be 'the substance of things hoped for, and the evidence of things not seen' (Heb. 11:1). If you would look at things invisible by reason of their nature, as God, or by reason of their distance, as the blessedness of the world to come, you must get faith. Nature is short-sighted. In things near at hand, reason is acute enough; in things that are afar off, we are stark blind. We see little of anything beyond this world to quicken us, to make that preparation that such eternal things deserve. Therefore the wisest part [people] of this world are taken up with toys and trifles. The sweetness of honours, and wealth, and pleasure is easily known. Few can see the worth of these unseen things, only those who can pierce above the clouds of this lower world to the seat of the blessed. The light of faith will make you see heaven, and glory, and happiness in the midst of deep pressures and afflictions.

3.7 To make us humble ourselves under God's mighty hand, owning sin as the cause of all our miseries. Two things compose the heart to quietness and submission to the will of God, to see the cause of afflictions, and the end of afflictions. The cause of afflictions is sin: 'I will bear the indignation of the Lord, because I have sinned against him' (Mic. 7:9); 'If then their uncircumcised hearts be humbled, and they then accept of the punishment of their iniquity' (Lev. 26:41). When God is angry, it is our duty to stoop humbly under his afflicting hand. The end of afflictions is for our good: 'We have had fathers of our flesh which corrected us, and we gave them reverence; shall we not much rather be in subjection to the Father of spirits, and live? For they verily for a few days chastened us after their own pleasure, but he for our profit, that we might be partakers of his holiness' (Heb. 12:9-10). We must be contented with God's methods, and submit to his discipline, let him take what way and course he pleaseth to do us good.

8

The Effects of Faith

I now will speak of the influence of faith upon obedience, and the duties of holiness.

Distinct beings have a distinct principle, by which their life is conducted and ordered; a beast liveth by sense, a man by reason, and a Christian by faith. By sense the beasts discern what is hurtful or useful, agreeing or disagreeing with their natures; mere human affairs are guided by reason; but all matters of Christianity and of a spiritual nature are directed and improved by faith. Therefore, as we have spoken hitherto of the influence of faith with respect to its objects and opposites; now of its effects, because the whole business of Christianity is conducted and quickened by it. Therefore I shall now treat of the influence of faith upon obedience, and show you: (1) what obedience is required of a Christian; (2) the necessity of faith as to this obedience; (3) what is the work of faith in order hereunto; (4) how we shall bring our hearts thus to live [be lively] in yielding obedience to God.

1. What obedience is required of us

It is needful to state that, that we may see it is no easy thing to walk with God. I think I need not go one step further back to prove that obedience is necessary, notwithstanding the grace of the gospel. In the kingdom of grace we are not our own masters, or at liberty to do what we will. Christ came, not only as a Saviour, but as a lawgiver, and accordingly hath given us laws to try our obedience. In Hebrews 5:9, the apostle telleth us: 'He is become the author of eternal salvation to all them

THE EFFECTS OF FAITH

that obey him.' Christ came not into the world to lessen God's sovereignty or man's duty, but to put us into a greater capacity to serve God; and though love be the great gospel duty (Rom. 13:10), yet by love is not meant a fellow-like familiarity, but a cheerful subjection to the will of God: 'This is love, that we keep his commandments, and his commandments are not grievous' (1 John 5:3). Therefore I think I need not go so far back, but shall take the rise of my discourse from the next step. And supposing that obedience is required, I shall show you what obedience is required and expected from us; and that I shall do by a short view of some few places of scripture.

The first place I shall mention is 1 Peter 1:15: 'But as he which hath called you is holy, so be ye holy in all manner of conversation.' No small things is required of Christians, but a conformity in some measure to the God whom they worship; the impression or stamp must be according to the engraving of the seal. If we own God as the supreme being, worthy of all that respect and worship that we give him, we must study to be like him. No other pattern is set before the eyes of the children of the Lord; the holiest upon earth is not sufficient copy for us to imitate. Now as God is holy, not only in regard of the purity of his essence, but also in regard of the rectitude of his administrations: 'The Lord is righteous in all his ways, and holy in all his works' (Ps. 145:15); so a Christian must not satisfy himself with an imaginary holiness within, but must really manifest the frame of his heart in his conversation and visible actings, that he may express God to the life, and be a perfect resemblance of his purity to all that see him, and are conscious to his walking. Yea, they must be holy in all manner of conversation – that is, in every creek and turning of his life. There is no part of his conversation which ought not to savour of holiness; not only his religious but even his common and civil actions ought to be done in the Lord and for his glory.

In all conditions he ought to prove himself a hater of what God hateth, and a lover of what God loveth. This is one place that expresses a Christian's duty, and the Lord help us to fulfil it. And as here our duty is expressed by holiness, and all manner of holiness, so the next place will acquaint us with the branches [aspects] of it. And that is in Luke 1:74-75: 'That being delivered out of the hands of our enemies, we might serve him without fear, in holiness and righteousness before him all the days of our lives.' Our duty there is made the end [in view] of our deliverance. Christ came to deliver us from the curse of the law, but not from the duty of the law; not that we might not serve God, but that we might serve him the more cheerfully, without fear, with peace of conscience, and joy of heart. But how will God be served? and wherein must we express our duty to him? There are two word: 'In holiness and righteousness.' Holiness denoteth our consecrated estate, and expresseth the duties of the first table; and righteousness the duties of the second table; and both grow together, universal obedience prescribed in both the tables of the moral law. Mark it, our duty lieth not in external shows [appearances] but in inward and substantial graces, expressed in a full conformity to the will of God. And this 'before him' means before the all-seeing God, to whom no hypocrite can be acceptable. And 'all the days of our lives'; not for a fit or start. We must be constant all our life. It is not enough to begin well, but we must hold out in such a course.

Take another place [text], Colossians 1:10: 'That ye might walk worthy of the Lord unto all pleasing, being fruitful in every good work, and increasing in the knowledge of God.' Still the work of a Christian groweth upon our hands; we are not only to be subject to God, but with such a subjection as will become such a Lord to exact or receive. And what is there not due to him? 'Worthy of the Lord,' so as the world

THE EFFECTS OF FAITH

may see there is no terror comparable to his frowns, no comfort comparable to his smiles, or the sense of his favour. There is a repugnancy [incongruity] and unbeseemingness [unfitness] in a slight, careless conversation [careless life lived] to so great a Lord as we profess to serve and obey. And as for this 'unto all pleasing', it is not enough to regard the *matter* of our actions, but also the scope and end of them. A thing done may be good for the matter, yet the end may be faulty; as a piece of money may be good for [in respect of] the metal, yet if it have not the king's stamp, it is not current [legal tender]. There must be in every action at least an habitual intention to please God, and in actions more solemn and weighty an actual purpose to please him by our obedient walking. 'Walk worthy of the Lord in all pleasing,' and that too with fruitfulness, that ye grow better every day: 'being fruitful in every good work'; praying better, bearing better, loving God more, and abounding in his work. And this not only in practising what we know, but searching that we may know more of his will concerning us: 'increasing in the knowledge of God.'

If all this begets not in you a sufficient sense of the duty that belongeth to a Christian, take one place [text] more, Hebrews 12:28: 'Wherefore, we receiving a kingdom which cannot be moved, let us have grace, whereby we may serve God acceptably with reverence and godly fear.' All the privileges of the gospel kingdom are given to us to oblige us 'to serve God'; and if we would serve God, we must 'have grace', that is, we must take fast hold of grace, otherwise we have neither heart nor hand to serve him. But how will God be served? 'Acceptable,' in a cheerful manner, as being persuaded of his acceptance and good-will to us in Christ. And then in the other part of this scripture our duty is expressed by two words: 'Reverence and godly fear.' 'Reverence,' in God's service looketh at his excellency and glorious majesty, that there may be due respect shown to him, and at our [own] unworthiness, and the infinite distance between him and us, that is a sense of our vileness to come near him, and to be concerned in anything that concerneth his glory, who is so great a God. And then with 'godly fear', that we may circumspectly handle and meddle with his service, with a care not to offend, but please him in all things; both with the greatest humility, with the greatest caution.

By this time I suppose you see what it is to serve God, and what obedience is required of us; that he will not be put off with everything. No, he requireth that men should be like him, walk worthy of him, in holiness and righteousness, all their days, and that with reverence and godly fear.

2. I shall show the necessity of faith as to this obedience. Faith is necessary: (1) as to God's acceptance; (2) and our encouragement; (3) from the nature of the thing itself.

2.1 It is necessary as to God's acceptance; for nothing can please God that is not done in faith: 'Without faith it is impossible to please God' (Heb. 11:6). It is so with respect to the person working, and it is so with respect to the work itself.

(i) With respect to the person working, because he is not within the covenant of grace till he believeth, 'but the wrath of God abideth on him' (John 3:36). Enemies' gifts are giftless; the services of wicked men are but glittering sins. In the covenant of grace God doth not accept of the person for the work's sake, but of the work for the person's sake, that is, because of his interest in Christ, in whom alone he is well pleased. And therefore whatever we do must be done in a believing state; for our obedience is not acceptable in itself because of much defect and imperfection in it, but in and through Jesus Christ.

THE EFFECTS OF FAITH

(ii) With respect to the work itself. For unless it be quickened by a true and lively faith, it is not acceptable to God; for it is but the carcass of a good work, without the life and soul of it. Superficially the selfsame things may be done by a believer and a carnal man; but that is but the body of a duty. That which should animate it is an obedient confidence, for all the motions, affections and inclinations of the soul are swayed and inclined by faith. All motion is inspired from the head, albeit we go upon our feet, and move with our hands. So a firm assent to God's good-will and pleasure revealed to us hath a sovereign command on every grace, to cause it to put forth an operation proper to it. All good acts regularly performed issue from faith, and therefore they are called 'the work of faith' (2 Thess. 2:11). Well then, to our acceptance, the person must be accepted before the work can please God. And that service is rightly qualified which proceedeth from faith in Christ, is conformable to the word, and tendeth to God's glory.

2.2 As to our encouragement, that we may serve the Lord readily and cheerfully, when we hear of so much duty, as was intimated before. Alas! what shall *we* do who are 'beset with sin' (Heb. 12:1)? What shall we do that find sin always 'present with us?', as Paul groaningly complains of it: 'I find then a law, that when I would do good, evil is present with me' (Rom. 7:21). Christians are often discouraged with the thought of their own weakness and vileness. The importunate returns [recurrence] of their lusts, makes them ready to say, 'We shall never do anything, or to any good purpose.' Therefore, till they be persuaded of God's help and grace, they do but coldly set upon the practice of holy duties, stagger much, and are off and on, often fainting at the difficulty of the work and dismayed at their manifold slips. Their service groweth tedious and troublesome, and their want of faith occasioneth doubts and fears, deadness and uncheerfulness, so that they drive on heavily in the Lord's work. But now faith, on the other side, keepeth us close to the commandment, and causeth us to rest upon the Lord for ability to do what he requireth, and comforts us with the acceptance of our sincere and unfeigned services, though weak and imperfect. So it causeth us to go about it with cheerfulness, life and vigour. Was it not an encouragement to Moses when God said unto him in Exodus 4:12: 'Now therefore go, and I will be with thy mouth, and teach thee what thou shalt say'? And was it not enough to encourage the disciples when Christ said, 'I will be with you always, to the end of the world' (Matt. 28:20)? And doth it not exceedingly quicken us to remember that God will help our infirmities, and accept of our sincere endeavours, and reward our sorry services with eternal life? What will put life and heart into us, except [unless] these promises do?

2.3 Faith is necessary from the nature of the thing itself, because of the inseparable connection between faith and obedience, as between the cause and the effect. Take faith either for assent, or for dependence, or a confident relying upon God's mercy in Christ, and still there is this connection between faith and obedience.

(i) Take faith for an assent. Faith produceth it where it is in any life and vigour; therefore it is called 'the obedience of faith' (Rom. 1:5; 16:26), as being begotten by it. Faith is not without obedience. There will be a reverent subjection to God if we believe he is [exists], and doth govern the world. Nay, there is not only such a connection between faith and obedience as there is between the cause and effect, but in some respects such a connection as between branches growing out of the same root, or acts of the same grace. The same grace that produceth assent produceth obedience; by faith we assent to every part of God's known will as good and fit to be observed by us. Now if this assent be real, you will assent to his commands as well as to his promises, and see a necessity of obeying the one as well as resting upon the other: 'Teach me good judgment and knowledge, for I have believed thy commandments' (Ps. 119:66). There is a faith that is conversant about the commands as well as the promises. These are part of his Word, and therefore must be believed. Faith is an assent to the whole doctrine of God, not only that part which concerneth our privileges, but that other part which concerneth our duty. The one part is as true as the other, and if we assent to it heartily, or 'receive the word gladly' (Acts 2:41), we are bound to acknowledge the precepts as well as to expect the graces and benefits of the new covenant.

(ii) If you take faith for dependence, or a confident relying upon God's mercy in Christ, still faith and holiness are near akin, and do imply the one the other. Partly because when we choose and accept of Christ, we choose and accept of him as a Lord and King, as well as a Saviour: 'Him hath God exalted with his right hand to be a Prince and a Saviour' (Acts 5:31), for Christ is the perfect antitype of Melchizedec, the king of Salem, which is by interpretation, king of righteousness, and after that, king of peace (Heb. 7:2). As a Saviour to beget peace, so a King to command the heart. So that if we take Christ with all his titles, we must necessarily mingle resolutions of duty with expectations of mercy; and as we thrive in the one, we grow in the other. Our confidence in God's mercy can be no greater than our fidelity to God's commands.

When love the world or the flesh tempts us to omit any part of our duty, or works any disorder in our souls, Satan will easily weaken our confidence thereby, and sin will breed distrust, when the soul is serious. Confidence and comfort follow grace, as heat doth fire; and fear and doubts follow sin, as pain doth the pricking of a needle, or some sharp thing wherewith a man goreth [pierces] himself. And partly, because faith in this sense is an act of obedience along with it; for we believe in Christ, because God hath commanded it: 'And this is his commandment, that we should believe on the name of his Son Jesus Christ' (1 John 3:23); and John 6:29: 'This is the work of God, that ye believe on him whom he hath sent.' Many times a poor soul hath no other motive and encouragement, but ventureth in the face of difficulties on the encouragement of a command; as Peter in Luke 5:5: 'We have toiled all night, and taken nothing; nevertheless, at thy command I will let down the net.' So say, Lord! I am an unworthy, poor, frail creature; yet at thy command I will believe.

Well then, I reason thus: That which is itself the obedience of a command cannot be the cause of disobedience. We must not pick and choose; the main work doth not exclude the rest, but enforce it. Certainly, if we believe on God's command, we will make conscience of other things that are commanded, as well as faith; for he is truly obedient to no precept who doth not obey all: 'Whosoever shall keep the whole law, and yet offend in one point, he is guilty of all' (Jas. 2:10). The same reason that maketh us believe, upon believing will make us obey God in other things, for all are enforced by the same authority. And partly, because this dependence of faith is the endeavour of a contrite or broken heart to come out of his misery, and to seek happiness of [from] God by Christ.

Now a broken heart cannot wax wanton against God. If we seek our relief by Christ, we cannot allow ourselves in rebellion against Christ. There is a contradiction in the thing; he cannot be an enemy to Christ, and hate him in whom he would trust. Among men dependence begets observance [respect]: 'Behold, as the eyes of servants look upon the hand of their

THE EFFECTS OF FAITH

masters, and as the eyes of a maiden on the hand of his mistress; so our eyes wait upon the Lord our God until that he hath mercy upon us' (Ps. 123:2); or rather: 'Work out your salvation with fear and trembling, for it is God that worketh in you both to will and to do' (Phil. 2:12-13). Men will not offend him from whom they look for their all. So that dependence and obedience mutually infer one another.

3. What faith doth in order to [foster] obedience

3.1 It urgeth the soul with God's authority, and chargeth the heart, as it will answer to him another day, not to neglect or despise the duty we owe to him. It is faith alone that doth acknowledge and improve God's sovereignty, and worketh the sense of it into the heart to any purpose. And that for these reasons:

(i) Because the governor is invisible, and we do not see him who is invisible but by faith: 'For he endured, as seeing him who is invisible' (Heb. 11:27). Temporal potentates are before our eyes; their terrors and rewards are matter of sense. That there is an infinite and eternal and all-wise Spirit who made all things, and therefore hath a right to command and give laws to all things, reason will in part tell us. But faith doth much more assure the soul of it, and impresseth the dread and awe of God as if it did see him with bodily eyes.

(ii) Because it must appear that this is the will of this Supreme Being. As the ruler is invisible, so none without faith can believe that those commands are *God*'s commands, holy, just and good. But without which persuasion there can be no obedience: 'When ye received the word of God, which ye heard of us, ye received it, not as the word of man, but as it is in truth, the word of God, which worketh effectually also in you that believe' (1 Thess. 2:13). There is need of faith to see that they be God's laws. For it is not a matter of sense, that the scripture is the expression [revelation] of God's commanding and legislative will, whereby he showeth to man what is holy, just and good, and bindingly determineth his duty. See Micah 6:8: 'He hath showed thee, O man, what is good; and what doth the Lord require of thee, but to do justice, and to love mercy, and to walk humbly with thy God?'

(iii) And partly because many of these commands are contrary to natural reason, and are not so evident by those common rules by which we judge of things. That it is contrary to natural reason is shown by Hebrews 11:17: 'And he that had received the promises offered up his only-begotten son'; and verse 30, they compassing Jericho seven days — to natural reason, it was a very unlikely means to make the walls fall down. So Abraham, contrary to natural affection, offered his son; and 'when he was called to go unto a place which he should after receive for an inheritance, obeyed; and he went forth, not knowing whether he went' (Heb. 11:8). There is *cultus naturalis* and *cultus institutus* (natural worship and instituted worship). An example of this is Naaman's washing seven times in Jordan (2 Kgs. 5:10). Some commands of God carry their own reason and evidence with them. Others stand only upon the authority of his institution, which no natural light could ever reveal to us, but only faith, giving credit to the work of God.

(iv) And partly, because we are not only to see God in the command and see it urgeth bindingly, but to receive it with that reverence that becometh so great a Lord. It is the command of God who 'is able to save and to destroy' (Jas. 4:12). He hath *potestatem vitae et necis*, do or die; so that *intuitus voluntatis* (1 Thess. 4:3, 18; 1 Pet. 2:15). The sight of God's will is reason enough, and instead of [as good as] all reasons to be believer. Thus to charge the heart, that we may not shift and distinguish ourselves out of our duty, there is need of

THE EFFECTS OF FAITH

faith, that we may shake off sloth and negligence, much more all deceit and fraudulency. A general dogmatical faith will not serve the turn.

3.2 It uniteth us to Christ as a fountain of grace, without whom we can do nothing: 'Without me ye can do nothing' (John 15:5). We can do nothing without Christ, nothing apart from Christ: 'Not that we are sufficient of ourselves to think anything as of ourselves but our sufficiency is of God' (2 Cor. 3:5). Christ is the fountain from whence all our supplies come: 'And of his fulness have we all received, and grace for grace' (John 1:16), and all by virtue of our union with him: 'Of him are ye in Christ Jesus, who of God is made unto us wisdom, and righteousness, and sanctification, and redemption' (1 Cor. 1:30). The band of this union is faith: 'That Christ may dwell in your hearts by faith' (Eph. 3:17). As the Spirit on Christ's part, so faith on ours; and the more we act [exercise] faith, the more clear and sensible it is: 'He that eateth my flesh and drinketh my blood dwelleth in me and I in him. As the living Father hath sent me, and I live by the Father; so he that eateth me, even he shall live by me' (John 6:56-57). So meat chewed and digested begets spirit and life, and is turned into the eater's substance.

Some do but taste Christ a little, and spit him out again. But in those that concoct [feed on] and digest him, that embrace Christ, and apply him by faith, and by a constant dependence, Christ doth abide by his constant influence and quickening virtue. By this spiritual union and mutual indwelling we are made partakers, not only of his righteousness and merits, in order to our justification, but also of his Spirit, in order to our sanctification. As the branches partake of the sap of the root, and as members of the body are partakers of the life of the soul by which the body is quickened; so whosoever is united to Christ, the Spirit of Christ dwelleth in him: 'Ye are not in the flesh, but in the Spirit, if so be that the Spirit of God dwell in you. Now if any man have not the Spirit of Christ, he is none of his' (Rom. 8:9); and if the Spirit of God dwell in us, he will not suffer us to be unholy and unfruitful.

3.3 Faith comforts and encourageth us by the promises of assistance, acceptance and reward.

(i) By the promises of assistance. Alas! in ourselves we are weak and of no strength and so our hearts are faint, and our hands feeble. Duty can never be done without God's sanctifying grace: 'Let us have grace whereby we may serve God acceptably, with reverence and godly fear' (Heb. 12:28). It must be so, or we are quite discouraged. There must be habitual grace, which giveth a general readiness and preparation of heart for the actions of the new life ('We are his workmanship, created in Jesus Christ unto good works', Eph. 2:10). A bowl is first made round before it can run round; we cannot act without a principle, without divine qualities infused. We need also actual grace, by which God doth excite that grace which is infused into us: 'The Lord make you perfect in every good work, to do his will, working in you that which is well-pleasing in his sight' (Heb. 13:21). God doth continually cooperate and work in us and with us. As providence is a continual creation, so is assisting grace a continuation of God's renewing work. He is at the beginning, middle and end of every good action: 'He worketh in us both to will and to do' (Phil. 2:13). Now this is a great encouragement to ply the oar, when we have wind and tide with us. The soul groweth into a confidence, and is much encouraged to lift up the feeble hands and strengthen the weak knees: 'Surely shall one say, In the Lord I have righteousness and strength' (Isa. 45:24). Comfort and spiritual ability increase as God strengthens us in the promise:

THE EFFECTS OF FAITH

'I can do all things through Christ that strengthens me' (Phil. 4:13). Assurance of help encourageth us to work.

(ii) By promises of acceptance. We drive on heavily when we know not whether God will accept of our work or not. As he that serveth a hard master that is always finding fault, hath no mind to his work. To take off this discouragement, God doth often promise to accept of what we do through the assistance of his Spirit: 'Present your bodies a living sacrifice, holy, acceptable to God (Rom. 12:1); 'Ye are an holy priesthood, to offer up spiritual sacrifices acceptable unto God by Jesus Christ' (1 Pet. 2:5). Our sacrifices are not sin-offerings, but thank-offerings; as the dedication of ourselves to God's service. 'Present your bodies a living sacrifice' (Rom. 12:1); penitent and humble supplications: 'The sacrifices of God are a broken spirit' (Ps. 51:17); and offering praise to God: 'By him therefore let us offer unto God the sacrifice of praise continually, that is, the fruit of our lips, giving thanks to his name' (Heb. 13:15); so charity to the saints: 'I have received the things which were sent from you, a sacrifice acceptable, well pleasing to God' (Phil. 4:18); and all these in testimony of our thankfulness to Christ in offering up himself as a sin-offering.

All spiritual sacrifices must be done in a spiritual manner. These are acceptable to the Lord, not for any worth that is in them or advantage that can be in them, but because they are presented to God by Jesus Christ, who taketh away the iniquity of our holy things: 'And he shall bear the iniquities of the holy things, which the children of Israel shall hallow in all their holy gifts, that they may be accepted before the Lord' (Exod. 28:38). He perfumeth our services with the incense of his merits: 'There was given unto him much incense, that he should offer it with the prayers of all saints' (Rev. 8:3).

Our iniquities are many, yet God's mercy is great, who will

accept us and our services that are unfeignedly [sincerely] performed to his glory. He owneth his gracious work in us when what we do is good, and done by a man in Christ, by strength drawn from Christ, and for God's glory, though in itself it be weak: 'Then shall the offerings of Judah and Jerusalem be pleasant unto the Lord, as in the days of old, and as in former years' (Mal. 3:4). They are acceptable when they are purified to be an holy priesthood unto God; so Isaiah 60:7: 'They shall come up with acceptance upon mine altar.'

Many such promises as these are everywhere in the word of God, which is a great encouragement to poor souls to do their utmost

(iii) By promises of reward. Hope doth excite and whet [sharpen] endeavours. We have no reason to be sluggish in God's service, for in the end it will turn to a good account: 'Be ye steadfast and unmovable, always abounding in the work of the Lord, forasmuch as ye know that your labour is not in vain in the Lord' (1 Cor. 15:58). He hath interposed his faithfulness, and laid his justice at pawn with [as a guarantee for] us; 'God is not unrighteous, to forget your work and labour of love' (Heb. 6:10). If God be a just God, we need not doubt; the rewards of religion are to come, but where they are apprehended as certain and evident, they do exceedingly encourage and strengthen the heart. It should be a shame to us that when we have such wages we are no more hard at work. When it is for the everlasting enjoyment of the ever-blessed God, shall we tire and wax faint?

Faith reasoneth and argueth in a most powerful and prevailing way, with such arguments that a believer cannot say nay [no] to them.

It reasoneth partly from what is past, and so all its arguments are dipped in love, or a sense of God's kindness to us

THE EFFECTS OF FAITH

in Christ, and then they must needs be forcible: 'For the grace of God that bringeth salvation hath appeared unto all men, teaching us, that denying ungodliness and worldly lusts, we should live soberly, righteously, and godly in this present world' (Titus 2:11-12); and Galatians 5:6: 'Faith worketh by love'; and Romans 12:1: 'I beseech you, by the mercies of God,' etc. Faith sets love to plead for God, and love beareth all before it: 'The love of Christ constraineth us' (2 Cor. 5:14). So too we have it in the text, 'Who loved me, and gave himself for me.' There is nothing like the pleadings of faith; he left heaven for our sakes, and took a body, and endured a cursed death, and is gone to heaven to plead our cause with God. He hath pardoned so many sins, and what wilt thou then not do for him? Faith will take no repulse.

And then faith reasoneth forward, partly from hope, and partly from fear. From the eternal recompenses; no hopes equal to the rewards it proposeth, no fears comparable to the terrors it representeth; no pleasure like the joys of heaven, no terrors like the torments of hell. So looking into the world to come, it breaketh the violence of every contrary inclination: 'For our light affliction, which is but for a moment, worketh for us a far more exceeding and eternal weight of glory' (2 Cor. 4:17), and so quickens the soul to follow hard after God, and overcometh the world and the great hindrance of keeping the commandments: 'This is the victory that overcometh the world, even our faith' (1 John 5:4).

4. What shall we do, that faith may have such an influence upon us?

4.1 Consider how just it is for God to command, and how reasonable it is that we should obey the supreme being. His will is the reason of all things, and therefore who should give laws to the world but the universal sovereign, who made all things out of nothing? Whatsoever you are, or have, you received it from the Lord; and therefore whatever a reasonable creature can do, you owe it to him to do it. You are in continual dependence upon him, 'for in him you live and move, and have your being' (Acts 17:28); and he hath bought you and redeemed you, and called you to life by Christ: 'You are not your own, for ye are bought with a price; therefore glorify God in your body and in your spirit, which are God's' (1 Cor. 6:19-20). You owe your time and strength, your life and love, and all that you are and can do to God.

4.2 He enjoineth nothing but what is good for us: 'And the Lord commanded us to do all these statutes, to fear the Lord our God for our good' (Deut. 6:24); and Deuteronomy 5:29: 'O that there were such an heart in them that they would fear me, and keep my commandments always, that it might be well with them, and with their children for ever.' God hath tempered his sovereignty to the reasonable creature, and doth not rule us with a rod of iron, but with a sceptre of love.

4.3 That God loveth all that are good, and hateth all that are evil, without any respect of persons: 'But in every nation, he that feareth God and worketh righteousness is accepted of him' (Acts 10:35); and Psalm 5:5: 'Thou hatest all the workers of iniquity.' God loves or else hates the greater of either kind the more, the lesser the less.

4.4 This must be laid up in the heart with a lively faith, and this belief must prevail with us so far as to submit ourselves to God's will, to like what he liketh and to hate what he hateth; to love that best which his word telleth us he loveth best, to hate that most which his word telleth us he hateth most, though

THE EFFECTS OF FAITH 199

otherwise pleasant to our natural inclination. But alas! we mistake opinion for faith, or a cold and dead assent for true believing. A hypocrite is not transformed by his faith; he talketh much of it, but he showeth little of the spirit of it; especially the fruit of obedience, which is most natural and proper to it, and without which all other pretences are to little purpose. Recall the three children in the furnace. The fire had no power over them nor was one hair of their head singed, nor their coats changed; no more power hath the word upon their hearts. A true believer is changed thereby: 'But we all, with open face beholding as in a glass the glory of the Lord, are changed into the same image from glory to glory, even as by the Spirit of the Lord' (2 Cor. 3:18); 'That I may know him, and the power of his resurrection, and the fellowship of his sufferings, being made comfortable to his death' (Phil. 3:10).

4.5 It is much better to obey the law of God than our own affections, the lusts of the flesh, or the law of sin: 'Not my will, but thine be done.' So our Lord said (Luke 22:42). By retaining any branch of our own wills unrenounced, or not resigned up into God's hands, we give Satan a hold of us, and he will never let go the hold till we cut off the member that offendeth. It is as an halter [rope] about an horse's neck, and we are as a bird that is caught by one claw, and as an ambassador pursuing but part of his instructions. Indispositions are so far from excusing, that they call for the more duty. Though we cannot command the wind, yet we are to fit [hoist] the sails.

9

The Life of Faith in Prayer

'But let him ask in faith, nothing wavering; for he that wavereth is like a wave of the sea, driven with the wind and tossed' (James 1:6).

Having spoken of the influence and use of faith upon obedience, or the duties of holiness in general, I shall now speak of the use of faith in prayer.

In the context there is an exhortation to prayer, and in the text an instruction how we should pray.

1. There is an exhortation to prayer in the fifth verse: 'If any man lack wisdom, let him ask it of God.' He presseth us to make an advantage of our wants, and to look upon them as so many occasions of recourse to God at the throne of grace; and he encourageth them, partly by the consideration of God's nature: 'Who giveth to all men liberally, and upbraideth not.' We need not make scruples of consulting with God upon every occasions; he is not backward to bestow grace, nor is he wont to reproach those to whom he giveth anything; though prayer putteth God to it [to act] never so often and never so much, yet he upbraideth none. And then he encourageth them partly by a promise: 'Let him ask, and it shall be given him.' It is said of Augustus[11] that he never sent away any from him sad; it is true of the Lord, he doth not send away his worshippers sad: 'Ask, and it shall be given you.' Prayer will not be a fruitless labour.

2. In the text there is an instruction how we should pray, which is laid down and enforced.

THE LIFE OF FAITH IN PRAYER

(i) It is laid down to prevent mistakes: 'Let him ask in faith.'

(ii) It is enforced by a reason *ab incommodo*, for the inconveniency of not asking in faith: 'For he that wavereth is like a wave of the sea, driven with the wind and tossed.' Wavering and doubting keep men in a perpetual tempest and agitation of mind, roving to and fro from one dependence to another, as the waves of the sea are carried hither and thither.

Doctrine. That none pray aright, but those that pray in faith. Faith is all in all in prayer: 'The prayer of faith shall save the sick' (Jas. 5:15). It is not prayer simply, but the faith in prayer that prevaileth with God for a gracious answer. So Matthew 21:21-22: 'If ye have faith, and doubt not, ... all things whatsoever ye shall ask in prayer, believing, ye shall receive.' The grant and answer is suspended upon that condition, for God will not exercise his power till we rest upon it. In short, faith and prayer are inseparable companions. Like Hippocrates'[12] twins, they live and die together. They are begotten together, and grow up together, and die together.

1. They are begotten together, for faith beginneth its life in crying unto God. The first grace that is acted is faith, and the first duty when grace is infused is prayer: 'I will pour upon them the spirit of grace and supplication' (Zech. 12:10); and as to Paul after his conversion, the first news we hear of him is, 'Behold, he prayeth' (Acts 9:11). As the new-born babe falls a-crying; so, as soon as we are born again, the first work that is set upon is prayer.

2. They grow up together, mutually strengthening and increasing, and setting one another a-work: 'Trust in the Lord at all times, pour out your hearts before him' (Ps. 62:8). Trust vents itself in prayer; and prayer increaseth trust, for in prayer the principles of confidence are solemnly drawn into the view of conscience.

3. Because they end together. When we come to die, faith is resolved into sight, and prayer unto an uninterrupted praise.

Now for the clearing of this point:

First, I shall show you what is that faith that is requisite in prayer. There are divers thoughts and opinions about it: I will not perplex you with them, but conceive it thus. It is a confidence that our prayers shall be heard; that is the faith that is required in prayer: 'And this is the confidence that we have in him, that if we ask anything according to his will, he heareth us' (1 John 5:14).

This confidence that we shall be heard containeth many things in it.

1. A believing that there is a God, or else why should we pray unto him? 'He that cometh to God must believe that God is, and that he is a rewarded or them that diligently seek him' (Heb. 11:6). Otherwise all our devotion will be but customary [routine] and for fashion's sake, or a compliance with the vulgar error. So someone called it, *Eamus ad communem errorem*, ['Let us go to the vulgar superstition] when he spake of the worship of God. Unless we have the persuasion that God is [exists] all is nothing.

2. That he is such an infinite being that he can supply all the wants of the creatures, and accomplish all their desires: 'Now unto him that is able to do exceeding abundantly above all that we ask or think, according to the power that worketh in us' (Eph. 3:20). This is a main prop of confidence in prayer, that God is able not only 'to exceed our prayers, but our conceptions and hopes'. So in 2 Chronicles 20:6 we read: 'And he said, O Lord God of our fathers! art not thou God in heaven? and rulest not thou over all the kingdoms of the heathen? and in thine hand is there not power and might, so that none is able to withstand thee?' Faith sets prayer a-work, and prayer sets the almighty power of that God a-work, and hath a universal empire and dominion over all the world, and all the events and affairs of the world. Therefore our Lord Jesus Christ layeth down this as a ground for prayer: 'Thine is the kingdom, the power and the glory.' He can set all things a-work for the glory of his name, and for the good of his people.

3. That he is omniscient as well as omnipotent. He knoweth what we do and speak, when and where any poor creature is praying to him: 'Arise, and go into the street that is called Straight, and inquire in the house of Judas for one called Saul of Tarsus, for behold he prayeth' (Acts 9:11). God observes you in your most private and secret retirements. In what corner of the house soever we are, he knoweth what we are a-doing, whether we are toying [wasting time] or praying, for it is said in what street Saul was, and in what house, and what he was doing. So Malachi 3:16: 'Then they that feared the Lord spake often one to the other, and the Lord hearkened and heard, and a book of remembrance was written before him for them that feared the Lord, and that thought upon his name.' God taketh notice of every word we speak to him, or of him, or for him. *We* cannot hear many speaking at one, because we are finite creatures, but God heareth all the world over, and knoweth how to interpret the secret groans and motions of the heart: 'He that searcheth the heart knoweth the mind of the Spirit' (Rom. 8:27). We do not speak to an absent God, but to one that looks into the secret corners of our heart, to one that is always present and near at hand.

4. That God is ready to hear and answer our prayers: 'O thou that hearest prayer, unto thee shall all flesh come' (Ps. 65:2). He hath taken the name upon him of a God hearing prayer. It is his nature and property; it is his work and constant practice; what hath God been doing for thousands of years, but receiving the addresses [prayers] of his people? It is his delight and glory; he will be known by it; therefore he is called the 'Father of mercies' (2 Cor. 1:3), as being the fountain of all grace, and 'rich in mercy to all that call upon him' (Rom. 10:12). He is more ready to give than we are to ask; yea, he giveth unasked, and more than we ask. His quarrel with us is, because we do not ask enough.

5. That God will stand to his word, which is the rule of commerce between him and his creatures. This assurance he hath given to the church: 'Thou hast magnified thy word above all thy name' (Ps. 138:2), that is, above all that is famed and spoken of God. You have him punctual in making good his promises. The heathen had two notions of their gods: that they always kept touch with their worshippers, and were ready to do them good. They are both true of the great and living God whom we serve in the spirit; we may put the humble challenge upon him, and mind him of his word: 'Remember thy word unto thy servant, upon which thou hast caused me to hope' (Ps. 119:49); and by this we exceedingly encourage ourselves to deal with him, when we have his promise to show for it: 'For thou, O Lord of Hosts, God of Israel, hast revealed unto thy servant, saying, I will build thee an house, therefore hath thy servant found in his heart to pray this prayer unto thee' (2 Sam. 7:27). The attributes of God apprehended at large have not such a force upon the soul as when he is obliged and bound by his promise. Therefore this is a great holdfast upon God.

THE LIFE OF FAITH IN PRAYER

6. That God will both accept of our persons and prayers in Christ, the Son of his love, in whom he is well pleased: 'Who hath accepted us in the Beloved, to the praise of his glorious grace' (Eph. 1:6). This is the proper ground of prayer. Christ was sparingly revealed in the Old Testament. When they prayed, they looked towards the temple, where were the figures and symbolical representations of Christ; yea, some of them spake out: 'Now therefore, O our God, hear the prayer of thy servant, and his supplications, and cause thy face to shine upon thy sanctuary that is desolate, for the Lord's sake' (Dan. 9:17). Jesus Christ was a mediator to the church in the Old Testament, but sparingly known. But now to us he is plentifully made known: 'In whom we have boldness, and access with confidence, by the faith of him' (Eph. 3:12). Our encouragement of [in] pleading, and our hopes of acceptance, must be grounded upon his merit and intercession, and the Father's love to him, and to poor sinners in and through him.

7. Out of all this there resulteth an actual reliance upon God, according to these terms, for the acceptance of our persons, and the answer of all our requests and supplications: 'And if we know that he hear us, whatsoever we ask, we know that we have the petitions that we desired of him' (1 John 5:15). Keep to the rule of prayer, ask the things that are agreeable to God's will and conducible to his glory, and fit for us to receive in our station [position in life], and then though they be ever so difficult, ever so many in number, ever so presently needed, we are confident we shall have the petitions [which] we ask. Indeed it doth not open a door for us to expect the fulfilling of all our desires and promises of our own making. If we interpret it in that way it is horrible presumption, just as you know it is to forge a bond. This maketh for God's dishonour, and is an ungrounded confidence. But ask regularly, according to

God's will, and you may be sure that God will grant what you ask.

But how can we thus rely upon God, and have confidence that we shall be answered in all our particular requests, since mercies asked are so various, some absolutely promised, and some only conditionally, and temporal things are not always granted in kind.

Answers
1. Prayer may be heard when it is not answered with success; Daniel was heard as soon as he prayed: 'At the beginning of thy supplications the commandment came forth' (Dan. 9:23); but yet there was some stop [delay], and some time before it could be brought about (Dan. 10:12-13). The Lord heareth presently [at once], but giveth in comfort afterwards. Prayer put up in Christ's name gets a hearing presently, and in time gets an answer. God will exercise our faith for a while to believe this, though we see it not; and he will exercise our patience for a while, to wait for his leisure, and in the meantime encourageth us to believe that prayer is heard, when it is not answered at all yet in kind. Therefore we must distinguish between God's hearing and answering the prayers of his saints. God will take his own way and time for giving answers of prayer to his people. Mordecai's name stood in Ahasuerus' books some time before his honour was conferred upon him. You may not hear of God for a good while, but you shall hear of him at length. Abraham prayed for a child, but many years intervened before he had him in his arms. Our Lord Jesus Christ was heard as to the success of his death, in the victory over his enemies, but not as to the taking away of the cup: 'Who in the days of his flesh, when he had offered up prayers and supplications with strong crying and tears unto him that

THE LIFE OF FAITH IN PRAYER

was able to save him from death, and was heard in that he feared' (Heb. 5:7).

2. We may be sure that prayers are granted, so far as they are asked regularly: 'And this is the confidence that we have in him, that if we ask anything according to his will, he heareth us' (1 John 5:14). What is it to ask according to his will? It concerns the person, the matter, the manner, and the end of prayer; *Si boni petant bona, bene, ad bonum* ['If good men seek good things it is well and will turn out well'].

(i) The person or the petitioner, he must be one that serveth God: 'And whatsoever we ask we receive of him, because we keep his commandments, and do those things that are pleasing in his sight' (1 John 3:22). He that serveth God and pleaseth God is sure to be accepted. So we read in James 5:16: 'The effectual fervent prayer of a righteous man availeth much.' What have others to do to come in Christ's name? Naturalists speak of a jewel of great virtue, which, being put into a dead man's mouth, loseth all its virtue; so prayer, though it be of wonderful use and virtue, yet put into the mouth of a dead man, one that is dead in trespasses and sins and is not made alive by Christ, it is of no virtue and efficacy with God.

(ii) For the matter, it must be according to the will of God. It must be good and lawful, such things as God seeth fit for us. It must be comfortable to his revealed will, and with submission to his secret will; not contrary to his word, nor against his decrees.

It must be according to his revealed will. The throne of grace is not set up that we may come and vent our sudden distempered passions before the Lord, or to set God a task to provide meat for our lusts. When the disciples would have called for fire from heaven, Christ saith unto them, 'Ye know not what manner of spirit ye are of' (Luke 9:54-55). We are soon transported into uncomely passions, but we would have enemies confounded. Many times a child of God goes on the devil's errand. We are his messengers when revenge sets us a-work.

With submission to his secret will: 'Father, if it be possible, let this cup pass from me; nevertheless, not as I will, but as thou wilt' (Matt. 26:39). Christ, as mediator, was subject to his Father's will. So we pray aright when we pray that if God see it good for us, he will give the thing we desire; if it be hurtful to us, God will not hear. In that case, denying is a greater mercy than granting. The heathens observed it too great a facility in their gods to grant men their wishes to their ruin. Herod was too lavish when he gave his minion [Salome] leave to ask what she would to the half of the kingdom.

(iii) The will of God falleth upon the manner too; it must be with fervency, that our hearts may be upon the work: 'Ask, and ye shall have; seek, and ye shall find; knock, and it shall be opened unto you' (Matt. 7:7). We must return upon God with renewed importunity.

(iv) The will of God falleth upon the end too: 'Ye ask, and receive not; because you ask amiss, to consume it upon your lusts' (Jas. 4:3). God will not provide meat for our lusts. This would be to debauch the throne of grace.

3. I answer, that faith is to be acted in prayer for temporal mercies; for both spiritual and temporal mercies and blessings are promised, and whatever is the matter of a promise is the object of faith. God will be as punctual in the lesser matters which concern the present life, as in the weightier matters that concern thy eternal happiness. He will either give them *in specie* (in kind) or in value. It is fit that God should judge whether a temporal enjoyment will be good for us, or when he will give something in lieu of it. We are to acquiesce in his good providence for our provision here, as well as our salvation hereafter. He is willing to take our care [away] from us (Phil. 4:6-7). He intends not our loss, but our ease. He will provide for us, and in the issue will give us a full account of his love and faithfulness.

4. To act faith in prayer for temporal mercies is not to believe that we shall have them *in specie*, in kind, but faith is to rely upon God's power, submitting to his will: 'If thou wilt, thou canst make me clean' (Matt. 8:2). Unbelief thinks little of an invisible hand, and saith, 'Can God prepare a table in the wilderness?' Doubting of God's power is the great thing that unbelief stumbleth at. We must not conclude against his will, but refer all things to his will, well knowing that he is a good God, and a wise God, not troubling ourselves about events, but determining that he will cast all things for the best. This is the faith that we are to have in conditional promises.

Let me show you the necessity of praying in faith

1. Without faith prayer is not acceptable to God: 'Without faith it is impossible to please God' (Heb. 11:6). God doth not look to the eloquence of a prayer. Carnal men, that have no grace, may have great gifts of speech and flowing of language. Nor doth God look merely to the ardour of affection, for lust may make men earnest, and beget in us rapid motions. But he looks to the prayer of faith.

2. No prayer hath life in it but what is made in faith: 'How shall they call on him, in whom they have not believed?' (Rom. 10:14). It is but a mocking of God, to pray to him, unless we expect good of it. We do but come and repeat words for fashion's sake if we do not pray in faith. Why should we address ourselves to him, if we make a question of his power and good-will to help us?

3. Faith is necessary, that we may not be dismayed with the difficulties and seeming impossibilities of obtaining what we need and ask according to God's will. Many times mountains must be removed: 'If ye have faith, and doubt not; ... If ye say unto this mountain, Be thou removed, and cast into the sea, it shall be done' (Matt. 21:21). It is true, not only in the age of miracles, but in all ages, there are still mountains of oppositions, difficulties which seem as impossible to remove as a mountain. Now this would shut up our mouths, and make us languish in despair, if there were not faith to remove these mountains. See Zechariah 4:7: 'Who art thou, O great mountain? before Zerubbabel thou shalt become a plain.' Faith apprehends nothing too hard for God. How contemptible are those difficulties to a lively active faith? 'Who art thou, O mountain?'

4. Faith is necessary, that we may resolve to stick fast to God, without carnal shifts, whatever cometh of it, and not to use any means of deliverance, but what are every way consistent with our duty to God. I take this to be the case of the text. He speaks this when Christians had divers cases to be resolved. Saith he, 'Let us pray in faith, nothing wavering'; and in verse 8, 'A double-minded man is unstable in all his ways'; he is divided between God and the world, and in doubt whether the ways of God be still to be adhered to and owned, and whether we should continue waiting upon God quietly, however things succeed with us, or else shift for ourselves. This man is in a wavering condition; and therefore to keep us in a close adherency to God, and in a quiet dependence upon him for the issue of all our troubles, there is need of faith. For he that cannot trust God cannot long to be true to him. Therefore 'let him ask in faith,' this is, adhering to God's all-sufficiency. He that is persuaded of God's power and good-will, and doth refer himself to him, to bear him out in his duty, this man will be faithful to God.

5. Faith is necessary, that we may wait God's leisure: 'The vision is for an appointed time' (Hab. 2:3). We must not be too hasty: 'He that believeth will not make haste' (Isa. 28:16). Precipitancy is the cause of much evil; Saul could not tarry till Samuel came, but would go and offer sacrifice himself, and that lost him his kingdom. So when we are hasty, and cannot tarry the Lord's coming, we miscarry [go wrong].

Use 1. Here is reproof:
1. To them that will not pray, when God alloweth us, yea, commands us, to pray in faith, and with a confidence that we shall speed the better. If there were but a loose possibility, we should pray: 'Repent therefore of this thy wickedness, and pray God, if perhaps the thought of mine heart may be forgiven thee' (Acts 8:22). It is a very great difficulty, yet pray; so Exodus 32:30: 'And it came to pass on the morrow, that Moses said unto the people, Ye have sinned a great sin, and now I will go up unto the Lord, peradventure I shall make an atonement for your sin'; so 2 Kings 19:4: 'It may be the Lord thy God will hear all the words of Rabshakeh'; so Joel 2:14, 'Who knoweth, but the Lord will return, and repent, and leave a blessing behind him?' Faith can stand upon one weak leg; if there be but a 'may be', we should go to the throne of grace.

2. It reproveth those that do not look for any success in prayer, but who pray only out of course, and throw away their prayers; as children shoot away their arrows, and never look after them any more; that do not gather up the fruit of their prayers: 'In the morning will I direct my prayer unto thee, and will look up' (Ps. 5:3). And 'I will stand upon my watch, and set me upon the tower and will watch to see what he will say unto me'

(Hab. 2:1). He was spying and observing what came in by his dealing with God in prayer. He was looking to see the blessing coming. Besides, when we do not look after the success of our prayers, we lose many gracious experiences that would confirm our faith: 'The word of the Lord is a tried word' (Ps. 18:30); I have found that it is not lost time to go and plead the promises with God. And it will awaken our love: 'I will love the Lord, because he hath heard the voice of my supplication' (Ps. 116:1). It will quicken us to holy living, and a life of praise.

3. It reproveth those that have many doubtings and dark thoughts about what they pray for, about the mercy and power of God; this is an evil incident to God's own children. There is a twofold unbelief: a reigning unbelief, and a doubting unbelief. The reigning unbelief is in those that were never acquainted with God: 'Ye have said, It is in vain to serve God, and what profit is it that we have kept his ordinances?' (Mal. 3:14). But then there is a doubting unbelief, which is a weakness left upon the saints, which though it make their prayers very uncomfortable, yet it doth not make void their prayers: 'O thou of little faith! wherefore didst thou doubt?' (Matt. 14:31). Peter ventured out of the ship at Christ's call, but his feet were ready to sink ever and anon. David was surprised with this unbelief, but the Lord heard him: 'I said in my haste, I am cut off before thine eyes: nevertheless thou heardest the voice of my supplication when I cried unto thee' (Ps. 31:22). If faith be weak, we must not cease to pray, but pray the more, that faith may be confirmed, and that we may be assured of God's favour, and may grow up into a confidence in his duty.

Use 2. Of exhortation, to persuade us to pray in faith. Now to this end, consider what encouragements there are.

THE LIFE OF FAITH IN PRAYER

1. Consider what assurance Jesus Christ hath given us: 'Verily, verily, I say unto you, Whatsoever ye shall ask the Father in my name, he will give it you' (John 16:23). There is a note of asseveration [confirmation], 'Verily, verily.' Whatever our doubts and temptations be about it, the word of God is to be tried. Do you think that Christ spake truth when he said, 'Verily, verily'? So John 15:7: 'If ye abide in me, and my words abide in you, you shall ask what you will, and it shall be done unto you.' If Christ hath subdued your desires to a submission to God's providence, and to the government of his laws, ask what you will, and it shall be given you. So John 14:13-14: 'Whatsoever ye shall ask in my name, that will I do, that the Father may be glorified in the Son. If ye shall ask anything in my name, I will do it.' Christ delighteth in despatching the affairs of his people. As the vision was double, and Pharaoh's dream was doubled for the greater assurance and certainty; so here Christ inculcateth his speech for the greater confirmation of it, that we may be confident that he meant what he spake.

2. In all your prayers to God consider how significant the name of Christ is in heaven. If you come in the sense of your own unworthiness, and desire alone to be accepted in him, you shall not be slighted or neglected. If you send a child or a servant to a friend for a thing in your name, the request is yours. He that denieth a child or a servant, denieth you. Jesus Christ hath sent you in his name, Go, ask in my name; so that in effect the request becomes Christ's request. God can no more deny your request in Christ's name than he can deny Christ himself.

3. Consider, how much God loveth you: 'For the Father himself loveth you, because ye have loved me' (John 16:27). His heart is upon the things you ask for his glory. Now this is a mighty encouragement; as when Joab perceived the king's heart was towards Absalom (2 Sam. 14:1), compared with the following verses. He made intercession by the woman of Tekoa. So when your desires are regulated according to his will, and subordinated to his glory, his heart is upon these requests.

4. Consider, the moans of the beasts and other dumb creatures are regarded by him, and will not the Lord hear the prayers and supplications of his people? 'The eyes of all things wait upon thee, and thou givest them their meat in due season. Thou openest thy hand and satisfiest the desires of every living thing' (Ps. 145:15-16). When the creatures gape for their refreshment, God satisfieth them. Now if the Lord hath respect to them, will he not hear his own children? 'Consider the ravens: for they neither sow nor reap; which neither have store-house nor barn; and God feedeth them: how much more are you better than the fowls?' (Luke 12:24). Such is the Lord's overflowing love, that all creatures have their wants supplied by his bounty.

5. Consider what kind of prayers have found acceptance with God. Solomon's dream was pleasing to the Lord (1 Kgs. 3:5, compared with verses 9-13). The workings of his heart in his sleep were pleasing to God. Many times through grief, and the prevalency of our distempers, we are hardly able to put prayer into language; but then faith can send sighs to heaven. Words are but the outside of prayer. It is the acting of grace that lieth nearer the heart that is the prayer. A dumb beggar can get an alms at Christ's gate by making signs. If we be not tongue-tied with sin, and carnal liberty hath not brought an indisposition upon us. Nay, a look finds acceptance with God: 'My voice shalt thou hear in the morning; in the morning will I direct my prayer unto thee, and will look up' (Ps. 5:3). And the breathing out our souls to God: 'Thou hast heard my voice; hide not thine ear from my breathing' (Lam. 3:5-6). Yea, broken words with spiritual affections will be accepted with God; nay, chattering, as Hezekiah chattered like a crane (Isa. 38:14). Our desires have a loud sound in God's ears: 'Lord, thou hast heard the desires of the humble' (Ps. 10:17). Desires make no sound with men, but with God they have an audible voice. All this being put together, is a great comfort to the soul that God will accept of a sigh, a groan, a look, a desire, a dream. These are more acceptable to him than the pen of a ready writer, more than when we flow in words without spirit, life and affection.

6. Consider the condescension of God, in parables relating to this matter (Luke 11:8); he speaketh there of a man that would not rise to give loaves to another because he was his friend; yet because of his importunity, he would not be gone else, he arose and gave him. So Luke 18:3-5, there was a clamorous widow and an unjust judge; he would not avenge her of her adversary for her sake, yet he did it, for his own sake, and for his own quiet, 'lest by her continual coming she weary me.' In these parables there is a condescension to our suspicious thoughts, as if God had said, 'I know you think me tenacious and hard-hearted, that I am not willing to give grace; I know these are your secret thoughts. Yet if I were so, see what importunity will do. Grant it that your supposition were true, yet it becometh you to pray, and to be earnest and instant, and see what I will do for you.'

Use 3. If none pray aright but those that pray in faith, then let us examine ourselves. Do we pray in faith? How shall we know that? Answer: By three things.

1. By the serenity and composure of your spirits in prayer. When Hannah had poured out her heart before the Lord, it is said, 'she went away, and her countenance was no more sad' (1 Sam. 1:18). So when thou hast made thy moan to God, thou findest a great deal of ease and comfort come of it. As when the wind is shut up in the bowels of the earth it[13] causeth terrible convulsions and earthquakes till it get a vent; so there are many tempestuous agitations and workings of heart in us; but then a believer can go to God, and there ease his heart by pleading his case before the Lord.

2. When thou continuest praying, though God seemeth to deny thee; when upon a denial thou dost return and fasten the more upon him; as the woman of Canaan cleaves the closer to Christ the more he seemed to thrust her from him. Christ says to her in Matthew 15:26: 'It is not meet to take the children's bread, and to cast it to dogs'; but she answers in verse 27: 'Truth, Lord, yet the dogs eat of the crumbs that fall from their master's table.' It is a sign you expect something from God when you will not be put off without it.

3. When you are satisfied with the promise before you enjoy the thing promised: 'In God I will praise his word' (Ps. 56:4). When you can praise God for his Word, though as yet you have not the performance; you see the blessing is the root, and this bears up your hearts.

10

The Life of Faith in Hearing the Word

'But the word preached did not profit them, not being mixed with faith in them that heard it' (Heb. 4:2).

I am now to show you the use of faith in hearing of the word.

It hath been sometimes said that there are many good laws, but there wanteth one good law to put them all in execution; so it may be said you often hear good sermons, but there wanteth one good sermon to persuade you to put the rest in practice. This is the design of this text.

The apostle is proving in the context that it concerneth us to take heed, by the example of the Israelites, that we do not miscarry [fail] through unbelief. The ground of the argument is, that we have an offer of rest as well as they, a merciful tender of eternal life, which he calleth 'a promise of entering into God's rest' (verse 1). Though many occasions of getting and doing be spent and gone, yet whilst it is today this offer is continued to us; and therefore we should stir up ourselves to lay hold of it in time. For we are in danger as well as the Israelites. Those that have like privileges may expect like judgments if they presume upon them or do not improve them. Yea, we are rather more in danger. The gospel was preached to them but darkly and implicitly, to us more clearly and fully. Canaan was but a type and figure of the heavenly inheritance or eternal rest to be obtained by Jesus Christ; yet their unbelief was heinous, and cost them dear. The sum of the apostle's reasoning is, that they had gospel as well as we, and we shall have judgments as well as they. He giveth a reason of their judgment for our warning. Though they had gospel in the wilderness, 'yet the word preached did not profit them,' etc.

In the words take notice: (1) of an event; (2) the reason of it.

1. The event: The word preached did not profit them: in which assertion we have:

(i) The subject – The word preached, the word of hearing, they did, or might hear it.

(ii) The predicate: 'Did not profit them'; that is, they got neither title to nor possession of eternal rest by it. That deserveth the name of profit, because it is the greatest good that God did ever give or man is capable of. All is nothing without this. It is loss rather than profit to the soul, whatever we get by it. If a man get knowledge by the word, or honour and credit by the word, by professing or preaching it, yet if he doth not get a title to heaven, or a right to enter into God's rest, he doth not profit by it. 'The word did not profit them.'

2. The reason of the event.
Some read the text, 'Because they were not united by faith to it'; so is the marginal note, and Chrysostom and many others go that way, and they explain it thus: the greatest part of Israel were not of the mind whereof Caleb and Joshua and others were who believed God's promise of bringing them into Canaan, and thereupon received no benefit by the promise. But I rather choose the text-reading: Not being mingled with faith, the word is taken from a potion, which, according to the ingredients put into it, is medicinal or else mortal [fatal]. The word is the potion; if it hath all its ingredients, if mixed with faith, it produceth its effect, and becometh the power of God to salvation; if not, it doth us no good, but hurt rather. Or as any liquor mingleth with the thing on which it is poured; or, as to make the seed fruitful it must be incorporated with the earth, and receive of the virtue and fatness of it. So the word must

not only be heard but digested by faith, or it will not be profitable, or stand them in any stead that hear it.

Doctrine. That though the word of God be so great a blessing, and so excellent a means of salvation, yet it doth no good, where it is not mixed with faith in the hearing: 'I am not ashamed of the gospel of Christ, for it is the power of God to salvation to every one that believeth' (Rom. 1:16).

Consider here: (1) the things mixed; (2) the necessity of this mixture in order to profit.

1. The things mixed; they are the word of God, and faith.

1.1 *The word of God.* A divine revelation is the proper object of faith. There is a human credulity when we believe anything spoken by man for the authority of the speaker; but no authority of man can be such a firm and sure ground of faith as the testimony of God, who neither can deceive nor be deceived. Therefore, 'if we receive the testimony of man, the testimony of God is greater' (1 John 5:9). Now the whole word is to be received and apprehended by faith; but chiefly the doctrine of the gospel, which containeth the offer of Christ and all his benefits. The whole Word is to be received, for faith hath a respect to all truths. There is the same reason for one as or all, because they are all revealed by God: 'Thy word is true from the beginning, and every one of thy righteous judgments endureth for ever' (Ps. 119:160). From beginning to ending there is nothing but truth; whatever is contained in the word is either history or doctrine, or precepts, or promises, or threatenings. Faith mingleth with all these.

(i) *The historical parts of the word.* These must be believed, because the doctrinal parts dependeth thereupon: as the creation of the world, the fall of man, the promise of the Messiah to Adam, the covenant made with Abraham. There is a harmony in the scripture, as in a concert [chord] all the notes agree, and suit one with another. The whole scripture suiteth with these historical passages, because they conduce much to our profit; for they are pawns and evidences of the possibility, yea, certainty of other things that are to come: 'My help cometh from the Lord, which made heaven and earth' (Ps. 121:2). The scripture is not only a register of what is past, but a prognostication [forecast] of what is to come. Yea, it serves for our caution: 'Now all these things happened unto them for ensamples, and they are written for our admonition' (1 Cor. 10:11). Now faith looketh upon these things in the word as if a-doing [they were happening] before our eyes.

(ii) *Doctrines*; as the mystery of the trinity, the union of the two natures in the person of Christ, the benefit of imputed righteousness, that we are healed by another's stripes, the doctrine of the resurrection, etc. All these mystical verities we receive upon God's revelation. They are properly the objects of faith, because without God's revealing them they cannot be understood and found out by the light of natural reason, and in these things, though we cannot so presently and fully see the reason of what we believe, yet we see reason enough why we should believe them, because they are revealed in the Word of God, which no otherwise appeareth to us to be his Word.

In these things reason must not be heard against scripture, or be set up as the highest judge in matters of religion. As reason corrects sense, so faith corrects reason. To appearance a star is but a little spark or spangle. But reason will tell us it is much bigger because of its distance from us. The work of grace is to captivate the pride of our thoughts and prejudices against God's revelation: 'Casting down imaginations, and every high thing that exalteth itself against the knowledge of God, and bringing into captivity every thought to the obedience of Christ' (2 Cor. 10:5).

THE LIFE OF FAITH IN HEARING THE WORD 221

Reason must be captivated to faith, though not to fancy. If it be revealed it must be believed, how absurd and unlikely soever it seem to us. This is 'receiving the kingdom of God as a little child' (Matt. 18:3). A child believeth as he is taught; I mean by God, not men. Thou art neither fit for heaven, nor the understanding of heavenly things, till thou hast denied thine own wisdom. That which is above reason cannot be comprehended by reason. All lights must keep their place: sense is the light of beasts, reason of men, and faith of the church. To consult with nature in supernatural things is all one as if you did seek the judgment of reason among the beasts, and determine human affairs by brutish instincts.

There are many things necessary to religion which the angels themselves could not know if they had not been revealed: 'That unto the principalities and powers in heavenly places might be known by the church the manifold wisdom of God' (Eph. 3:10). The way of salvation by Christ is such a mystery as could not have entered into the heart of any creature, no, not an angel.

In these things, believe God upon his word. Pills are to be swallowed, not chewed; if the sick man cheweth them, he spits them up when he tasteth the bitterness of them, and so loseth a wholesome remedy. Or to use Chrysostom's comparison: 'A smith that taketh up his red-hot iron with his hands, and not with his tongs, what can he expect but to burn his fingers?' So we destroy our souls when we judge of mysteries of faith by the laws of common reason.

(iii) *Precepts*. That is another part of the word to be propounded not only to our obedience, but to our faith; first to our faith, and then to our obedience. 'Teach me good judgment and knowledge, for I have believed thy commandments' (Ps. 119:66). It is not enough to grant them rational or wise directions, or good rules for the regulating of human nature, but we must see them as God's laws, as injunctions from the glorious and powerful sovereign of the world, which we cannot neglect without the greatest hazard. That is to believe the commandments.

Many will catch at promises, but do not regard precepts. They smile upon the promise, but frown when the command puts them in mind of their duty. Faith owneth our obligation to God, and maketh us see the necessity of obedience, as well as it representeth the comfort of the promises, and to perform our duty, how contrary soever it be to our interest and carnal affections. But otherwise, without faith, when the commandments are crossing to our corrupt humours they are questioned, slighted, and shifts [expedients] studied by defiled consciences to divert the thoughts of duty. Therefore we need expressly to see that this is the will of God.

(iv) *Promises*; these are only received by faith: 'Faith is the substance of things hoped for' (Heb. 11:1). So the promissory part of the word is there in brief described. These are a principal object of faith: 'To us are given exceeding great and precious promises, that by these you might be made partakers of the divine nature' (2 Pet. 1:4). The Lord worketh saving grace at first by these promises, enabling the guilty, graceless and cursed sinner to believe, and apply the pardon, grace and blessedness freely offered in them. As soon as he gets grace to believe and apply these promises, God beginneth to apply and make out upon his heart the things promised, stamping his own image upon him, that the sinner beginneth to look like God his Father for holiness, wisdom and purity. These promises have a fitness to purify the heart as well as pacify the conscience, and must be used to both ends.

If we respect promises, we must respect all promises. The honour of God is as deeply engaged to perform one promise as another. God's failing in any one promise would be the

THE LIFE OF FAITH IN HEARING THE WORD 223

breaking of the whole covenant; as on our part the breach of one point maketh us guilty of the breach of the whole law: 'Whosoever shall keep the whole law, and yet offend in one point, he is guilty of all' (Jas. 2:10). Promises for pardon, and promises for sanctification, you must regard both, and put both in suit; promises for this life, and of a better. Many live by their wits in the world, and yet pretend to live by faith for heaven. You must trust God for all things, your names and estates as well as for your souls; only you must not be a stranger to the main promises, for herein lieth the life and heart of religion.

(v) There are *threatenings* in the word of God, and these are part of the object of faith; for God is faithful and true in his threats as well as in his promises, and therefore equally to be believed in both. The threatenings should work with us as if already accomplished. Josiah rent his clothes when he heard the words of the law: 'And it came to pass, when the king heard the words of the law, that he rent his clothes' (2 Chr. 34:19). We are not like [as deeply] affected when the judgment is threatened, as when it is come upon us: 'But to this man will I look, even to him that is poor, and of a contrite spirit, and trembleth at my word' (Isa. 66:2). So Noah prepared for a flood many years before it came: 'By faith Noah, moved with fear, prepared an ark, to the saving of his house' (Heb. 11:7). Tell many of the wrath of God, and they look upon it as a vain scarecrow; tell them of judgment to come, which is enough to make a heathen tremble (Acts 24:25), but they are no more moved at it than with a dream or a vain fable. All is for want of faith; but they that will not believe, shall feel.

Thus you see the whole Word is the object of faith: faith in the histories, for our warning and caution; faith in the doctrines, to increase our reverence and admiration; faith in the threatenings, for our humiliation; faith in the precepts, for our subjection; and faith in the promises, for our consolation. They all have their use: the histories to make us wary and cautious; the doctrines to enlighten us with a true sense of God's nature and will; the precepts to direct us, and to try and regulate our obedience; the promises to cheer and comfort us; the threatenings to terrify us, to run anew to Christ, to bless God for our escape, and to add spurs to our duty. Thus faith maketh use of the Word of God, and all things contained therein.

But especially the truths of the gospel, and that good thing which is offered in those truths is that mainly which saving faith doth close with [fasten on] and rely upon, and is fully satisfied withal. This is that which is most mysterious in itself, and remote from vulgar [secular] knowledge: 'Flesh and blood hath not revealed it to thee, but my Father which is in heaven' (Matt. 16:17). It is most profitable to lost sinners: 'Who gave himself for us, that he might redeem us from all iniquity' (Titus 2:14). It doth most set forth the praise of God: 'All the promises of God in him are Yea, and in him Amen, unto the glory of God by us' (2 Cor. 1:20). It is that to which all the rest tendeth: 'Thy testimony of Jesus is the spirit of prophecy' (Rev. 19:10), the life and heart of religion, the most blessed news that could come from heaven. Faith findeth death in the threatenings and a burden of work in the precepts; but in Christ and the gospel it findeth the way to heaven laid open, a way how a sinner may be saved and divine justice not wronged. This is that which 'the angels desire to look into' (1 Pet. 1:12). So excellent and ravishing is the saving of lost sinners by Christ incarnate, they study it and pry into it.

Once more, the Word is considered as dispensed in the ordinance of teaching and hearing: 'The word preached did not profit them.' God doth not only work by the word, but by the word preached: 'It pleased God by the foolishness of preaching to save them that believe' (1 Cor. 1:21). To hope to gain the world by the preaching of a few contemptible per-

THE LIFE OF FAITH IN HEARING THE WORD 225

sons was looked upon as a ridiculous confidence; but it pleased God to make use of that way, which pierced farther and conquered more than the Roman armies ever could. *Britannorum inaccessa Romanis loca, Christo tamen patuere* ['The regions of Britain which were inaccessible to the Romans were thrown open to Christ'].

So Ephesians 1:14: 'In whom ye also trusted, after that ye heard the word of truth, the gospel of your salvation.' The hearing of the word is the ordinary means whereby faith is wrought and exercised; so 1 Peter 1:25, 'The word of the Lord endureth for ever. And this is the word, which by the gospel is preached unto you.' That Word is the seed of the spiritual life; that Word endureth for ever in the effects of it; that Word must be mingled with faith in the hearing; not only the Scripture in the general, but the particular messages that are brought to you, and delivered from and according to that Word by the Lord's servants, whom he hath sent. Many men will not declaim against the written Word, but they have a slender esteem of those portions of truth which God carveth out to them by the messengers whom he sendeth to them. God, who instituted prophets and apostles to write Scripture, did also institute pastors and preachers to explain and apply Scripture: 'He gave some apostles, and some prophets, and some evangelists, and some pastors and teachers' (Eph. 4:11). And when they go to work, *clave non errante* ['with the proper key'], their messages are the Word of God.

But you will say, Must we believe all the dictates of fallible men?

Answer. Yes, in what accordeth with scripture, and is rightly deduced and inferred thence. Consequences [the inferences drawn from scripture] are the Word of God, and bind as well as the express Scripture. Jesus Christ proves the resurrection by this consequence [deduction] that 'God was the God of

Abraham, and the God of Isaac, and the God of Jacob' (Matt. 22:32). We are to search: 'They received the word with all readiness of mind, and searched the scripture daily whether those things were so' (Acts 17:11-12). Therefore many of them believed. The Scriptures we receive upon their divine evidence, and other doctrines upon their consonancy [agreement] to the Scripture: 'To the law and to the testimony, if they speak not according to this word, it is because there is no light in them' (Isa. 8:20). We must not be light of belief, but weigh things in the balance of the sanctuary; nor yet obstinate and contemptuous off what is delivered in the way of an ordinance.

2. *Faith.* Nothing less will serve the turn. That whereby the soul receiveth the Word is faith; that whereby it receiveth it effectually is sincere faith. There ever have been and still are three sorts of men in the world.

(i) Some men, who break out into open opposition of the gospel; that are so far from being Christians, that they are scarcely men: 'That ye may be delivered from unreasonable, and wicked men, for all men have not faith' (2 Thess. 3:2). Infidels are unreasonable and absurd, and never oppose the laws of Christ but they also violate the principles of nature.

(ii) There are some who are neither hot nor cold, that do not oppose the gospel nor yet accept it. That assent which they seem to have, is not so much an actual assent as a non-refusal, or non-opposition, or rejection of the counsel of the word. Some indeed stand in full contradiction, and actually reject the counsels of God: 'But the Pharisees and lawyers rejected the counsel of God against themselves' (Luke 7:30); and Psalm 2:3: 'Let us break their bands asunder, and cast away their cords from us.' But these though they make some profession of the gospel, yet they are careless, idle and secure. These the apostle speaketh of in Hebrews 2:3: 'How

THE LIFE OF FAITH IN HEARING THE WORD 227

shall we escape if we neglect so great salvation'; compare this with Matthew 22:5: 'And they made light of it.' They do not deny, but excuse themselves. *Non vacat* ['The time is not right'] is the sinner's plea; but *non placet* ['I have no wish to'] is the real disposition of his heart.

(iii) There is a third sort, who do not only make profession of the name of Christ, but receive the truth in the love of it and in the power of it, and transfer it into practice: 'They received not the love of the truth, that they might be saved' (2 Thess. 2:10). There is a receiving truth in the light of it by conviction, but there follows no conversion. And then they receive the truth not long in love, but in power. The gospel is the ministration of the Spirit and power: 'Our gospel came not to you in word only, but also in power, and in the Holy Ghost, and in much assurance' (1 Thess. 1:5); 'My speech and my preaching was not with the enticing words of man's wisdom, but in demonstration of the Spirit, and of power' (1 Cor. 2:4). And they transfer it into practice: 'If ye continue in my word, then are ye my disciples indeed' (John 8:31); and Matthew 7:21: 'Not every one that saith unto me, Lord, Lord, shall enter into the kingdom of heaven, but he that doth the will of my Father which is in heaven.'

Christ's real worshippers are known, not by compliments and external respects, but the inward constitution of their hearts, and the course and uniformity of their practice and conversations; they are those that do so carefully and constantly attend unto God's Word that they lay it up in their hearts: 'Thy word have I hid in my heart, that I might not sin against thee' (Ps. 119:11). They make it the rule of their whole lives: 'As many as walk according to this rule' (Gal. 6:16). They obey his commands: 'Ye have obeyed from the heart that form of doctrine that was delivered you' (Rom. 6:16); rely upon his promises: 'Remember thy word unto thy servant, on which thou hast caused me to hope' (Ps. 119:49); fear his threats: 'To this man will I look, even to him that is poor, and of a contrite spirit, and trembleth at my word' (Isa. 66:2). A carnal man doth not tremble even under God's strokes [punishments], but believers tremble under his Word and engage themselves to continue with God in well-doing, and in the pursuit of everlasting happiness: 'To them who, by patient continuance in well-doing, seek for glory, honour and immortality, eternal life' (Rom. 2:7).

To make this evident unto you, I shall show you:

(1) How many things come short of faith, or that true and unfeigned assent that must be mingled with the Word, to make it a sovereign remedy for our souls.

(2) What true faith is which doth so believe.

1. Many things come short of faith, or that true and unfeigned assent which maketh the word effectual. There are several degrees of assent.

(i) There is conjecture, or a lighter inclination and propension [propensity] of the mind to the gospel or Word of God, as possible or probably true; a suspicious [conjectural] knowledge or guess at things, when we go no higher than an 'it may be so'. The generality of careless professors [professing Christians] go no further. It may be true, for aught they know, that there is a rest remaining for the children of God; and these do walk according to the trade of Israel, and conform to the current opinions and practices that are a-foot [that is, they conform outwardly to gospel practice].

(ii) There is beyond this opinion, when the mind is strongly inclined to think it true, but not without fear of the contrary. They are so rationally convinced of the truth of the gospel that they are not able rationally to contradict it. They can dispute for it, but it is mere opinion. They can plead for it and defend

THE LIFE OF FAITH IN HEARING THE WORD

it, as a dead, rotten post may support a living tree; yet it doth not sink so deep unto them as to enter into the heart: 'When wisdom entereth into thine heart, and knowledge is pleasant to thy soul' (Prov. 2:10). They live in suspense and uncertainty in matters of religion, and do not know 'truly': 'Surely, that Christ came out from God' (John 17:8), and 'assuredly': 'Let all the house of Israel know assuredly that God hath made that same Jesus whom ye have crucified, both Lord and Christ' (Acts 2:36).

(iii) There is a higher degree, and that is dogmatical faith or a naked assent unto, or a persuasion of the truth of God's Word; but it is such an enlightening as is without taste and without power. It worketh no thorough change in the heart or practice. Many men make no doubt of the truth of the gospel, yet they do not feel the power of it. This is spoken of in James 2:19-20: 'Thou believest that there is one God, thou dost well; the devils also believe and tremble. But wilt thou know, O vain man, that faith without works is dead?' They have so much light as may disturb their peace, but not so much as doth comfort the conscience and overpower their carnal affections. Well then, this is not the kind of faith which must be mingled with the Word. It is not the Word and conjecture; not the Word and opinion; not the Word and dogmatical faith that rests in a dead naked assent, but it must be a believing with all the heart, a cordial assent: 'If thou believest with all thy heart, thou mayest be baptized' (Acts 8:37).

(iv) There is presumption, or a snatching at the promises, without considering the terms. There is no man that hath a conscience, and some loose persuasion of the truths of the gospel, but he apprehends it to be a good word, suitable to the necessities and desires of a guilty and indigent creature. But it hath no prevailing efficacy to purge the heart and subdue him to God: 'Yet they will lean upon the Lord and say, Is not the Lord among us? none evil shall come upon us' (Mic. 3:11). The leaning of a carnal presumer and the leaning of a broken heart differ, as the leaning of a drunkard that is not able to go alone, and the leaning of a wounded man who is ready to faint. Now a man who in compassion would lend his arm to someone wounded, and whose life is dropping out [ebbing away] by degrees, would not lend his arm to a reeling drunkard who is defiled with his own vomit. So the claims of mercy that a bold sinner maketh to the grace of God in Christ are rejected, when the dependence of a broken-hearted creature is justified. We have a comfortable promise: 'Call upon me in the day of trouble, and I will deliver thee' (Ps. 50:15). But a guard is set about it, so that no disobedient wretch should gather its sweet fruit: 'But unto the wicked, God saith, What hast thou to do to declare my statutes, or that thou shouldst take my covenant into thy mouth, seeing thou hatest instruction, and castest my words behind thee?' (verses 16-17).

You have the same thing in Psalm 68:19-20: 'Blessed be the Lord, who daily loadeth us with his benefits, even the God of our salvation, Selah. He that is our God is the God of salvation, and unto God the Lord belong the issues from death.' We can never speak enough of the mercy of God to poor broken-hearted sinners; it is here twice repeated; but bold and daring sinners, who continue in their rebellion and enmity against God, have no share in it, nor can they lay claim to it. See verse 21: 'But God shall wound the head of his enemies, and the hairy scalp of such a one as goeth on still in his trespasses.' Christians who live loosely, as pagans, shall not find grace to be a sanctuary to them. It was Origen's answer to Celsus, who said that Christianity was a sanctuary for wicked profligate persons said: 'No. It is not a sanctuary for them, but an hospital to cure them.'

THE LIFE OF FAITH IN HEARING THE WORD

What is the true faith which must be mingled with the Word?
1. It is a *lively* faith or assent to the doctrine of God. The scripture speaketh of a dead faith (James 2:20); and a lively faith, and of a lively hope: 'Who hath begotten us again unto a lively hope' (1 Pet. 1:3); such as quickens them to the use of all due means to attain what they believe and hope for:

> 'But this I confess unto thee, that after the way which they call heresy, so worship I the God of my fathers, believing all things which are written in the law and the prophets; and have hope towards God, which they themselves also allow; that there shall be a resurrection of the dead, both of the just and unjust. And herein do I exercise myself, to have always a conscience void of offence toward God and toward men' (Acts 24:14-16).

A drowsy inattentive assent prevaileth nothing, but such as hath life and affection in it. To many people faith is no more than non-denial, or a negative assent; they do not contradict the truth, but it doth not affect their hearts, of excite them to pursue and look after the things represented to them.

Faith is acted and exercised about what we hear, as about matters wherein we are deeply concerned. It is enough to have faith, but it must be exercised and put forth. Such a faith engrafteth the Word into us: 'Receive with meekness the engrafted word, which is able to save your souls' (Jas. 1:21). It is not only pleased with the notions [doctrines] as matter of opinion, but receiveth and layeth up the Word as the seed of life. It changeth the disposition of the soul into the nature of the Word: 'But God be thanked, that ye were the servants of sin; but ye have obeyed from the heart the form of doctrine which was delivered to you' (Rom. 6:17); or, into which form of doctrine ye were delivered; its lively character is enstamped upon us: 'Whereby are given unto us exceeding great and precious promises, that by these you might be partakers of the divine nature' (2 Pet. 1:4). What effect hath the Word upon the soul, to transform us unto the image of God?

2. It is an *applicative* faith. We do not only believe God's Word and all things contained therein to be a truth, but we believe it as a truth that concerneth us in particular, and thereupon apply it to ourselves. Meat will feed, if it be eaten; water will quench thirst, if we drink it, and receive it into our bodies; yet if we neither eat the one nor drink the other, we may perish for hunger and thirst. So the applying and urging the heart with the word preached doth profit us: 'Hear it, and know thou it for thy good' (Job 5:27); and 'What shall we then say to these things?' (Rom. 8:31); and 'How shall we escape, if we neglect so great salvation?' (Heb. 2:3).

3. It is an *obediential* confidence, such as doth not take one part of the Word and set it against the other; the precept against the promise, or the promise against the precept. It does not hope to take liberty now and then, to break a commandment without forfeiting a claim to the promises, or, like mountebanks [quack doctor], who offer poison for a cure: 'What shall we say then? Shall we continue in sin, that grace may abound? God forbid! How shall we that are dead to sin live any longer therein?' (Rom. 6:1-2) Such people are not encouraged to duty, but to sin by hopes of grace: 'Turning the grace of God into lasciviousness' (Jude 4). These debauch the principles of the gospel. It teacheth other things, where it is rightly apprehended: 'For the grace of God that bringeth salvation, hath appeared unto all men, teaching us, that denying ungodliness and worldly lusts we should live soberly, righteously, and godly in the present world' (Titus 2:11-12). Others are not sensible of the necessity of yielding obedience to God.

THE LIFE OF FAITH IN HEARING THE WORD

The necessity of this mixture in order to profit. This I shall make good, for otherwise the ends of the gospel cannot be obtained. I prove it thus:

1. It is agreeable to the wisdom of God, that as there should be a means to offer, so there should be a means to receive his grace. The Word doth only offer grace, but it is faith that doth receive it; therefore, as without the Word there can be no faith, so without faith the Word can have no power. To a good crop, or a fruitful harvest, there is required, not only good seed, but *sabactum solum*, a prepared soil and ground (Matt. 13). The seed was the same, but the ground was different: some fell on the highway, some on the stony ground, some on the thorny ground, some on the good ground, which alone thrived and prospered: 'He that receiveth the seed into the good ground, is he that heareth the word, and understandeth it, which also beareth fruit, and bringeth forth, some an hundred, some sixty, some thirty-fold' (verse 23).

Well then, there must be receiving as well as offering, and a kindly [glad] receiving. A plaster doth not heal at a distance till it be applied to the sore. It is our souls which were wounded, and so it is our souls which must have the cure. The light that illuminateth must shine into the place that is enlightened; the life that quickeneth must be in the substance which is quickened by it. If the bare discovery and offer of grace, without the applying of grace, or receiving of grace, were enough, the gospel would save all alike, the despisers of it as well as those that submit to it. Therefore there must be receiving: Christ must not only be offered, but received: 'To as many as received him, to them gave he power to become the sons of God' (John 1:12). And the covenant is not only tendered [offered] to us, but accepted by us: 'Then they that gladly received his word were baptized' (Acts 2:41).

Blood shed will not avail us, unless it be blood sprinkled: 'And to the blood of sprinkling, that speaketh better things than the blood of Abel' (Heb. 12:24). Christ's making the atonement is not effectual to salvation, unless it be received, owned, and applied: 'We joy in God through our Lord Jesus Christ, by whom we have received the atonement' (Rom. 5:11). General grace must some way be made particular, or else it cannot profit us. Christ doth not save us at a distance, but as received into our hearts, or else why are not all justified, all adopted, all saved? There is the same merciful God, the same sufficient Saviour, the same gracious covenant. The reason is that some apply this grace, others do not: 'After ye heard the word of truth, the gospel of your salvation' (Eph. 1:13). It is not enough to know the gospel to be a doctrine of salvation in the general, but we must look to this, that it be a doctrine of salvation to ourselves in particular. What doth it profit us if it be a doctrine of salvation to others and not to ourselves? Therefore we must receive and apply the promises to our own souls, that these promises may stir up joy, thankfulness and praise and quicken and enliven our obedience, and in due time our interest in them be determined to our joy and comfort.

2. That the proper grace to receive the word is faith. Here I shall show: (i) the necessity of it; (ii) the efficacy of it, that without it the ends [aims] of the gospel cannot be obtained; that by it they are powerfully and effectually obtained.

First, *the necessity of it*, because without it the ends of the gospel cannot be obtained; and this with respect to God, Christ, the gospel, or Christian religion, and the believer himself.

(i) *With respect to God.* Holiness and love to God are required *sub ratione finis* [as ends], and faith *sub ratione medii* [as the means], as a means to make us holy and to love God. That

THE LIFE OF FAITH IN HEARING THE WORD

this is the great end of the gospel institution is plain from Scripture: 'Now the end of the commandment is charity, out of a pure heart and a good conscience, and faith unfeigned' (1 Tim. 1:5). The end and scope of the gospel is love to God, and faith in Christ our Redeemer is the great means which conduceth [leads] to it. So Christ giveth us an account of the words which he heard from his Father. The sum of it is, that our great duty is to God and our great happiness to be beloved by him (John 14:21-23). The gospel revelation was set up for this end and purpose, to represent to us the goodness and amiableness of God, that he might be more lovely to us and be loved by us. The great design of reconciling and saving lost man by Christ, and his wonderful condescension in his incarnation, life, sufferings and death, is all to reveal this love of God in Christ, and to work up our hearts to love God again. To this end also tend his merciful covenant and promises, all the benefits given to his church, and the privileges of the saints: the Spirit, pardon, peace, glory. All these tend to warm our hearts with love to God; and faith is appointed to look upon all these, to consider them, and improve them: 'Faith worketh by love' (Gal. 5:6). The principal use of faith is to kindle the love of God in our souls, that knowing and believing the love which God hath to us in Christ, we may love him in return and thankfully obey him. Now if this be not enough for you, take an argument or two, thus:

The great end of Christ's coming is to bring us to God: 'For Christ also hath once suffered for sins, the just for the unjust, that he might bring us to God' (1 Pet. 3:18); and John 14:6: 'Jesus saith unto him, I am the way, and the truth and the life; no man cometh to the Father but by me'; and Hebrews 7:25: 'Wherefore he is able to save them to the uttermost that come unto God by him.' But if this be the end of Christ's coming, to bring us to God – that is, to turn us in heart and life to him from whom we had fallen, surely love to God is the great end of the Christian religion. Therefore faith, which is to receive and improve it, is the means to this end.

Again, if heaven and eternal blessedness be perfect love, then the end of the gospel is love; for the gospel is appointed to make us everlastingly happy. Therefore it was written, therefore did the Son of God come to bring us to this perfect estate. Heaven is the love of God and perfection in holiness; and to be blessed in heaven is to be happy in the perfect love of God, to see him as he is and to be like him. A perfect love to God is maintained by perfect vision, and on our part a perfect receiving his love to us. Then surely that is the end, and faith is the means, to take notice of and be persuaded of the love of God that shineth to us so graciously in Christ.

Well now, how can the end of the gospel be obtained, which is to love God, and be beloved of him, if either we have no faith, and do not believe this wonderful demonstration of God's love in Christ; or if we only have a dead faith and do but slightly reflect upon it with cold and narrow thoughts? Surely, though the gospel be such a notable institution to teach us the art of loving God, and so sovereign a remedy against our corrupt self-love, yet it will not profit unless it be mixed with faith in the hearing.

(ii) *With respect to Christ*. In the gospel he is represented as clothed with the office of a mediator between God and us, an office which he executeth in that three-fold function of a prophet, priest and king. Now the great duty of the gospel is to own him in all these and to submit to him, that these offices may have their perfect effect upon us. Hear him as a prophet: 'This is my beloved Son, in whom I am well pleased; hear ye him' (Matt. 17:5). Receive him as lord and king: 'As you have received Christ Jesus the Lord, so walk ye in him' (Col. 2:6).

Consider him as a priest: 'Consider the apostle and high priest of our profession, Jesus Christ' (Heb. 3:1).

Now how can any of this be done without faith, or a sound belief that he is the Son of God, who cometh in all these qualities [offices] to us? Can we learn of him whom we take to be a deceiver? Or obey him whom we believe not to be our true and rightful Lord? And if we believe not his merits and sacrifice as a priest, can we be comforted with his glorious promises and covenant, and come to God with the more boldness and hope of mercy upon that account, especially in a dying hour? Surely Christ must lie [idly] by and the fruits of his offices be neglected, unless we believe that he is authorised and fitted for all these things.

But he is the teacher sent from God to show us the way of life; his sacrifice offered through the eternal Spirit is of full merit and value to expiate our sins; and he is Lord of life and glory, able to protect us till he hath brought us to heaven: 'I know whom I have believed, and I am persuaded that he is able to keep that which I have committed unto him against that day' (2 Tim. 1:12). We must be persuaded of his authority, sufficiency, readiness, willingness to do us good, before we can trust ourselves and our eternal interests in his hands. Who will take physic [medicine] from a physician whom he does not trust? Or go to sea with a pilot whose skill he questioneth? Surely before we can heartily consent, or resolvedly put ourselves into his hands to be reconciled to God, and saved from sin and punishment and finally brought to perfect happiness and glory, we must be persuaded what he is, and that he is able to do all this for us. 'Believe ye then that I am able to do this?' Christ asks of the blind men. They answer, 'Yea, Lord' (Matt. 9:28).

So when you consider Christ's glorious offices and the blessed effects of them, believe that he is able to so these things. Ask yourself: 'Will he indeed show me the way to heaven? Hath he paid such a ransom for my captive soul? Will he protect me so powerfully in the way of salvation?' Let faith work such a thorough persuasion of his ability and fidelity, as may extort a full resignation from you of yourselves into his hands, that by his own methods he may lead you to everlasting glory.

(iii) *With respect to the Word itself,* or those sacred oracles wherein the gospel of the Christian religion is contained, you will see the truth there recorded cannot well be apprehended and digested without faith, because there are things written which do concern matters past, present and to come. And all these have difficulties which can be only removed by faith.

Matters past; as the creation of the world; the providence of God towards his church and people throughout all successions of fore-going ages, till the Scriptures were written and completed; the keeping of the promise of the Messiah still a-foot [unfulfilled] till his coming in the flesh; the birth, life, death and resurrection of Jesus Christ. These were things of necessity to be confined to some determinate time and place. It was not necessary that Christ should be always dying and always rising, in every age and place, and in the view of every man. These things can therefore only be apprehended by faith, for *we* saw them not. They are believed upon some competent and sufficient testimony.

Things present are those which concern our present duty. They pre-suppose our accepting of Christ and self-denying obedience. Both require faith, yea, a strong faith.

The accepting of Christ for our Lord and Saviour. Now this is hard, yea, impossible to be done, without a sound persuasion of the truth of that doctrine which concerneth our redemption by Christ, for this is a rare and wonderful mystery. 'Great is the mystery of godliness' (1 Tim. 3:16). Those 'natural apostles' [the created universe], which are gone forth into all lands to preach up an infinite and eternal power, I mean the sun, moon, and stars, these natural preachers are dumb and silent, say not a word concerning Christ, or God manifested in the flesh. Angels could not find out this mystery by all their excellency of wisdom and knowledge. But they admire it, as they study it, and see it in God's dispensations to the church: 'To the intent that now unto the principalities and powers in heavenly places might be known by the church the manifold wisdom of God' (Eph. 3:10); and 1 Peter 1:12: 'Which things the angels desire to look into.' When a messenger was sent from heaven to tell the blessed virgin Mary of this mystery, though he was an extraordinary messenger, and though she so nearly [closely] concerned [in the matter], she said: 'How shall this be?' (Luke 1:34). The conception of a virgin, the death of the Son of God, who was life itself, are not matters so easily apprehended and improved, unless the Lord gives us faith. How can we build upon this foundation with any confidence?

Self-denying obedience. Men are addicted to their own wills and lusts, and will not easily suffer themselves to be persuaded to change heart and life, especially when this change is likely to cost them dear in the world, and they must forfeit those things which they see and love for a God and glory which they never saw. Naturally [By nature] the spirits of men are yokeless and libertine [love complete freedom]: 'Let us break their bands asunder, and cast away their cords from us' (Ps. 2:3). And when temptations come, we consult with the flesh, and so we do not easily believe the necessity of this self-denying obedience, but we cavil [argue] and wriggle and distinguish ourselves [excuse] out of our duty. Unless a firm assent lays a strong obligation upon us, we shall cast off yoke after yoke, till we leave Christ but an empty name.

Things future in the unseen world. We have to do with an invisible God, who hath propounded hopes in an invisible world. Now what shall we do without faith, which is 'the evidence of things not seen' (Heb. 11:1)? We are apt to take up with [be interested in] things present, and are little affected with [not fond of] things unseen and above our senses. Nothing but a strong faith will engage us to look after [take an interest in] these things or to venture all that we are and have, depending upon these things.

(iv) *With respect to the party who is to receive these truths*, faith is necessary. We may consider the true believer as to his mind, heart and life, all of which are bettered and profited by the Word.

iv.1 As to his *mind*, which must be enlightened and awakened. Corrupt and carnal reason is such a stranger to God and heavenly things that unless the Lord gives us a new light, which may direct and quicken us, we shall not much mind either God or heaven. Therefore, for our cure, the understanding must be enlightened and awakened, and it is done in both cases by faith.

(a) Enlightened rightly to the discerning of these things: 'The natural man received not the things of the Spirit of God, for they are foolishness unto them; neither can he know them, because they are spiritually discerned' (1 Cor. 2:14). Supernatural matters must be discerned by a supernatural light, spiritual matters by a spiritual light. Other things are determined by sense and reason, but *our* light in these things is by faith, by which we see those excellent and high things which are above the reach of the natural man. Faith serveth for the government [directing] of the soul, as the eye does for the body.

By it we see God: 'By faith he saw him that is invisible' (Heb. 11:27). Hereby we see Christ: 'That every one that seeth the Son, and believeth on him, may have everlasting life' (John 6:40); and we see heaven: 'While we look not to the things which are seen, but to the things which are not seen; for the things which are seen are temporal, but the things which are not seen are eternal' (1 Cor. 4:18). Till God openeth the eye of our minds, we neither see God ('Without faith it is impossible to please God; for he that cometh to God must believe that he is', Heb. 11:6); nor do we see Christ ('Unto you therefore which believe he is precious', 1 Pet. 2:7); nor do we see heaven ('Receiving the end of your faith, the salvation of your souls', 2 Pet. 1:9). Therefore must we mind [intend to get] saving faith, which is spiritual sight. Deal seriously with God about it: 'The eyes of your understanding being enlightened, that you may know what is the hope of his calling, and what the riches of the glory of his inheritance in the saints' (Eph. 1:18).

(b) The understanding or mind must be excited and awakened to regard and consider these things which we see and are convinced of. For otherwise, in seeing we see not, and in hearing we hear not. As when you tell a man of a business [matter] when his mind is taken up about other things. He mindeth it not, regardeth it not, or carrieth himself as if he minded it not. They do not think of God or Christ or heavenly things; they mourn for sin as if they mourned not, rejoice in God as if they rejoiced not, seek after heaven as if they sought not after it. Now to cure this inadvertency [carelessness], or to bring us to a more attentive consideration of these things, requireth a lively faith. The same light and Spirit that doth open the eyes of the mind to discern heavenly things doth also awaken us to the minding of them: 'Whose heart the Lord opened, that she attended to the things that were spoken of Paul' (Acts 16:14). Many precious truths lie [idly] by, and are lost for want of consideration. Non-attendance is the bane [curse] of the professing [religious] world: 'They made light of it' (Matt. 22:5). People do not allow their minds to dwell upon these things, so as to consider what is true misery, and what is true happiness.

iv.2 That which is next to be considered in the entertainment [reception] of truth, or of the gospel is the *heart*, which is to be subdued to God: 'But God be thanked, that ye were the servants of sin, but ye obeyed from the heart that form of doctrine which was delivered to you' (Rom. 6:17). How shall we without faith? To win over the heart to a holy and heavenly life, which is naturally so averse from it? The credulity and belief required of Christians is for the matters which are presented to our belief. Christianity, which is mostly conversant about things practical, must be received not only with the mind, but the heart: 'If thou shalt confess with thy mouth the Lord Jesus, and shalt believe in thine heart, that God raised him from the dead, thou shalt be saved; for with the heart man believeth unto righteousness, and with the mouth confession is made unto salvation' (Rom. 10:9-10); so Acts 8:37: 'If thou believest with all thy heart thou mayest be baptized.'

You must receive the truth in the love of it: 'They received not the love of the truth, that they might be saved' (2 Thess. 2:10). That which was made for the heart must be admitted into the heart. Till it is there it is not in its proper place. It is rejected, even though it seemeth to be received. For if you be convinced of the truths of the gospel, and do not admit them to come into your hearts, you are false to them and yourselves, and cannot expect them to profit you. This is the difference between the unsanctified and the regenerate. The one receiveth the truth in the light of it by a mere speculation, but shuts up his heart against it; the other receiveth it in the love of it, openeth his heart to it, and admitteth it to its proper place and work. The one imprisoneth it in unrighteousness, the other entertaineth it with love and regard.

Now this is the true receiving, and that which is proper to faith, to receive all holy truths with a practical intent so to work them upon your hearts according to their nature, weight and use. Now if it be so, we may see how little we profit by the gospel till we mingle it with faith when we hear it. We must apprehend and believe the truth so as to get the *heart* affected with it.

iv.3 The life is bettered and overruled by the Word received. For a believer is to be considered as to his head, heart and life. When the mind is enlightened and the heart sanctified, the truth must show itself in the conversation [outward life]. The life must be holy and obedient: 'As obedient children, not fashioning yourselves according to the former lusts in your ignorance. But as he which hath called you is holy, so be ye holy in all manner of conversation' (1 Pet. 1:14-15). Now how shall this be done without faith? It may be done by a lively faith.

How dare you neglect Christ if you believe that he is the Son of God, who must be your judge? How dare you indulge the flesh, or be mindless of heavenly things if you believe the necessity of self-denial and the reality of the world to come? There is a great deal of difference between the name, title and profession [of faith] of a believer, and the real efficacy of true faith.

A true believer must get the truth of the gospel into his mind, heart and life. That truth which enlighteneth his mind doth also purify his heart: 'Purifying their hearts by faith' (Acts 15:9); so that by it not only mistakes are discovered, but lusts subdued. And it doth not only purify the heart, but overcomes the world: 'This is the victory whereby we overcome the world, even our faith' (1 John 5:4). And it produceth a good conversation, not discouraged with tribulations, nor diverted from the pursuit of eternal happiness by the baits and allurements of the flesh. Yea, it putteth us upon a bold and an open profession of the name of Christ, and respect to his ways, however discountenanced [unpopular] in the world: 'We having the same spirit of faith, according as it is written, I believed, and therefore have I spoken; we also believe, and therefore speak' (2 Cor. 4:13).

Now this being the case with the person which is to receive and entertain the gospel, to receive it into his mind, heart and life, certainly there is a necessity for faith. For it is the office of faith to do all these things.

Secondly, the efficacy of faith. To this end I shall show: (1) that all efficacy is ascribed to faith; (2) whence it hath its power and force.

That all efficacy is ascribed to faith; for till the gospel be owned as a divine and infallible truth, it hath no effect upon us: 'Ye received the word of God, which ye heard of us, not as the word of men, but (as it is in truth) the word of God, which effectually worketh also in you that believe' (1 Thess. 2:13). The truths of the gospel concerning God, Christ, sin, grace, hell and heaven are of such weight and moment as that they might move a rock. Yet they shake not, they stir not the heart of a carnal professor, because they receive the Word in word only. But where it is received in faith, it is not received in word only, but in power. And there it worketh effectually: 'Our gospel came not to you in word only, but also in power, and in the Holy Ghost, and in much assurance' (1 Thess. 1:5). To believe the truth of God's Word is the ready way to make it effectual. It is slighted because it is not credited [believed]. A man may give high and cogent reasons against his lusts and yet still follow them, if the truth be not rooted in his heart.

All graces are set a-work by faith. These include: reverence for the Word; some tremble at the Word when it convinceth of sin (Isa. 66:2), because they know it is the Word by which they shall be judged at the last day. The same is true of repentance; some humble themselves at God's warnings and threatenings. It is the fruit of their faith: 'The people of Nineveh believed God and proclaimed a fast, and put on sackcloth' (Jon. 3:5). Some prize Christ as he is offered in the new covenant, but this is from faith: 'To you that believe he is precious' (1 Pet. 2:7). When faith representeth him in all his loveliness, then the soul prizeth him. Some are ready to the duties enjoined: 'I have believed thy commandments' (Ps. 119:66). Faith doth all, and enliveneth all truths, and maketh them operative.

Whence hath faith this power?

1. Because it qualifieth us for the gift of the Holy Spirit: 'That we might receive the promise of the Spirit through faith' (Gal. 3:14); and John 7:39: 'This he spake of the Spirit, which they that believe in him should receive.' The Spirit begets faith and actuates faith, and then faith doth enliven all truths.

2. From the matter propounded to faith and apprehended by it, which is God's Word, and hath a stamp of his wisdom, goodness and power left upon it. There we see his divine authority, charging and commanding us under pain of his displeasure to mind and regard such things. It is the Lord who hath spoken it: 'Ye received it not as the word of men, but (as it is in truth) the word of God, which effectually worketh also in them that believe' (1 Thess. 2:13). And it is enforced upon us in the most strong and potent way of argumentation:

as from the equity and excellency of what he hath commanded: 'I have written to them the great things of my law, but they were counted as a strange thing' (Hos. 8:12);

from his great love in Christ: 'The love of Christ constraineth us' (2 Cor. 5:14);

from the strict day of accounts, as we will answer it to him another day: 'In the day when God shall judge the secrets of men by Jesus Christ, according to my gospel' (Rom. 2:16);

from the importance and unspeakable concernment of those things to us, our salvation or damnation depending thereupon: 'He that believeth and is baptized shall be saved; but he that believeth not shall be damned' (Mark 16:16).

The danger of refusing him is no less than everlasting death, and the happiness of complying with his motions no less than everlasting life and complete blessedness. Now since everlasting life and death are involved in this matter, we had better be serious.

3. The way of faith's working about these things. The apprehension is clear, the consideration serious, the assent strong, the application close. Men are pierced to the quick where this faith prevaileth, and are deeply affected with what they hear. The apprehension is clear: 'Faith is the substance of things hoped for, and the evidence of things not seen' (Heb. 11:1). The consideration serious; they attend, they search: 'They searched the scriptures daily' (Acts 17:11). The assent strong: 'Let the house of Israel know assuredly' (Acts 2:36); and John 17:8, 'They have known surely.' And the application close: 'What shall we say to these things?' (Rom. 8:31),

THE LIFE OF FAITH IN HEARING THE WORD

Objection:
How can faith be necessary to make the Word effectual since faith itself cometh by hearing, and is ordinarily wrought by the Word: 'So then faith cometh by hearing, and hearing by the word of God' (Rom. 10:17)?

Answer
1. At first God by his preventing [prevenient] grace taketh hold of the heart, and maketh it to believe. At the first creation light was made before the sun; and the first man was made out of the dust of the ground. Afterwards Adam propagateth and bringeth forth after his kind. So the first work is exempted from the common rule; yet not the subsequent works.

2. Faith is wrought in and by the hearing, as the gospel doth propound and make known to our understanding the object of saving faith. The Lord doth at the same time work the grace of faith in the hearts of the elect: 'And a certain woman named Lydia, a seller of purple, which worshipped God, heard us, whose heart the Lord opened, that she attended unto the things spoken of Paul' (Acts 16:14). Without this the Word would not profit.

3. One faith maketh way for another, the dogmatical faith for the saving faith, and common and general grace for a particular and saving work of God's Spirit; just as the priming [undercoat of paint] on the woodwork maketh it receptive of other colours.

Use 1
For information, to show the reason why there is so little profiting under so much preaching. It is because there is no faith; the cause is from ourselves or in ourselves. Alas! We may complain: 'Who hath believed our report?' (Isa. 53:1). Most men have not that general faith so as to incline their hearts and ears to take notice of what God saith.

Use 2. Reproof of various types:

1. *Some do not hear;* they neglect the seasons of grace, and refuse to go where the sound of the gospel may be heard. But we are commanded 'to be swift to hear' (Jas. 1:19). Others sleep while the word is preaching; as Eutychus fell asleep: 'While Paul was long preaching, he sunk down with sleep, and fell down from the third storey, and was taken up dead' (Acts 20:9). It was a sin, and God punished him, though he was only a youth. The sermon was after supper and was of great length. It went on till midnight. It was an infirmity, but infirmities are punished by God. Others talk, or suffer their minds to be diverted by every trifle: 'And they come unto thee as the people cometh, and they sit before thee as my people, and they hear thy words, but they will not do them; for with their mouth they show much love, but their heart goeth after their covetousness' (Ezek. 33:31). A child's eye is off his book if a butterfly do but come by. The devil findeth them other work. How often do we mingle sulphur with our incense! Those that hear in jest will find hell hot in good earnest. 'He that hath an ear, let him hear what the Spirit saith to the churches' (Rev. 2:7).

2. *Some do not understand what is outwardly heard by the ears of the body:* 'When any one heareth the word of the kingdom, and understandeth it not, then cometh the wicked one, and catcheth away that which was sown in his heart' (Matt. 13:19); and Jeremiah 5:21: 'Hear now this, O foolish people, and without understanding! Which have eyes and see not, which have ears and hear not.'

3. *Some do not believe what they understand.* But that is the great requisite. 'That the gentiles by my mouth should hear the word of the gospel and believe' (Acts 15:7).

THE LIFE OF FAITH IN HEARING THE WORD

4. *Some do not obey what they seem to believe*: 'But they have not all obeyed the gospel; for Esaias saith, Lord, who hath believed our report?' (Rom. 10:16); and Matthew 7:26-27: 'And every one that heareth these sayings of mine, and doth them not, shall be likened unto a foolish man that built his house upon the sand; and the rain descended, and the floods came, and the winds blew, and beat upon that house, and it fell, and great was the fall of it.'

5. *Some do not persevere in what they undertake to obey*: 'Go thou near, and hear all that the Lord our God shall say, and speak thou unto us all that the Lord our God shall speak unto thee, and we will hear it, and do it. And the Lord heard the voice of your words, when ye spake unto me; and the Lord said unto me, I have heard the voice of the words of this people which they have spoken unto thee; they have well said all that they have spoken. Oh that there was such an heart in them that they would fear me, and keep all my commandments always, that it might be well with them and with their children for ever' (Deut. 5:27-29).

Use 3. Is to press and excite you:

First, In the general, to entertain [accept] the gospel with a sound and lively faith.

1. Without it no sin can be conquered. The first sin was unbelief: 'Yea, hath God said, Ye shall not eat of every tree of the garden?' (Gen. 3:1). And still unbelief is the cause of transgressing, for the flesh is importunate to be pleased, and the temptations of the world will hurry us to evil: 'Take heed, brethren, lest these be in any of you an evil heart of unbelief, in departing from the living God' (Heb. 3:12). The flesh is fed with the baits of sense, but the spirit is encouraged and strengthened by the supports of faith.

2. Without it no grace can be thoroughly exercised: 'Without faith it is impossible to please God' (Heb. 11:6). All graces are set a-work by faith. Repentance: 'The people of Nineveh believed God, and proclaimed a fast, and put on sackcloth' (Jon. 3:5). To believe the truth of God's Word when it is spoken is the ready way to make it effectual. Their repentance was no more than legal, but it was as good as their faith was. All is quiet in the soul. There is no news of repentance, nor noise of any complaining against sin till faith sets the conscience a-work. So there is no prizing of Christ without faith. He and all his graces lie by as a neglected thing till we believe: 'To them that believe he is precious' (1 Pet. 2:7). When faith represents him in his loveliness to the soul, then the affections are stirred.

3. No worship can be seriously performed with it. This is so of prayer: 'O thou that hearest prayer, unto thee shall all flesh come' (Ps. 65:2). When we believe him, then we come cheerfully into his presence. So for hearing the Word. It is this prayer – hearing God bindeth the ear to hear: 'We are all here present before God, to hear all things that are commanded thee of God' (Acts 10:33); and it bindeth the heart to reverence: 'To him will I look, who is of a humble and contrite heart, and trembleth at my word' (Isa. 66:2).

4. Without it no acts of justice and mercy can be well done: 'But this I confess unto thee, that after the way which they call heresy, so worship I the God of my fathers, believing all things which are written in the law and the prophets; and have hope towards God, which they themselves also allow, that there shall be a resurrection of the dead, both of the just and of the unjust. And herein do I exercise myself, to have always a conscience void of offence toward God and toward men' (Acts 24:14-16).

THE LIFE OF FAITH IN HEARING THE WORD

But what shall we do to get this faith?

1. Beg it of God. It is his gift: 'By grace ye are saved, through faith; and that not of ourselves, it is the gift of God' (Eph. 2:8). He must open the eyes of our minds: 'That the God of our Lord Jesus Christ, the Father of glory, may give unto you the Spirit of wisdom and revelation in the knowledge of him; the eyes of your understanding being enlightened, that ye may know what is the hope of his calling, and what the riches of the glory of his inheritance in the saints' (Eph. 1:17-18).

2. Study the grounds [basis] of faith. Many truths revealed in scripture are agreeable to the light of nature, and known by it; as that there is one God, the first causes of all things, of infinite power, wisdom, and goodness; that it is reasonable that he should be worshipped and served, and that according to his will; that we have faulted with [sinned against] him. We have rebelled against his will declared in his law and so are obnoxious to his wrath and displeasure. Faith says that reasonable [rational] creatures have immortal souls, and die not as the brute beasts; that true happiness is not found in those things wherein men ordinarily seek it, namely, in things grateful [pleasing] to the animal life. All these and such like things are taught by faith. The business of the Christian religion must needs lie in three things.

(i) In declaring to us more fully the nature, will and worship of God.

(ii) In finding out a remedy for the Fall, or expiating the faults and sins of men, which is done by the incarnation, death and resurrection of Christ.

(iii) In propounding a fit happiness for an immortal soul. Now think with yourselves with what congruity [fitness] and evidence these things are done in the gospel. Here are prophecies to usher in this doctrine, miracles to confirm it, valuable testimony to recommend it to us. How agreeable all these are to the nature of God and our necessities!

3. Attend upon the means whereby faith is wrought. Listen to the ministry of the Word: 'Who is Paul, and who is Apollos, but ministers by whom ye believed?' (1 Cor. 3:5). There is some consideration or other given out to beget or strengthen our faith, for God is not wanting to his ordinances, and we go on by degrees in believing, the sincere soul still finding more evidence in the Word continually, and more experience in his own heart: 'He that believeth on the Son of God hath the witness in himself' (John 5:10).

4. Get a prepared heart. To this end:

(i) See that there be no carnal bias: 'How can ye believe that seek honour one of another, and seek not the honour that cometh from God only?' (John 5:44). Indulgence to any sensual affection, to the honours, riches and pleasures of the world, maketh men unfit either to believe or consider the truths of the gospel.

(ii) Let there be no wilful, heinous sin: 'Holding the mystery of faith in a pure conscience' (1 Tim. 3:9). Men are loth to believe in their torment, as malefactors cannot endure to think of the assizes [courts of justice]. An honest and good heart doth best receive the good seed. Sin doth weaken our faith, and wilful sins breed horror in our minds and make us wish the gospel were not true, that there were no God, no day of judgment, no hell for the wicked and ungodly. If that were true, then it is your interest to be an unbeliever.

5. Are you willing to unwilling to believe? If willing, wait upon God. He will not fail the waiting soul: 'Grace and truth came by Jesus Christ' (John 1:17). But if you are unwilling, Christ

THE LIFE OF FAITH IN HEARING THE WORD 253

will not give his grace to them that despise it, or make folks believe whether they will or no, or when they would rather not believe. If God out of his secret grace will surprise you, you cannot expect it.

Secondly, in every particular message that is brought to you in the way or an ordinance, regard God's providence in it. Christ hath a greater share in it than the teacher. Remember now that in every important truth your faith is tried: 'Believest thou this?' (John 11:26), and in every duty which God enforces your obedience is tried. Now let faith be lively and applicative, and the closer the application the better. The promise of pardon and life is universal and includeth you as well as others, if you will believe in Christ, for all true believers shall be saved. But this is to excite your faith and obedience, not to assure your interest, which dependeth upon your sincerity in faith, love and obedience. There is the application of faith and the application of assurance. The application of faith is a particular application of Christ and the promise to ourselves, so as to excite us to look after the benefits and ends for which Christ is appointed: 'To you is the word of this salvation sent' (Acts 13:26).

It is our duty to make general grace particular. The application of assurance is, when I actually determine that my own sins are pardoned, that I am adopted into God's family, and appointed to eternal life. This cannot be without some sense of my sincerity, because the promises of God require a qualification and performance of duty on the part of the person to whom the promise is made: 'We know that we have passed from death unto life, because we love the brethren' (1 John 3:14). And as you are to stir up your faith, so you are to set about the duties which the Word calleth for. On the first opportunity fall a-practising [stand to practice what the Bible teaches] for this is a message sent from God to try your obedience. By doing this continually you will insensibly habituate yourselves to the practice of godliness, and so grow up into comfort and peace.

References
1. This is a popular but not an accurate view of Mary Magdalene's earlier life.
2. The idea of heaven held by the ancient Greeks.
3. Reference not known.
4. A metaphorical explanation of earthquakes.
5. Rather, Asaph.
6. Bernard of Clairvaux (1090-1153).
7. Augustine of Hippo (354-430).
8. Cajetan: a Dominican Cardinal, opponent of Luther (1464-1534).
9. Two famous libraries, at Oxford and Rome.
10. Rather, Asaph.
11. The first Roman Emperor.
12. Siamese twins (?)
13. See footnote 4
14. How often do we offer to God a sinful worship!